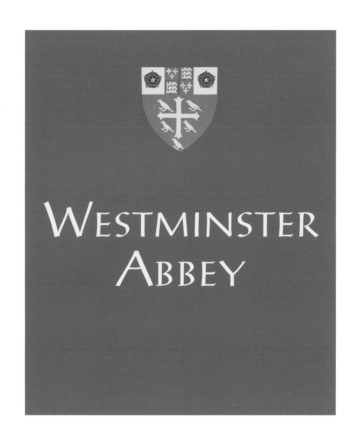

WESTMINSTER ABBEY

OFFICIAL GUIDE

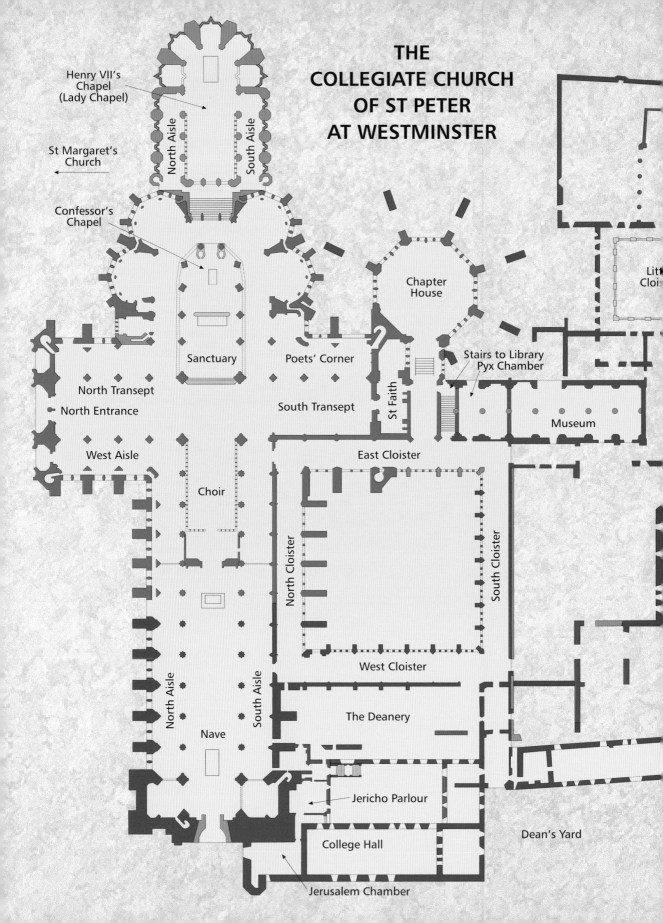

THE
COLLEGIATE CHURCH
OF ST PETER
AT WESTMINSTER

Henry VII's Chapel (Lady Chapel)

North Aisle

South Aisle

St Margaret's Church

Confessor's Chapel

Chapter House

Sanctuary

Poets' Corner

Stairs to Library
Pyx Chamber

North Transept

South Transept

St Faith

Museum

North Entrance

West Aisle

East Cloister

Lit
Cloi

Choir

North Cloister

South Cloister

North Aisle

South Aisle

West Cloister

The Deanery

Nave

Jericho Parlour

Dean's Yard

College Hall

Jerusalem Chamber

Contents

Dimensions of the Abbey

Exterior length:
530 feet/161.5 metres
Interior length:
511 feet 6 inches/155.9 metres

Height of nave:
101 feet 8 inches/31 metres
Height of west towers:
225 feet 4 inches/68.7 metres

- ■ 11th Century
- ■ 12th Century
- ■ 13th Century
- ▨ 14th Century (first half)
- ■ 14th Century (second half)
- ☐ 15th Century
- ■ 16th Century (first half)
- ☐ 17th Century

10 20 30 40 50   100ft

15   30m

Illustrations

Plans

An asterisk against a numeral on the plan key denotes that this marks the grave of someone whose memorial is elsewhere in the Abbey, e.g. Charles James Fox. An asterisk only on the plan (e.g. 32*) indicates the position of the grave of someone whose monument is some distance away on the same plan. A name printed in italics is that of a person whose monument or grave is marked on the plan but who has no entry in the text of the Guide.

Text © 1997 Dean and Chapter of Westminster

All photographs are copyright © Dean and Chapter of Westminster excepting those on pages 42, 48, 77, 81, 107 and 114 which are copyright © Jarrold Publishing, Norwich

First edition 1965; revised 1969; further revised 1971, 1973; new and revised edition 1977; further revised 1988; reprinted 1992

This edition 1997

ISBN 0–7117–0381–7

Printed and bound in Great Britain by Jarrold Book Printing, Thetford, Norfolk 9/97

Foreword

The Westminster Abbey Guide – or rather The Deanery Guide was first compiled in 1885 by two daughters of Dr G. G. Bradley, Dean of Westminster from 1881 to 1902. The original co-authors afterwards became Mrs Alexander Murray Smith and Lady Birchenough; their book was inspired by Dean Stanley's Historical Memorials of Westminster Abbey, a work which told the story of Westminster Abbey, emphasising the events in the Abbey's history and stressing the links between the persons buried or commemorated here and the history of the British Isles.

Mrs Murray Smith added to and amended the Guide until her death in 1946. Subsequent revisions embodying notices of additional monuments, corrections, and discoveries resulting from scholarly research followed the pattern of the earlier editions. In 1965 the Guide appeared in a new format with numerous photographs, revised plans, extensively rewritten text, and a somewhat more detailed treatment of the monuments.

In 1977 a further revision was undertaken by the Keeper of the Muniments, Nicholas H. MacMichael. This involved a great deal of rewriting, and greater emphasis was placed on the post-medieval monuments. It must, however, be stated that not every monument was listed or described and the Guide did not, and can not now claim to mention every burial within the Abbey church and precincts; of that there is nothing approaching a complete record.

Nicholas MacMichael was engaged on another extensive revision at the time of his death in November 1985, and his work was brought to completion in 1987 by Enid Nixon (Assistant Librarian 1983–93). It is appropriate also to record the lasting contribution made to the Guide by Lawrence Tanner (Librarian and Keeper of the Muniments 1926–72).

In undertaking the present revision I have been enormously helped by my colleagues Christine Reynolds and Richard Mortimer, and by all those associated with Westminster Abbey who have suggested amendments and additions.

Tony Trowles
March 1997

The Bayeux Tapestry: Westminster Abbey with funeral procession of King Edward

Introduction

For close on twelve hundred years – perhaps for longer – it is believed that a religious community has existed in the area we think of today as 'Westminster Abbey' and its precincts.

Over the centuries the constitution of 'the Abbey' has changed several times, and within each major period of its history there have been gradual alterations in the life and activities of those who visit the church of Westminster or work for the Abbey in one capacity or another. The degree to which we can state this with confidence depends mainly on two factors: the distance in time and the survival of historical, architectural or archaeological evidence. For the earliest periods, until the Norman Conquest, the remoteness in time and the almost total lack of records combine together, so that very little can be said of the Abbey's history. But our knowledge of Westminster from the twelfth century until 1540, during which time it was a Benedictine abbey, and from 1560 until today, is very detailed. Only in the two periods of religious and political disturbance (in the middle years of the sixteenth and seventeenth centuries) is the evidence scanty, although not entirely wanting.

Nevertheless, continuity there has been. Divine service has been celebrated within the walls of the Abbey church on its present site for nine hundred years, and Westminster School, which had its origin in the monastic school, remained even when the Chapter had been expelled during the Commonwealth. There are other centuries-old links: the Benedictine tradition of welcome to visitors; the coronation church of all the crowned sovereigns of England since William I in 1066, perhaps since Harold II (in the same year); the burial place of royalty, of the great in peace and war, of the lesser men and women who have served the Abbey, of those who have been benefactors or who simply have lived near by.

But while these separate traditions have been carried on changes have been and are made: the very building of the Abbey church and precincts has been transformed, the uses made of its component parts have been altered. Great assemblies of Church and State were held within the precinct walls; in the now-ruined Chapel of St Catherine in the monastic infirmary bishops were consecrated; the Commons met in the monks' Chapter House or in their refectory; when, after the dissolution of the monastery, the Chapter House no longer had its old function, it was used as a repository for State records; the great room where the monks had slept was turned part into a library and part into a school-room; the ancient granary, in what is now Dean's Yard, became a dormitory for the Westminster Scholars; the lodgings and offices of the monastery were adapted as houses for the clergy and others. Some of these buildings remain almost intact or easily recognisable; some exist although partly altered inside and out; some have gone altogether.

The church and the great cloister almost certainly have changed the least, and it is probably safe to say that the exterior of the Abbey church today would be easily recognised by anyone familiar with it in the last days of the monastery. Inside, however, although the general plan is essentially the same, the wall-surfaces have been transformed. We know the dedications of many of the medieval altars in the church, but today there are only eleven altars. The Chapels of St Andrew, St Michael, St John the Evangelist, Our Lady of the Pew, St John the Baptist, St Paul, St Nicholas, St Edmund and St Benedict are chapels only in name, and the places where their altars stood are occupied by tombs or memorials. These changes resulting from the Reformation have given the Abbey one of the features for which it is most celebrated: the place of burial and of commemoration of the great and famous. But it is a mistake to think that, for an individual to have a monument or grave in the Abbey church or cloisters, he or she must be greatly distinguished. From early times a person connected with the Abbey, either as abbot or a senior monk, might be included; during the Middle Ages laymen and women of comparative obscurity could be buried within the walls of the church. From the sixteenth century, when more monuments were added and records of the epitaphs are known, and from 1607 when the burial register begins, we know the names of many more. It was common practice then for College servants and members of their families to be buried in the cloisters, together with some of the clergy, and not unknown for some laymen who held Abbey offices to have graves in the church.

The presence of a particular monument in the Abbey, or why (at any one time) an individual was buried here, is more a comment on the social, political, and cultural history of that age. The memorials themselves can be studied in many ways and all can be found to have interest or merit. An idea prevails now that some writer, some statesman or some scientist deserves the honour of at least an Abbey memorial if not actual burial; it is as if Poets' Corner or the Musicians' or Scientists' Aisle is incomplete without such an addition. By the eighteenth century this notion was apparent: Milton (d. 1674), excluded for years on political grounds, was accorded a memorial in 1737, and, perhaps the most surprisingly belated of all, Shakespeare (d. 1616) not until 1740. The inclusion of Nelson's wax effigy among those of persons who actually were buried in the Abbey was because those whose perquisites of office included the 'Tomb Money' were annoyed at the knowledge of the crowds flocking to the Admiral's grave at St Paul's. Nelson's own words, 'Victory, or Westminster Abbey', suggest that he expected for himself an Abbey monument or grave.

This book is not intended as a history of 'Westminster Abbey', either as a monastery or as 'the Collegiate Church of St Peter, Westminster'. It is primarily a guide-book to the internal fabric and fittings, the altars, the ornaments, the tombs, and the memorials. A summary of the main stages of the building follows this section, and lists of abbots and deans are given. By looking up their names in the index the reader can trace the Abbey's history from details dispersed in the main text of the book.

Chronology & Building History

ORIGINS

As is the case with many ancient institutions there is no short answer to the question 'How old is the Abbey?' Medieval legends variously told of Westminster's origin in a church founded (i) by 'King Lucius', (ii) by 'a rich citizen of London', and (iii) by Sebert, king of the East Saxons in AD 604. Sebert, an historical character who died about 616, was the nephew of Ethelbert, the king of Kent who in 597 received St Augustine and his mission from Pope Gregory.

The foundation by King Sebert of what was to become Westminster Abbey may be fairly dismissed as a myth. But 'the Isle of Thorns' or 'Thorney' – the old name for Westminster – was a not unlikely place where a typical Anglo-Saxon 'minster' church may have been built and grown up possibly in the late seventh and eighth centuries. No archaeological evidence of it has been found, but Roman remains have been discovered both in the Abbey precincts and in Whitehall. References to the Abbey before Edward the Confessor are sparse and difficult to assess. A few charters of varying degrees of authenticity (in their present form) survive. Among the Abbey muniments is a charter which *may* be original but if not it probably does embody a genuine tradition; it purports to record a grant made in 785, by the Mercian King Offa (d. 796), of land at Aldenham in Hertfordshire 'to St Peter and the needy people of God in Thorney in the terrible [aweful] place which is called "aet Westmunster"'. It has been suggested that, since Aldenham is some distance away from 'Westmunster', Thorney was by 785 of more than local, though not outstanding, importance and that then it was not new.[1]

We are told that St Dunstan, about 960, when bishop of London, brought twelve Benedictine monks to Westminster. King Edgar (ruled 957–75), perhaps in 961, granted land to the Abbey, and in his charter refers to an existing church with ruined chapels.[2] The first few Benedictine abbots apparently were: Ælfric (960?–973?), St Wulfsige (973?–995?), and Ælfwig II (995?–1017?), and the names handed down as those of the rulers of the earlier foundation are: Siward, Ordbriht, Ælfwig I, Ælfgar, Adymer, and Ælfnod.

ST EDWARD'S FOUNDATION

The story of this is related below (p. 43). The king, we are told, planned to make the new Abbey his burial-place adjacent to his new palace, much as some of the royal private foundations on the continent were, but it seems possible that Westminster already did have a close relationship with the

ruling dynasty. King Harold 'Harefoot', King Canute's bastard son, had been buried at Westminster, and King Athelstan (924–39), Edgar, Ethelred 'the Unready' (979–1016), Canute himself (1016–35), and his Queen Emma had all shown the Abbey favour by presenting relics. Edward certainly built an entirely new church to the east of the early one, planned a monastery for a greatly increased number of monks and liberally endowed it with land. Nothing remains *in situ* and visible above the present floor levels of the church; but bases of the great columns have been found towards the west end of the present nave and other bases and the lower courses of three columns survive beneath the present sanctuary pavement. Beyond the altar screen beneath the pavement in the Confessor's Chapel an arc of a circle also exists and has been interpreted as the apse of Edward's new church. In style the building was the Norman form of Romanesque, which Edward had the opportunity of seeing during his years of youthful exile in Normandy but of the three master masons whose names can be connected with the building, Teinfrith, Leofsi Duddeson, and Godwin Gretsith, the two latter have English names.[1] From a life of the Confessor and from the representation of the church on the Bayeux Tapestry (see above, p. 5) we know that it had a central tower and transepts, and that the roof was covered with lead.[2] Wulfnoth was abbot (from *c.* 1020) when Edward's church was begun, but he died in 1049; his successor was Abbot Edwin.

28 December 1065: consecration of King Edward's church. **5 January 1066**: death of King Edward; buried before the High Altar. **Christmas Day 1066**: coronation of William I. **1102**: King Edward's tomb opened. **1140**: unsuccessful attempt to canonize King Edward. **1161**: bull of canonization from Alexander III. **13 October 1163**: first translation of the Confessor. *Temp.* Abbot Laurence (d. 1173): Westminster made a mitred Abbey. **1216**: accession of Henry III and his first coronation at Gloucester. **16 May 1220**: foundation-stone of Lady Chapel laid by Henry III. **17 May 1220**: coronation of Henry III at the Abbey. **1222**: Award of papal judges making Westminster Abbey exempt from the Bishop of London and the Archbishop of Canterbury, and subject directly to the Pope.

HENRY III'S BUILDING

The Gothic Lady Chapel started by Abbot Humez in 1220 stood to the east of the Confessor's church. There is a hint that this chapel was the beginning of an intended total rebuilding of the old church in the new Gothic style but that such an ambitious scheme was soon found to be beyond the Abbey's financial resources.[3] The successor of Humez, Abbot Berkyng (d. 1246), was buried in the Lady Chapel; Widmore thought that, from the posts Berkyng held – one of the King's Council, Chief Baron of the Exchequer and then Lord Treasurer – and the favour shown him at Court, 'his persuasions helped at least to determine the King' to undertake the rebuilding and to do so 'in the stately manner

1 C. A. Ralegh Radford, 'Westminster Abbey before King Edward the Confessor', *Westminster Abbey Occasional Papers*, No. 15 (1965), pp. 1–7, especially p. 4.
2 *Ibid.*, p. 3.

1 R. D. H. Gem, 'The Romanesque Rebuilding of Westminster Abbey', in *Proceedings of the Battle Conference* (1980), p. 39.
2 F. Barlow (ed.), *Life of King Edward the Confessor* (1962), pp. 45–6, especially the footnotes.
3 H. M. Colvin (ed.), *History of the King's Works*, vol. 1 (HMSO, 1963), pp. 131–2.

Thirteenth-century sculpture of censing angel, south transept

in which we now see it'.[1] Three master masons supervised Henry's works: *Master Henry 'de Reyns', Master John of Gloucester*, and *Master Robert of Beverley*. It is not known whether *Master Henry* was English or French; 'de Reyns' could derive from an English place-name or from Reims in France, but the architect of the Gothic Abbey at Westminster was greatly influenced by the new buildings at Reims, Amiens, Paris (Sainte-Chapelle), Chartres, and Beauvais. The plan of the apse with its radiating chapels derives from Amiens, and the recessed portals of the north transept at Westminster come from the west front at Amiens. From Reims the master mason took the form of the apsidal chapels with their tall windows, and wall-arcades. Further conspicuous French features are the flying buttresses, the rose windows in the transepts (p. 9), the bar-tracery of the other windows, the iron tie-bars linking the columns, and the superbly sculpted censing angels (*see above*). The design of the church is based on the continental system of geometrical proportion, but it is built in some respects on an English plan, with single, not double, aisles and with a long nave and widely projecting transepts. The Englishness of the Abbey is also apparent in the elaborate mouldings of the main arches, the prominence and lavish use of polished Purbeck marble, the method of filling the stone vaults, and the overall sculptured decoration.

The early part of the building, following the demolition of the eastern part of the Confessor's church in 1245, was done

1   R. Widmore, *History of . . . Westminster Abbey* (1751), pp. 40–2.

while *Master Henry* was in charge. Space was restricted: to the east by the Lady Chapel; to the west by the Norman nave; to the south by the Norman cloister and other buildings; the east-west axis of the new church was determined by that of the Lady Chapel. The north transept was given single aisles and the great height (by English standards) of the vault was made to seem higher by making the aisles narrow following the proportions of a double-aisled church. This simple device gave the Abbey the effect of extreme verticality which is one of its most pronounced architectural features. On the south side the cloister intruded into the transept on the west, but by placing the present Muniment Room *above* part of the east cloister, the south transept was widened and in effect given a western aisle to match that of the north transept. The ritual choir was built west of the crossing, and a large central area under the lantern was provided as a coronation theatre in the sight of people in both transepts.

The whole eastern arm of the church, the ambulatory and chapels, the transepts, and the Chapter House appear to have been built by 1259. *Master Henry* was succeeded in 1253 by *Master John of Gloucester*, who died in 1260. *Master Robert of Beverley*, who was in charge between 1260 and 1272, continued the work west of the crossing according to the work already done, but with variations in details which may have been his own. By 1269 the choir and eastern part of the nave were virtually complete, and the new shrine for the Confessor was ready for his second translation on 13 October. By 1272, the year of Henry III's death, five bays of the nave were finished except that the fifth (westernmost) bay lacked its clerestory and vault.

After Henry's death the west end of the Norman nave remained attached to the far higher Gothic building to the east for over a century.

CONTINUATION OF THE NAVE

The western part was carried on by Abbot Litlyngton, who laid the foundation-stone on 3 March 1376 in the name of Cardinal Langham (q.v.), who gave money during his life and left the residue of his estate to the Abbey. **1376–1387**: demolition of the Norman nave, the new outside walls in the process of being erected. **1387–1403**: Langham, eager to see his work advanced, had urged that if need be a stone less expensive than marble should be used for the nave columns. It was probably Litlyngton who insisted that the columns should be of Purbeck and that the general design of Henry III's master masons was followed. His successor Abbot Colchester continued the work; by 1403 all the columns were in place and the walls complete to triforium level. Richard II gave £1,685 towards the cost. Within this period *Henry de Yevele* was master mason and made only minor alterations in the architectural details. **1413–1422**: Henry V provided regular royal finance once more; he gave £3,861, promising 1,000 marks (£666 13s. 4d.) yearly. Richard ('Dick') Whityngton and Brother Richard Harweden (representing the Abbey) were appointed Surveyors of 'the New Work'. **Mid fifteenth century**: Henry V's Chantry Chapel built under *Master John Thirske*, probably also responsible for the altar screen. Nave proceeded slowly. **1468**: Prior Thomas Millyng, who became abbot in 1469, continued the nave. His affording sanctuary to Queen Elizabeth Woodville (1470) led to royal assistance following Edward IV's recovery of the

The North Front

throne in 1471. Elizabeth Woodville built the Chapel of St Erasmus adjoining the Lady Chapel; Millyng was made a bishop. **1471–1498**: Millyng and his successor, Esteney, roofed in the nave and constructed the west window. **1500–1517**: Abbot Islip completed the nave vaulting and glazed the west window. West towers remained unfinished.

LATER WORKS

1503: Foundation-stone of Henry VII's Chapel laid; Chapels of St Erasmus and Our Lady demolished. By Henry VII's death (April 1509) £14,856 had been paid to abbot and convent towards the cost of the chapel. Shortly before he died Henry gave a further £5,000 to finish the work; Henry's will, **1509**, suggests the structure was nearly complete. The decoration, glazing, etc., probably continued until about **1512**. The names of the master masons responsible for the design and construction have not been established. It is not unlikely that they were among the following: *Robert Vertue, William Vertue, John Hylmer* (or *Aylmer*), *Robert Janyns, Henry Redman*, and *John Lebons*. **Before 1532**: The Islip Chantry Chapels built. **1698–1745**: *Sir C. Wren* appointed Surveyor, undertook restoration and designed west towers. His designs for the latter were modified by *N. Hawksmoor* and completed by *J. James* in 1745. **1808–1822**: Restoration of Henry VII's Chapel. **1849–1906**: *Sir G. G. Scott* appointed Surveyor (1849); restoration, notably of the Chapter House, carried

out by him. His successors *J. L. Pearson* (q.v.) and *J. T. Micklethwaite* (q.v.) restored the north transept.

RECENT RESTORATION

1973–1995: an intensive programme of restoration began, entirely funded through private contributions raised by the Westminster Abbey Trust. Between 1973 and 1988 under the surveyorship of *J. P. Foster* the north and south fronts were cleaned and restored. Under *D. Buttress* (appointed Surveyor in 1988) work began on the west front; a new gable cross was added (a memorial to T. Thompson of the Westminster Abbey Trust, d. 1991) together with six new statues, and a commemorative inscription unveiled by HRH The Duke of Edinburgh in March 1993. Work on the exterior of Henry VII's Chapel, the final phase of the restoration, was completed during 1995 [1] **1996**: four statues of allegorical figures depicting the virtues for which Christian martyrs have laid down their lives were installed above the great west doors. From north to south they represent Truth, Justice, Mercy and Peace. Carved by *T. Crawley*. A further ten statues depicting martyrs of the twentieth century will be installed in the remaining niches in 1998.

---

1 For a detailed account of this and earlier restorations see Thomas Cocke and Donald Buttress, *900 Years: the Restorations of Westminster Abbey* (1995).

Abbots & Deans

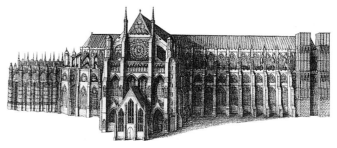

The Benedictine monastery was surrendered to the Crown by deed dated 19 January 1540 and signed by Abbot Boston and twenty-four monks. The same year Henry VIII erected Westminster into a cathedral church with a bishop, dean, and twelve prebendaries. The bishopric was surrendered on 29 March 1550 and the diocese reunited with London, Westminster being made by Act of Parliament a cathedral church in the diocese of London. The Benedictine monastery was restored by charter from Mary I in 1556. Upon the accession of Elizabeth I the religious houses revived by Mary were given by Parliament to the Crown, and the abbot and monks removed in July 1559. The foundation charter of the present Collegiate Church, exempt from the jurisdiction of the Archbishop of Canterbury and the Bishop of London, is dated 21 May 1560.

BISHOP OF WESTMINSTER

Thomas Thirlby	1540–50

DEANS OF WESTMINSTER

William Benson (formerly Abbot Boston)	1540–49
Richard Cox	1549–53
Hugh Weston	1553–56
William Bill	1560–61
Gabriel Goodman	1561–1601
Lancelot Andrewes	1601–05
Richard Neile*	1605–10
George Montaigne	1610–17
Robert Tounson	1617–20
John Williams	1620–44
Richard Steward (never installed)	1644–51
John Earle	1660–62
John Dolben*	1662–83
Thomas Sprat*	1683–1713
Francis Atterbury*	1713–23
Samuel Bradford*	1723–31
Joseph Wilcocks*	1731–56
Zachary Pearce*	1756–68
John Thomas*	1768–93
Samuel Horsley*	1793–1802
William Vincent	1802–15
John Ireland	1816–42
Thomas Turton	1842–45
Samuel Wilberforce	1845
William Buckland	1845–56
Richard Chenevix Trench	1856–64
Arthur Penrhyn Stanley	1864–81
George Granville Bradley	1881–1902
Joseph Armitage Robinson	1902–11
Herbert Edward Ryle	1911–25
William Foxley Norris	1925–37
Paul Fulcrand Delacour de Labilliere	1938–46
Alan Campbell Don	1946–59
Eric Symes Abbott	1959–74
Edward Frederick Carpenter	1974–85
Michael Clement Otway Mayne	1986–96
Arthur Wesley Carr	1997–

also Bishop of Rochester

ABBOTS OF WESTMINSTER SINCE THE CONQUEST

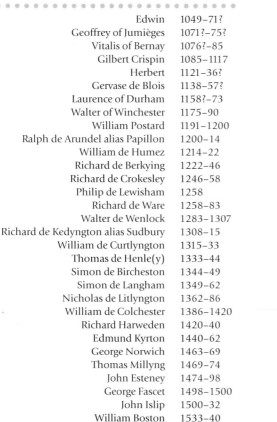

Edwin	1049–71?
Geoffrey of Jumièges	1071?–75?
Vitalis of Bernay	1076?–85
Gilbert Crispin	1085–1117
Herbert	1121–36?
Gervase de Blois	1138–57?
Laurence of Durham	1158?–73
Walter of Winchester	1175–90
William Postard	1191–1200
Ralph de Arundel alias Papillon	1200–14
William de Humez	1214–22
Richard de Berkying	1222–46
Richard de Crokesley	1246–58
Philip de Lewisham	1258
Richard de Ware	1258–83
Walter de Wenlock	1283–1307
Richard de Kedyngton alias Sudbury	1308–15
William de Curtlyngton	1315–33
Thomas de Henle(y)	1333–44
Simon de Bircheston	1344–49
Simon de Langham	1349–62
Nicholas de Litlyngton	1362–86
William de Colchester	1386–1420
Richard Harweden	1420–40
Edmund Kyrton	1440–62
George Norwich	1463–69
Thomas Millyng	1469–74
John Esteney	1474–98
George Fascet	1498–1500
John Islip	1500–32
William Boston	1533–40
John Feckenham	1556–59

The Nave

See plan, page 12

• •

Outside the great west doors, at the foot of the north-west tower, a slab of green Cumberland slate within a radiating circle of York stone commemorates the **Innocent Victims of Oppression, Violence and War**. The memorial was designed by *K. Thompson* and unveiled by HM The Queen on 10 October 1996.

The inner **west doors** of engraved glass, designed by *D. Peace* and *S. Scott*, were dedicated in June 1990. They were the gift of Barclays Bank, whose eagle symbol, cast in bronze by *Sir D. Hughes*, features in the central door-pulls.

The sixteen crystal-glass **chandeliers** in the nave and transepts, designed by *A. B. Read* and *S. E. Dykes Bower*, were given by members of the Guinness family in 1965 to mark the Abbey's 900th anniversary. They were handblown at Waterford and each weighs two and a half hundredweight.

THE UNKNOWN WARRIOR
• •

At the west end of the nave is the Grave of the **Unknown Warrior**, whose body was brought from France to be buried here on 11 November 1920. The grave, which contains soil from France, is covered by a slab of black Belgian marble from a quarry near Namur. On it is an inscription, written by Dean Ryle, which embodies the text 'They buried him among the Kings because he had done good toward God and toward his House'. The burial was attended by King George V and many other members of the Royal Family. There were also present the Prime Minister, members of the Cabinet and the Service Chiefs, and a guard of honour of a hundred VCs lined the nave.

The idea of such a burial seems first to have come to a chaplain at the Front, the Reverend David Railton, when he noticed in 1916 in a back garden at Armentières, a grave with a rough cross at its head on which were pencilled the words 'An Unknown British Soldier'. In August 1920 he wrote to Dean Ryle, through whose energies this memorial, which captured the imagination of the world, was carried into effect. From the day of the funeral the grave has become a place of pilgrimage for people from all over the world. 'The Padre's Flag' which originally covered the coffin, now hangs in St George's Chapel.

On the pillar near by to the south hangs the ship's bell from HMS *Verdun*, the destroyer on which the body of the Unknown Warrior was brought from Boulogne to Dover. Given in 1990 by Commander J. D. R. Davies, RN.

On the corresponding pillar to the north is placed the highest honour which can be conferred by the United States of America: the **Congressional Medal**. On 17 October 1921 it was delivered into the keeping of the Dean by General Pershing, the Commander-in-Chief of the United States Army.

In a case farther west is a copy of **Rudolph Ackermann's** *History of the Abbey Church of St Peter's Westminster*, 1812.

The only copy printed on vellum, it contains original watercolours by eight different artists. In 1926 the book was given to the Dean and Chapter by King George V, Queen Mary, Edward, Prince of Wales, the Duke and Duchess of York, the Princess Royal and her husband, Prince Henry (Duke of Gloucester), and Prince George (Duke of Kent), who have all signed it.

Between the Grave of the Unknown Warrior and the west door a green marble stone, incised arrestingly with the words 'Remember Winston Churchill', commemorates **Sir Winston Leonard Spencer Churchill, KG, OM, CH, FRS**, b. 1874, d. 1965, statesman, twice Prime Minister, and writer. After opening his career in the Army, he entered Parliament in 1900 and during his long political life held most of the principal Government offices. He was Home Secretary in 1910–11 and was then appointed First Lord of the Admiralty, a post which he held until 1915. After a brief period of renewed Army service he returned to politics and held high-ranking posts on and off until 1929. For ten years he served simply as an MP but in 1939 became once more First Lord of the Admiralty and on 10 May 1940, after Neville Chamberlain's resignation, became Prime Minister. In this position his oratory inspired Britain at war and through his doggedness and determination led his country and her allies to victory in 1945. After a period of socialist government Churchill became Prime Minister again, from 1951 until April 1955 when he resigned. He was made KG in 1953. Churchill died on 24 January 1965 and, after a State Funeral at St Paul's Cathedral, was buried at Bladon, Oxon. This memorial in the Abbey was unveiled by HM The Queen on 19 September 1965, twenty-five years after the Battle of Britain, the subject of Churchill's perhaps most-remembered words: 'Never in the field of human conflict was so much owed by so many to so few.' Sculptor: *R. Stone*.

Grave of the Unknown Warrior

The Nave, St George's Chapel and North-West Tower

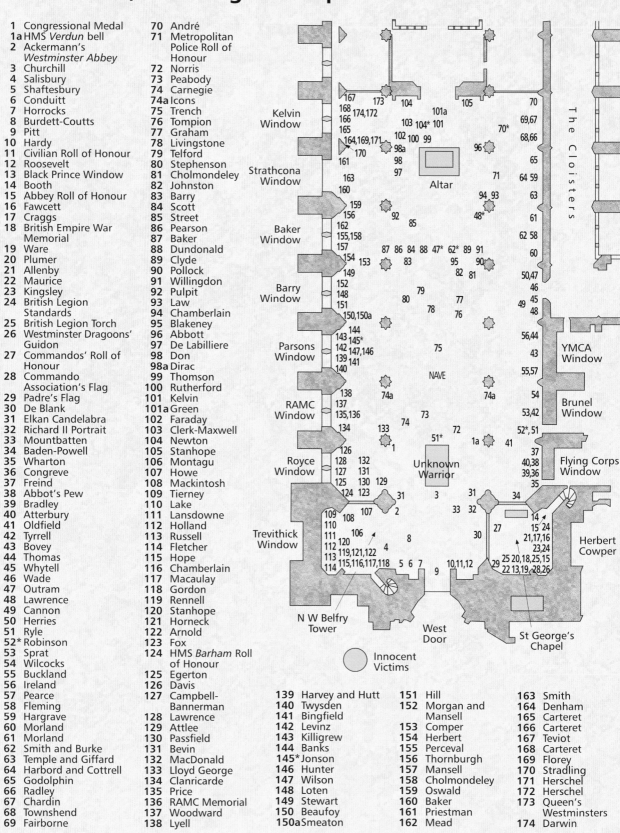

WEST END OF NAVE

Robert Arthur Talbot (Gascoyne-Cecil), 3rd Marquess of Salisbury, KG, b. 1830, d. 1903, statesman and thrice Prime Minister. The black marble monument designed by *G. F. Bodley* and executed by *W. Goscombe John*, was erected by Parliament in 1909; the recumbent bronze effigy is misleading, for in fact Lord Salisbury was buried at Hatfield, Herts. He was Master of Trinity House, Lord Warden of the Cinque Ports, Chancellor of Oxford University, and High Steward of Westminster, and shields of arms appropriate for these offices are at his head and feet. On the sides of the memorial are statuettes of his father, the 2nd Marquess and his mother; also of his great ancestors, William (Cecil), Lord Burghley and Lady Burghley, with their son, Robert (Cecil), 1st Earl of Salisbury, and his wife; the earl is holding a model of Hatfield House.

A statue by *Sir J. E. Boehm*, of the philanthropist, **Anthony (Ashley-Cooper), 7th Earl of Shaftesbury, KG**, b. 1801, d. 1885, was erected here in 1888. He concerned himself with the reform of the lunacy laws, protection of colliery workers and chimney-sweeps, the reclamation of juvenile offenders, and better housing for the poor. Funeral at the Abbey, but buried at Wimborne St Giles, Dorset.

North of the west door – **John Conduitt**, b. 1688, d. 1737, scientist. He married Sir Isaac Newton's niece and succeeded him as Master of the Mint. Conduitt preserved a mass of Newton's personal papers and anecdotes of his life. His monument with portrait bust on medallion, by *Sir H. Cheere*, looks towards Newton's memorial. Buried close to Newton's grave.

After the transit of Venus in 1874 a tablet with inscription by Dean Stanley was added to Conduitt's monument in memory of **Jeremiah Horrocks**, b. 1617, d. 1641, astronomer. A clergyman, Horrocks was a youthful prodigy as a theoretical astronomer, and predicted from his own observations the transit of Venus across the Sun in 1639. Buried at Toxteth Park, near Liverpool.

Near Shaftesbury's statue lies the body of **Angela Georgina (Burdett-Coutts), Baroness Burdett-Coutts**, b. 1814, d. 1906. A close friend of Charles Dickens, she used her considerable fortune to initiate numerous philanthropic ventures, especially among the poor of London's East End. She founded the bishopric of British Columbia and paid for the building of St Stephen's church in Rochester Row, Westminster.

The Rt Hon. William Pitt, b. 1759, d. 1806, 'the Younger Pitt' and Lord Chatham's second son; statesman and Prime Minister. He became Prime Minister astonishingly young (aged twenty-four) in 1783, and remained in office, with a break of only three years, until his death. He died insolvent

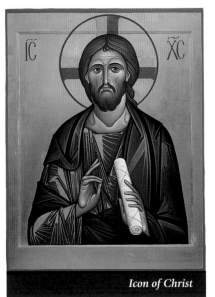

Icon of Christ

and was buried at the public expense but in recognition of his services to the country Parliament voted £40,000 to pay his debts. Above the west door on his monument (1807–13), by *Sir R. Westmacott*, Pitt the Orator declaims as the muse History records his words and Anarchy (the French Revolution – a chained naked male) crouches at his feet. Buried in the north transept in his father's grave.

South of the west door – **Rear-Admiral Sir Thomas Hardy**, b. 1666, d. 1732; served under Admiral Sir George Rooke at Cadiz (1702) commanding the *Pembroke* and afterwards, for his contribution to Rooke's victory over the Spanish fleet at Vigo Harbour, was knighted by Queen Anne. On the monument, executed by *Sir H. Cheere*, the epitaph proclaims his descent from the Jersey family of Le Hardy, which aided the future Henry VII when in exile.

South of Hardy's monument in a case are seven volumes which contain a **Roll of Honour of the Civilian War Dead** (1939–45).

Above this case is a memorial plaque to **Franklin Delano Roosevelt**, b. 1882, d. 1945. 'A faithful friend of freedom and of Britain, four times President of the United States. Erected by the Government of the United Kingdom'. Unveiled by the Prime Minister (Clement Attlee) and by the Leader of the Opposition (Churchill) on 12 November 1948. Sculptor: *H. W. Palliser*.

A **Burma Book of Remembrance** (1939–45), a copy of the books of remembrance in Rangoon Cathedral, is in the keeping of the Dean's Verger.

ST GEORGE'S CHAPEL
(The Warriors' Chapel)

In this place the Consistory Courts of the Peculiar Jurisdiction of the Dean and Chapter were formerly held; the judge's seat still remains on the south wall. The chapel was also at one time the baptistery, but the font has been removed to Henry VII's Chapel (see p. 66).

The arch through which the chapel is now entered from the nave was blocked by the large monument to Captain James Cornwall, RN (q.v.), and against the original screen which separates the chapel from the south aisle was placed the Craggs monument, which was originally much larger.

The chapel was remodelled and, on 24 June 1932, Edward, Prince of Wales, attended its dedication to the memory of the men and women who died in the First World War. The alterations to the chapel and the decorations were designed by *Sir J. N. Comper* (q.v.) and the work was carried out by *B. Pegram* and *W. F. Knight*. The cost was defrayed mostly by a gift from Mr John Denham of Johannesburg; the remainder was collected by the Mothers' Union from women of the British Empire, and from private donations.

A new **glass screen**, designed and executed by *D. Peace*, was erected in 1978.

The glass in the west window is a composition partly medieval (late fourteenth or early fifteenth century) and partly later. A seventeenth-century drawing shows that the figure represents **Edward, Prince of Wales** ('the Black Prince'), b. 1330, d. 1376.

The **altar** was dedicated to St George on 23 April 1944; east of it are remains of the ancient stone screen.

Over the door in the south-east corner is a bust of **William Booth**, b. 1829, d. 1912, founder of the Salvation Army. Unveiled 2 July 1965.

On the wooden panelling at the back of the seats are the names of the twelve **Abbey servants** who were killed in the First World War and of the nine who died in the Second World War.

Henry Fawcett, b. 1833, d. 1884, statesman. He was Postmaster-General (1880–4), and established parcel post (1882). Monument erected in 1887; bronze figures by *Sir A. Gilbert*. Also a memorial to his wife **Dame Millicent Garrett Fawcett**, b. 1847, d. 1929, who supported the movement for women's suffrage. Unveiled 1932. By *Sir H. Baker*.

Above on the south wall is the monument to **James Craggs**, b. 1686, d. 1721. Craggs became a Privy Counsellor and Secretary of State before he was thirty-two, but his brilliant career was cut short by smallpox at thirty-five. He was a friend of Addison but survived him by less than two years. Pope, who had a great admiration for Craggs, wrote the epitaph:

> Statesman, yet friend to truth of Soul sincere,
> In Action faithful and in Honour clear,
> Who broke no Promise, serv'd no private end,
> Who gain'd no Title, and who lost no Friend;
> Ennobled by Himselfe, by All approv'd,
> Prais'd, wept, and honoured, by the Muse he lov'd.

The monument, no longer in its original position and much reduced in size, was designed by *J. Gibbs*; *G. B. Guelfi* was the sculptor, assisted by *F. Bird*. Buried in Henry VII's Chapel.

Before the dedication of the chapel the Prince of Wales, President of the Imperial War Graves Commission, unveiled (19 October 1926) the tablet on the west wall in memory of the **Million Citizens of the British Empire** who died in the First World War. Designed by *Lt.-Col. P. H. C. de Lafontaine*. An additional inscription commemorates those who died in the Second World War.

Beneath this tablet is another small one, unveiled in 1950, to **Major-General Sir Fabian Ware**, KCVO, b. 1869, d. 1949, Vice-Chairman Imperial War Graves Commission.

The first interment in this chapel in recent years took place on 18 July 1932, when **Field-Marshal Herbert Charles Onslow (Plumer), 1st Viscount Plumer, GCB**, b. 1857, d. 1932, was buried here. He served in the Sudan and South Africa and was a distinguished commander in the First World War; High Commissioner for Palestine (1925–8). Here also rest the ashes of another famous First World War commander: **Field-Marshal Edmund Henry Hynman (Allenby), 1st Viscount Allenby, GCB, GCMG**, b. 1861, d. 1936; principally remembered for his recapture of Jerusalem.

Two busts commemorate (1) **Frederick Denison Maurice**, b. 1805, d. 1872, Christian Socialist preacher and writer. Buried at Highgate. And (2) **Charles Kingsley**, b. 1819, d. 1875, writer and poet, Canon of Westminster (1873–5); 'disciple' of F. D. Maurice. As a writer Kingsley's best-known books are probably *Hereward the Wake*, *The Water Babies*, and *Westward Ho!*. Buried at Eversley, Hants, of which place he was rector. Bust by *T. Woolner*.

On either side of the Craggs monument are **standards of the Royal British Legion**, and on the west wall is the **torch** presented by the Legion to commemorate the 900th anniversary of the consecration of the Confessor's Abbey church.

On 25 November 1961 the **guidon of the Westminster Dragoons**, presented to the Regiment by Edward VII in 1909, was laid up here.

The Roll of Honour of the Combined Operations Command ('the Commandos'), in the form of a book containing the names of the Officers and All Ranks who fell 1940–5, is preserved in this chapel, together with the **Commando Association's Battle Honours Flag, 1940–5**, unveiled 1 May 1971 by HM Queen Elizabeth the Queen Mother.

Above hangs the Union 'Jack' known as the **Padre's Flag**, presented by the Reverend David Railton. At the burial of the Unknown Warrior it had covered the coffin, as it also had for many of those killed on Vimy Ridge, on the Ypres Salient, on the Somme, and elsewhere; it was also used as an altar-cloth at many services on the Front. On 11 November 1921 Dean Ryle dedicated the Flag 'to the memory of all those who gave their lives' in the First World War.

Outside the entrance to the chapel is buried **Joost de Blank**, b. 1908, d. 1968, Canon of Westminster 1963–8, previously Suffragan Bishop of Stepney, and Archibishop of Cape Town (1957–63). The inscription on the stone over his ashes includes the words 'indomitable fighter for human rights' in allusion to his strenuous opposition as Archbishop of Cape Town, to the policy of apartheid. Beneath an adjacent stone rest the ashes of the Bishop's sister, **Bartha de Blank**, b. 1906, d. 1975.

Close to the westernmost free-standing columns in the nave are the two **bronze candelabra** designed by *B. Elkan* and presented to the Abbey by Arthur Hamilton (Lee), 1st Viscount Lee of Fareham (1868–1947) in 1939 and 1942. Their subjects are taken from the Old and New Testaments respectively.

On the pillar just outside St George's Chapel is now placed the contemporary **portrait of Richard II**. It used to hang over the Lord Chancellor's stall on the south side of the choir, but it suffered damage there allegedly from the wigs of the occupants of the stall. The painting was removed to the Jerusalem Chamber in 1775, but Dean Stanley in the following century replaced it in the Abbey church (in the sanctuary). This wooden panel-painting is the earliest known contemporary painted portrait of an English sovereign. The suggestion has been made that the artist was *André Beauneveu*, portrait-painter to Charles V of France. Beauneveu is known to have visited the English court about 1398. The picture was restored by *George Richmond* in the nineteenth century, at which time the pattern of raised and gilt gesso work had already disappeared. The vivid colours of the costume still remain unimpaired: the green vest powdered with the golden letter R, the crimson robe lined with ermine, the ermine cape, the vermilion socks, and gilt shoes.

At the foot of the pillar is a joint memorial of Belgian fossil marble, inlaid with brass and stainless steel, to **Admiral of**

Portrait of Richard II

SOUTH AISLE

A stone in the floor at the west end of the aisle, next to the screen of St George's Chapel, unveiled in 1947 commemorated **Robert Stephenson Smyth (Baden-Powell), 1st Baron Baden-Powell**, b. 1857, d. 1941, the founder of the Scout Movement. A new joint memorial to him and **Lady Olave Baden-Powell, GBE**, World Chief Guide, b. 1889, d. 1977, was unveiled on 12 February 1981. Lord Baden-Powell died at Nyeri, Kenya, and the ashes of both are buried there. Above the memorial stone are placed the flags of the Boy Scouts' and Girl Guides' Associations.

Near by in the south wall a door leads into the Deanery. Directly above the doorway a tablet commemorates **Henry Wharton**, b. 1664, d. 1695, scholar and divine, rector of Chartham and vicar of Minster-in-Thanet, Kent. The best known of his writings, *Anglia Sacra* is still used by historians. Buried in the south aisle. Archbishop Tillotson attended his funeral for which Purcell composed the anthems.

Next is a wall monument to **William Congreve**, b. 1670, d. 1729, dramatist. His most successful plays were *Love for Love* (1695), *The Mourning Bride* (1697), and *The Way of the World* (1700). Before his funeral his body lay in state in the Jerusalem Chamber, and the Prime Minister was one of the pall-bearers. Henrietta, Duchess of Marlborough, to whom Congreve left the bulk of his fortune, erected the monument and wrote the epitaph. She spent the legacy on (among other things) a statue of Congreve in ivory moved by clockwork, and had it set daily at her table where she talked with it as if it were alive. The monument, executed by *F. Bird*, consists of a sarcophagus (on which are theatrical emblems) and above on an oval medallion a bust based on Kneller's portrait of Congreve in the Kit-Kat series.

Dr John Freind, b. 1675, d. 1728, eminent physician, chemist, and scholar, favourite of George II and Queen Caroline. Imprisoned in the Tower for his friendship with Dean Atterbury, and released through Dr Richard Mead's influence with Sir Robert Walpole. His brother Robert, Head Master of Westminster School, wrote the epitaph. Monument designed by *J. Gibbs*, bust executed by *J. M. Rysbrack*. Buried at Hitcham, Bucks.

Above the last three monuments is a small wooden gallery known as **the Abbot's Pew**. It leads out of the Deanery and was built in the time of Abbot Islip (1500–32).

Beneath gravestones in the floor are buried:

George Granville Bradley, DD, b. 1821, d. 1903; Dean (1881–1902). He was Master of Marlborough College (1858–70); Master of University College, Oxford (1870–81). At Westminster he officiated at the jubilee of Queen Victoria (1887) and at the coronation of King Edward VII and Queen Alexandra (1902). He died 13 March 1903, having resigned the deanery. The brass was presented by the Dean and Chapter and carried out by *Messrs Clayton and Bell*.

Francis Atterbury, DD, b. 1663, d. 1732; Dean of Westminster; King's Scholar, Westminster School, under Dr Busby, and Scholar and Fellow of Christ Church, Oxford; the famous Jacobite Bishop of Rochester noted as a brilliant orator and controversial writer. Under Atterbury the school dormitory was rebuilt, and he also left his mark on the structure of the Abbey. He chose the subjects for the rose window in the north transept, and himself superintended the

the Fleet Louis Francis Albert Victor Nicholas (**Mountbatten**), **1st Earl Mountbatten of Burma, KG, PC, GCB**, etc., b. 1900, d. 1979, and **Edwina Cynthia Annette** (*née* **Ashley**), **Countess Mountbatten of Burma**, b. 1901, died 1960 in North Borneo, on tour as Superintendent-in-Chief, St John Ambulance Brigade. After a distinguished naval career spanning two world wars Lord Mountbatten became Viceroy of India in 1947 and Governor-General from August 1947 to June 1948, during the difficult period of transition when British India was divided into the separate republics of India and Pakistan. Subsequently he returned to naval duties, becoming Commander-in-Chief, Mediterranean, 1952–4. First Sea Lord, 1955–9, and Chief of UK Defence Staff from 1959 to 1965. Together with other members of his family, he was assassinated on 29 August 1979 in an IRA terrorist attack on his family yacht in Mullaghmore Harbour, Co. Sligo. 'He was a man of fiery enthusiasm and total commitment,' who, meteor-like, 'flared brilliantly across the face of the twentieth century.'[1] Funeral at Westminster Abbey, buried at Romsey Abbey, Hants. Memorial designed by *C. Ironside*.

---

1   Philip Ziegler, *Mountbatten* (1985), p. 702.

repairing of the north front by Wren, then Surveyor of the Abbey. A High-Churchman and a Tory, he lost favour under the Hanoverian dynasty, although he officiated at the coronation of George I. He was sent to the Tower charged with conspiracy to place the Pretender on the throne, deprived of his offices, and condemned to perpetual exile in 1723. Nine years later he died in Paris, and was buried here by his own desire, expressed in a letter to Alexander Pope, 'as far from Kings and Caesars as the space will admit of'. Also buried under the stone are his wife **Catherine**, d. 1722; his daughters **Elizabeth**, d. 1716, and **Mary**, wife of William Morice, High Bailiff of Westminster. Mary Morice died at Toulouse in 1729 and was buried here on 21 February 1730.

In a grave near by lies **Ann Oldfield**, b. 1683, d. 1730. She was considered to be the chief actress of her day, excelling in both tragedy and comedy on the London stage and creating original roles in more than fifty plays, including works by Steele, Vanbrugh and Congreve. Her body lay in state in the Jerusalem Chamber before a magnificent funeral.

Filling part of the next window east of Dr Freind's monument and above that to Dean Sprat is a much-cut-down monument by Roubiliac's pupil and assistant *N. Read* to **Rear-Admiral Richard Tyrrell**, d. 1766, nephew of Sir Peter Warren (q.v.) and like Warren a member of an Irish family. Before its mutilation this memorial could not have been easily understood, but in its present state it is even more confusing. Originally the Admiral's soul – represented as a slightly veiled naked body – was to be seen on its way from the sea (where his body was buried) to Heaven. Two descending angels with trumpets heralded his approach. Beneath is commemorated Tyrell's defeat of three French men-of-war in 1758 when he commanded the *Buckingham*. Hibernia, with an Irish harp, leans on a globe and points to Tyrell's watery grave flanked by Hope and the Angel of Remuneration. HMS *Buckingham* is shown grounded on a coral reef and the inscription is carved on the rocks. Opinions were divided upon the merits of the Tyrrell monument: Nollekens derided it; Brayley detected some points to praise; John Wesley thought it and Roubiliac's Nightingale monument (see p. 52) had no others worthy of comparison.

Mrs Katherine Bovey, b. 1669, d. 1727, has a memorial erected by Mrs Mary Pope to mark their forty-year friendship. The ladies were caricatured by Addison as the 'Perverse Widow' and her 'Malicious Confidante' in *The Spectator*. The monument, designed by *J. Gibbs* and executed by *J. M. Rysbrack*, consists principally of a sarcophagus, with the figures of Faith and Prudence sitting on it, and a portrait bust on a medallion. Mrs Bovey was buried at Flaxley, Glos., where Mrs Pope put up another monument.

John Thomas, b. 1712, d. 1793, succeeded Pearce as Dean of Westminster (1768), and became also Bishop of Rochester. In his time the festival of the centenary of Handel's birth was held in the nave of the Abbey (1784). Thomas was an advocate of Catholic emancipation. The sculptor of the bust, *J. Bacon, Jun.*, based it on a portrait by Reynolds. Buried at Bletchingley, Surrey.

In the next bay east is a monument to **Ann Whytell**, d. 1788, of Gilmonby, Yorks., by *J. Bacon*, dated 1791. An urn on a pedestal is flanked by statues of Innocence and Peace. It formerly stood in the north aisle between the monument to Governor Loten and Captain Stewart.

A monument by *L. F. Roubiliac* commemorates **Field-Marshal George Wade**, b. 1673, d. 1748; Lieutenant-General of the Ordnance; Governor of Fort William, Fort Augustus, and Fort George after the 1745 Rebellion. He is now, perhaps, chiefly remembered for the good roads he made in the Highlands and the lines:

> If you'd seen these roads before they were made
> You would hold up your hands and bless Marshal Wade

Buried in the centre of the nave. Roubiliac's monument exhibits a medallion portrait bust of Wade above which Fame repels Time who advances to destroy a column or trophy which bears a suit of armour and other martial emblems.

Lieutenant-General Sir James Outram, Bt, b. 1803, d. 1863. His name is connected with the defence of Lucknow, and he ranks as one of the heroes of India during the Indian Mutiny. The bas-relief represents the scene at the Residency when Lord Clyde (Sir Colin Campbell) relieved Lucknow. General Havelock stands between Outram and Clyde. Monument by *M. Noble*, erected by the Secretary of State for India in Council. Buried in the centre of the nave.

John Laird Mair (Lawrence), 1st Baron Lawrence, GCB, b. 1811, d. 1879, Governor-General of India (1864–9). Lawrence served as Chief Commissioner of the newly formed province of the Punjab from 1853 to 1859. He reformed the agricultural economy, built roads and canals, and introduced a stable and fair administration. During the Indian Mutiny of 1857 Lawrence's clear thinking and military acumen (though he was never a soldier) played a crucial part in the recapture of Delhi. Bust by *T. Woolner*.

Robert Cannon, b. 1663, d. 1722. Prebendary of Westminster (1715–22) and Dean of Lincoln (1721–2).

Charles Herries, b. 1745, d. 1819. Colonel of the London and Westminster Light Horse Volunteers. Monument with bas-relief designed by *Sir R. Smirke*, and executed by *Sir F. Chantrey*. Buried in the centre of the nave.

Above the doorway leading to the Dean's Verger's office in 1928 was placed a tablet, designed by *O. Cheadle*, in memory of **Dr Herbert Edward Ryle, KCVO**, b. 1856, d. 1925, Dean of Westminster (1911–25); Bishop of Exeter (1901–3); Bishop of Winchester (1903–11). Ryle officiated at the 1911 coronation and was Dean throughout the First World War. Before the war the installation ceremony for the Knights of the Bath was revived. Dean Ryle was greatly involved in the burial of the Unknown Warrior (1920) and in many memorial services. He also took part in several royal weddings including that in 1923 of Albert, Duke of York (later King George VI) and Lady Elizabeth Bowes-Lyon (now Queen Elizabeth the Queen Mother). He started an appeal fund which bears his name. Buried in the centre of the nave east of the Unknown Warrior.

The monument, by *J. Settle*, to **Sir Lumley Robinson, 2nd Bt**, d. 1684, which formerly stood here, is now in the triforium. Buried in the south aisle; his widow **Anne**, d. 1690, daughter of John Laurence (q.v.), and secondly the wife of William Foulis, afterwards a Baronet, is also buried in the Abbey.

Close by is the monument by *F. Bird* to **Dr Thomas Sprat, FRS**, b. 1635, d. 1713, Dean of Westminster (1683–1713), and Bishop of Rochester. Sprat was not only an original Fellow of the Royal Society but the author of the first printed account of the Society's foundation, objects, and achievements. Dr John Freind (q.v.) erected this monument which was moved from St Nicholas's Chapel to make room for the Northumberland monument. Dean Sprat was buried in that chapel, and beside him also lies his son **Thomas Sprat**, d. 1720, Archdeacon of Rochester, Canon of Westminster, Rochester, and Winchester. Archdeacon Sprat is commemorated on his father's monument.

Joseph Wilcocks, b. 1673, d. 1756, Dean of Westminster (1731–56) and Bishop of Rochester for twenty-five years, during which extensive repairs to the Abbey's fabric were carried out, and the western towers built. The Dean was so proud of the towers that he caused a representation of them to be placed upon his monument, and chose his grave beneath the south-west tower. Sculptor: *Sir H. Cheere*.

A monument with a bust, by *H. Weekes*, of **William Buckland, FRS**, b. 1784, d. 1856; Dean of Westminster (1845–56), and a noted eccentric. He was one of the best geologists of his day and twice President of the Geological Society. While Dean he initiated a programme of stone restoration and used his scientific expertise to devise a more effective system of drains for the precincts. Buried at Islip, Oxon.

John Ireland, b. 1761, d. 1842; Dean of Westminster (1816–42); founder of the theological professorship and the Ireland Scholarships at Oxford. Bust by *J. Ternouth*. He officiated at the coronations of George IV and William IV but was too infirm to attend that of Queen Victoria. Buried in the south transept.

Zachary Pearce, b. 1690, d. 1774, Dean of Westminster (1756) and Bishop of Rochester. Pearce was a Queen's Scholar at Westminster School and rector of St Martin-in-the-Fields during the building of the present church. He resigned the deanery in 1768 and bequeathed his books to the Chapter Library. Buried at Bromley, Kent. Monument with bust by *W. Tyler*, executed about 1777. Inscription by Dean Thomas.

Major-General James Fleming, b. 1682, d. 1751, and his friend **Lieutenant-General William Hargrave**, b. 1672, d. 1751, Governor of Gibraltar, are buried not far from the choir gates. Fleming had been wounded at Blenheim (1704) and distinguished himself later at Falkirk and Culloden (1746). They both have monuments by *L. F. Roubiliac* high up in adjacent windows. General Fleming's memorial has, like Field-Marshal Wade's, a portrait bust, emblems of war, and allegorical figures: at the base Hercules (Valour), using great Strength and with help from Minerva binds – rather oddly – her serpent (Wisdom), and a looking-glass (Prudence) to his club. On the Hargrave monument, in the next window east, the Christian theme of the resurrection from the dead, and the pagan Time and Eternity are combined. The General, casting away his shroud, rises from his tomb obedient to the call of the Last Trumpet. At the angel's blast the pyramid of Time collapses; Time with bedraggled wings breaks the dart of Death, who, losing his crown, falls headlong down.

Carola (*née* Harsnett), d. 1674, and **Ann** (*née* Filding), d. 1680, two of the wives of **Sir Samuel Morland**. He was Oliver Cromwell's secretary, writer of the *History of the Evangelical Churches of Piedmont*; inventor of the speaking-trumpet, and improver of the fire-engine. He has displayed his learning in the Hebrew, Greek, Ethiopic, and English inscriptions which commemorate his wives. Sculptor: *W. Stanton*.

Between Morland's wives' monuments is one, designed by *J. Gibbs* and executed by *J. M. Rysbrack*, to **John Smith, Esq.**, b. *c.* 1651, d. 1718, a Commissioner of Excise. An allegorical figure of a weeping female, her right hand on a medallion on which is a portrait bust, sits on a sarcophagus and clasps her head with grief. Smith's memorial is also that of his grandson the **Hon. John Burke**, b. 1716, d. 1719, buried in his grandfather's grave in the centre of the nave.

A tablet records the burial in the nave of **Sir William Temple, 1st Bt**, b. 1628, d. 1699, statesman, diplomat, man of letters, and Master of the Rolls in Ireland; and of his wife **Dorothy**, b. 1629, d. 1695, daughter of Sir Peter Osborne of Chicksands, Beds. Her love-letters to her husband are well known. Also buried and commemorated here are their daughter **Diana Temple**, b. 1665, d. 1679, and Temple's sister **Dame Martha Giffard**, b. *c.* 1638, d. 1722, widow of Sir Thomas Giffard, Bt (d. 1662), of Castle Jordan, Co. Meath. Lady Giffard is described in contemporary journals as having been 'maid, wife, and widow, in one day, her husband dying on their wedding day'.

Beneath Hargrave's monument is a joint memorial to two friends killed together at Sole Bay on 28 May 1672 in the third Dutch War: **Sir Charles Harbord**, aged thirty-two, son of the Surveyor-General to Charles II, and **Clement Cottrell**, aged twenty-two, son of the Master of the Ceremonies. Cottrell was a volunteer and Harbord the First Lieutenant of the *Royal James*, Lord Sandwich's flagship. The monument includes an interesting bas-relief of the last moments of the *Royal James*. To the right is a Dutch division and to the left the English flagship caught between a fireship and the Dutch Admiral's ship. The *Royal James* sank two fireships but was blown up by a third. Of Harbord the inscription says he '(though he swome well) neglected to Saue him selfe as some did, and out of perfect Loue of that Worthy Lord . . . Dyed with him'; and of Cottrell, that having boarded a Dutch ship and 'pulled downe the Ensigne of it with his owne hand', he returned unwounded to his ship and perished with it. Harbord's father, Sir Charles Harbord, put up this monument, and left 40 shillings annually to the poor of Westminster, as long as the memorial remained whole or undefaced in the Abbey church.

Sidney (Godolphin), 1st Earl of Godolphin, KG, b. 1645, d. 1712, High Treasurer of England. He held office under Charles II, James II, and William III, and was chief minister during Anne's reign. Burnet calls him 'the silentest and modestest man that was perhaps ever bred in a court', but though he spoke little his judgement was 'always to the purpose'. Buried in the aisle. A fine bust by *F. Bird*.

A small baroque cartouche in the window commemorates (**Mrs**) **Bridget Radley**, d. 1679, wife of Charles Radley, Gentleman Usher to Charles II.

Sir John Chardin, b. 1643, d. 1713, a French merchant, who became court jeweller to Charles II, and was sent by him as Minister Plenipotentiary to Holland. He published some volumes of travels describing his early adventures in the East. Sculptor: *Sir H. Cheere* (1746). Buried at Albany, New York.

Lieutenant-Colonel the Hon. Roger Townshend, d. 1759, aged twenty-eight; killed reconnoitring the French lines on the second expedition to Ticonderoga. This is a distinguished monument, designed by *R. Adam* (q.v.) and *L.-F. Breton* and executed by *B. and T. Carter II*. Two Pequot Indians support a sarcophagus on which is a bas-relief (executed by *J. Eckstein*)[1] The scene represents the fort, showing a skirmish between French and British, who are in classical armour. In the foreground is the death of Colonel Townshend.

Sir Palmes Fairborne, b. 1644, d. 1680. Killed defending Tangier, of which he was Governor, against the Moors. The monument, which was erected by his widow, has been cut down; according to Brayley it originally incorporated a bas-relief of 'Moorish towns'. Designed and executed by *J. Bushnell*, with an inscription by Dryden. Buried at Tangier.

Major John André, b. 1751, d. 1780, Adjutant-General of the British forces in America. André was sent on a secret mission to General Benedict Arnold to negotiate the surrender of West Point to the British. However, he was captured within the American lines, in civilian dress, with incriminating papers about him, and taken before General Washington. In spite of every effort made to obtain his pardon, he was hanged as a spy on 2 October 1780, aged twenty-nine. Forty years later his remains were, at the Duke of York's request, brought from America, and buried with the funeral service, near this monument, which had been erected at the expense of George III. The chest in which his bones were enclosed is still in the triforium. On a sarcophagus

---

1   See *The Connoisseur* (July 1962), pp. 163–71.

Monument to Major John André

Britannia reclines mournfully and at her feet is a similarly sorrowful lion. On the bas-relief Washington is portrayed receiving the petition, in which André vainly implored for a soldier's death, and André is seen on the way to execution. The heads of both André and Washington have been often broken away. Designed by *R. Adam* (q.v.) and executed by *P. M. Van Gelder*.

In July 1950 a Roll of Honour to the members of the **Metropolitan Police Force** who lost their lives in the First and Second World Wars was unveiled by King George VI. Now in a case at the west entrance to the south choir aisle.

CENTRE OF NAVE

East of the Unknown Warrior's Grave is that of Dean Ryle (q.v.). Near him lies his successor, **William Foxley Norris, KCVO**, b. 1859, d. 1937, Dean of Westminster (1925–37). Officiated at the coronation of King George VI and Queen Elizabeth (1937).

Near by a stone in the floor commemorates **George Peabody**, b. 1795, d. 1869, the American philanthropist. His remains rested beneath this stone for a few days, and were afterwards reinterred in his native state of Massachusetts. His name is preserved in the houses built by his generosity for the London poor.

Gravestones record the burials of:

William Hartley Carnegie, b. 1859, d. 1936, Canon and Sub-dean of Westminster, and rector of St Margaret's (1913–36). Also his wife, **Mary** (*née* Endicott), d. 1957, whose first husband was Joseph Chamberlain (q.v.).

Richard Chenevix Trench, b. 1808, d. 1886, Dean of Westminster (1856–64), Archbishop of Dublin (1864–84), writer and philologist. Trench was the son of Richard Trench and the author Melesina Chenevix, 1786–1827. He instituted at Westminster evening services in the nave on Sundays. In 1857 at a meeting of the Philological Society a suggestion of his became a resolution which resulted in the scheme for *The Oxford English Dictionary*.

Two **icons**, before which votive lamps may be lit, are a reminder of the Abbey's primary role as a place of Christian worship. They are the work of the Russian painter *S. Federov* and depict the Mother of God *Hodegitria* ('she who points the Way') and Christ *Pantocrator* ('the all-ruling Lord'). Steel frames designed by *D. Buttress*, made by *R. Quinnell*. Dedicated on the Feast of the Annunciation 1994.

Two great mechanical engineers lie in the same grave: **Thomas Tompion**, b. 1638, d. 1713, and his pupil and later partner **George Graham, FRS**, b. 1673, d. 1751. Tompion, known as 'the father of English watchmakers', has been called 'the finest clockmaker of all time', his products possessing high precision as well as great beauty. He was made free of the Clockmakers' Company and in 1704 was Warden. Graham came from Quaker parents in Cumberland and was apprenticed in 1688 to a London clockmaker, Thomas Aske, being made free of the Clockmakers' Company in 1695 and Warden in 1722. Graham, who married Tompion's niece Elizabeth and succeeded to his business, was the maker of the most accurate astronomical instruments yet seen in Europe. His inventions included the temperature-compensated pendulum and the first planetarium.

North of Tompion and Graham lies **David Livingstone**, b. 1813, d. 1873, the African explorer and missionary. After

twice crossing the entire continent he died in the centre of Africa. His faithful servants carried his body through months of toil and danger to Zanzibar, whence it was shipped to England and interred in the Abbey on 18 April 1874, eleven months after his death.

The gravestone in the centre of the aisle to **Thomas Telford** (q.v.) was replaced in 1974 by a metal one given by the Institution of Civil Engineers. At his own request **Robert Stephenson, FRS**, b. 1803, d. 1859, civil engineer, was buried next to Telford beneath a brass, designed by *Sir G. G. Scott*, the effigy unusually portrayed in contemporary dress.

East of Telford are buried: **General the Hon. James Cholmondeley**, b. 1708, d. 1775, Governor of Chester Castle and Colonel of the Inniskilling Dragoons; and **General James Johnston**, b. *c.* 1731, d. 1797, Governor of Quebec and Colonel of the Inniskilling Dragoons.

At the feet of Stephenson are four fine Victorian brasses to distinguished architects of the Gothic Revival:

Sir Charles Barry, RA, FRS, b. 1795, d. 1860, architect. His chief work, the new Palace of Westminster ('the Houses of Parliament') is represented in plan on the brass and also, in elevation, the Victoria Tower. Although Barry was primarily a classicist, for the Palace he successfully followed the late Gothic style in England. Brass made by *Hardmans of Birmingham*.

Sir George Gilbert Scott, RA, b. 1811, d. 1878, architect; Surveyor of the Fabric of the Abbey (1849–78). Perhaps the foremost of the Gothic Revivalists; designer of many churches and secular buildings and restorer of many more. While Surveyor here he restored the Chapter House and drew up designs for the restoration of the north front. He studied the Abbey fabric deeply and wrote his valuable book *Gleanings from Westminster Abbey* (second edition 1863). Brass designed by *G. E. Street*, and executed by *Messrs Barkentin and Krall*. Scott's pupil **George Edmund Street, RA**, b. 1824, d. 1881, architect, is buried directly east. His chief work is the Royal Courts of Justice in the Strand. Brass designed by *G. F. Bodley* and executed by *Messrs Barkentin and Krall*.

John Loughborough Pearson, RA, b. 1817, d. 1897, architect; succeeded Scott as Surveyor of the Fabric. As Surveyor he practically rebuilt the north front, and refaced much of the exterior of the whole building, a work continued by his successors. Pearson's greatest original work is probably Truro Cathedral. Brass designed by *W. Caroë*.

North of Pearson is **Sir Herbert Baker, RA**, b. 1862, d. 1946, architect of Church House, on the south side of Dean's Yard. He designed the Government House at Pretoria, the Rhodes Memorial on Table Mountain, some of the government buildings at New Delhi, and many other buildings.

Admiral Thomas (Cochrane), 10th Earl of Dundonald, GCB, b. 1775, d. 1860, a naval commander of brilliance, is buried south of Scott. As Captain Lord Cochrane, RN, MP (for Westminster), he had been made a KB in 1809 and installed in 1812 as a supernumerary Knight until the death (January 1814) of Sir Thomas Trigge (q.v.). He had already exposed abuses at the Admiralty, and was placed on half-pay for further attacks; thereby he made enemies in high places. He was prosecuted and wrongfully convicted of fraud, imprisoned, lost his seat in Parliament and, regardless of its Statutes, was expelled from the Order of the Bath. His stall-plate was removed from Henry VII's Chapel and his banner kicked down the steps and he was expelled from the Royal Navy. His Westminster constituents immediately re-elected him, whereupon he was harassed by the government with fines and imprisonments (1814–16). His fines being paid by penny subscriptions, he accepted command of the Chilean Navy, and (1819–22) secured the independence of Chile and Peru from the Spanish; in the former country his memory is still honoured; as Admiral of the Brazilian fleet he secured the independence of Brazil (1823–5); Admiral of the Greek Navy (1827–8). Cochrane succeeded to the Dundonald earldom in 1831, was reinstated in the Royal Navy and promoted Rear-Admiral. He first used steam-power in warships and later (1843) urged the adoption of screw-propellers. Prince Albert became interested in Lord Dundonald's case and he was reinstated as a GCB (1847). Commander-in-Chief, North American Station (1848), and Admiral (1851).

South of Lord Dundonald are the graves of several famous for their connections with India: Sir James Outram (q.v.) and south of Outram, Lord Clyde. Lord Lawrence (q.v.) is to the east of Clyde.

Field-Marshall Colin Campbell (*né* M'Liver), **1st Baron Clyde, GCB**, b. 1792, d. 1863. He served as an Ensign under Sir John Moore (1808) and distinguished himself in the Peninsular War; was in India (1846–53), KCB (1849) after second Sikh War; in the Crimea as Major-General commanded the Highland Brigade the First Division; GCB (1855). Commander-in-Chief, India (1857–60). Remembered especially for his part in suppressing the Mutiny and in the Relief of Lucknow.

West of Clyde lies **Field-Marshall Sir George Pollock, 1st Bt. GCB**,. b. 1786, d. 1872. Pollock served in India for over forty years. His Afghan campaign, which culminated in the recapture of Kabul in 1842 was a model of mountain warfare. His funeral procession was led by ten warders of the Tower of London, of which he had become Constable in 1871.

Near by are buried **Freeman (Freeman-Thomas), 1st Marquess of Willingdon, GCSI, GCMG**, b. 1866, d. 1941; Viceroy of India (1931–6); Governor-General of Canada (1926–31); Lord Warden of the Cinque Ports (1936–41); and his widow **Marie**, b. 1875, d. 1960.

The early sixteenth-century hexagonal **pulpit** (formerly in Henry VII's Chapel) with linenfold panelling replaces a marble pulpit by Scott presented in 1862 and subsequently given to Belfast Cathedral (it has since been destroyed). There is a tradition that Archbishop Cranmer preached from it at the coronation of King Edward VI.

The ashes of two Prime Ministers are buried to the south of the nave altar:

The Rt Hon. Andrew Bonar Law, b. 1858, d. 1923, statesman and Prime Minister, Canadian by birth and Scottish by descent. Law entered Parliament first in 1900; Leader of the Conservative Opposition (1911–15); Colonial Secretary in first Coalition Government (1915); Chancellor of the Exchequer in Lloyd George's War Cabinet; Lord Privy Seal (1919–21); Prime Minister, 1922–3 (resigned).

The Rt Hon (Arthur) Neville Chamberlain, b. 1869, d. 1940, statesman and Prime Minister (1937–40). Only son of Joseph Chamberlain (q.v.) by his second wife. Entered Parliament in 1918; promoted in Baldwin's ministry. As

Prime Minister declared war on Nazi Germany in 1939. Resigned premiership in 1940.

The ashes of **Dr Eric Symes Abbott, KCVO**, b. 1906, d. 1983, Dean of Westminster (1959–74), are close by; Dean of King's College, London (1945–55); Chaplain to King George VI (1948–52) and to Queen Elizabeth II (1952–9); Warden of Keble College, Oxford (1956–60); Extra-Chaplain to Queen Elizabeth II from 1974. In 1965–6 the 900th anniversary of the Abbey's consecration was celebrated. For this, the theme of 'One People' was adopted and numerous events, exhibitions, and special services took place. An official history of the Abbey, entitled *A House of Kings*, edited by Canon Edward Carpenter (Dean 1974–85), was also published. The theme of 'One People' introduced by Dean Abbott, continued to develop under Dean Carpenter. The 900th anniversary also saw the introduction of the continuing practice of short prayers at every hour when there is no service taking place, to remind visitors that they are in a Christian church. Stone cut by *M. Harvey*.

In this area is buried **General William (Blakeney), 1st Baron Blakeney, KB**, b. 1672, d. 1761. Born in Co. Limerick, he served under the Duke of Marlborough and is reputed to have been the first to drill troops by signal of drums or colours. In 1745 he defeated a Jacobite assault on Stirling Castle, and in 1747 became Lieutenant-Governor of Minorca, where he was in effective command for ten years. Blakeney surrendered Minorca to the French in 1756, but his gallant defence of the island assured him of popular acclaim for the remainder of his life.

North of the nave altar are buried two Deans; **Dr Paul Fulcrand Delacour de Labilliere**, b. 1879, d. 1946, Dean of Westminster (1938–46); Suffragan Bishop of Knaresborough (1934–8). He took a deep interest in the history of the fabric and in the traditions of the Abbey, and he aimed to enhance its beauty and to increase the dignity of the services. The placing of an altar once more in the nave was due to Dean de Labilliere. During the Second World War the Dean remained on the spot despite the fact that in May 1941 much of the Deanery was destroyed by bombs, and his personal possessions were lost. He bore both these blows with very great courage. De Labilliere lived to see peace and that the Abbey church had emerged with very little damage. His wife **Ester**, d. 1954, is buried with him.

Dr Alan Campbell Don, KCVO, b. 1885, d. 1966, Dean of Westminster (1946–59), Provost of Dundee Cathedral (1921–31); Chaplain to Archbishop Lang of Canterbury (1931–41); Chaplain to King George VI (1937–46); Canon and Sub-dean of Westminster, rector of St Margaret's (1941–6). The greatest event of his decanate was the coronation of HM The Queen on 2 June 1953, and in that year was launched a great appeal for funds to save the Abbey fabric. In Dr Don's time also the Deanery was restored after bomb damage and the Nurses' Memorial Chapel and the Lower Islip Chapel were fitted up. The Dean himself gave the window (q.v.) as a thank-offering for peace and in memory of Abbot John Islip and his own predecessor Dean de Labilliere. Dr Don's wife **Muriel Gwenda** (née McConnel), d. 1963, is also buried here.

Immediately to the east a stone of green slate commemorates **Paul Adrien Maurice Dirac, FRS**, b. 1902, d. 1984, theoretical physicist and Lucasian Professor of Mathematics at Cambridge University. The stone depicts Dirac's Equation which describes the behaviour of the electron. Buried at Tallahassee, Florida. Unveiled November 1995; executed by *L. Cardozo*. Near by are buried three other great physicists:

East of the altar lies **Sir Joseph John Thomson, OM, PRS**, b. 1856, d. 1940, Master of Trinity College, Cambridge, the discoverer of what we now call 'electrons'. This discovery was announced in 1897, and from then modern atomic physics began. Thomson was awarded the Nobel Prize for Physics in 1906. His wife Rose, d. 1951, is buried with him. Near Thomson is buried **Ernest (Rutherford), 1st Baron Rutherford, OM, PRS**, b. 1871, d. 1937, Cavendish Professor of Experimental Physics, Cambridge University; Director of the Royal Society Mond Laboratory, Cambridge; he continued Thomson's work on atomic physics, and after much work on radioactivity moved to the study of the structure of the atom. He received the Nobel Prize for Chemistry in 1908. **William (Thomson), 1st Baron Kelvin, OM, PRS**, b. 1824, d. 1907, physicist and inventor. He is best known for his work, in combination with Joule, on the laws of thermodynamics, and for the invention of navigational and electrical measuring instruments.

Adjoining Kelvin is a memorial to **George Green**, b. 1793, d. 1841, mathematician and physicist. His father built the windmill at Sneinton, Notts. depicted on the stone. Green pioneered the application of mathematics to physical problems, and theorems derived from his work on electricity and magnetism are used in modern nuclear and solid state physics. Buried at Sneinton. Stone designed by *D. Buttress*; executed by *J. Hutchinson* and *D. Reid*. Unveiled July 1993.

To the north of Rutherford and Kelvin in the floor are metal plates, both redesigned by *J. P. Foster* and executed by *Messrs Morris Singer* in 1976 and given (as replacements for stone) by the Institution of Civil Engineers to commemorate: **Michael Faraday**, b. 1791, d. 1867, physicist and chemist. With early encouragement from Sir Humphry Davy, he investigated the composition of steel and the making of optical glass, but his greatest achievements were his studies in electricity and magnetism. Buried at Highgate Cemetery. Near to Faraday's metal plaque is one to **James Clerk Maxwell**, b. 1831, d. 1879, mathematician and physicist; Cavendish Professor of Physics, Cambridge University. Although greatly interested in optics and colour, Maxwell is most celebrated for his mathematical work on electromagnetic fields, which in turn led to modern radio-communication.

Against the choir screen, to the north of the entrance to the choir, is the monument to the man whose burial here has attracted to him the graves and memorials of these great scientists:

Sir Isaac Newton, PRS (1705–27), b. 1642, d. 1727, philosopher and mathematician. Newton is most commonly known for his conception of the law of universal gravitation, but his other discoveries and inventions in mathematics (e.g. the binomial theorem, differential and integral calculus), optics, mechanics, and astronomy place him in the very forefront of all scientists. His study and understanding of light, the invention of the reflecting telescope (1668), and his revelation in his *Principia* of the mathematical ordering of the universe are all represented on the monument. Newton's effigy loosely clad in classical costume, reclines on a sarcophagus with his elbow upon his great works labelled

 Monument to Sir Isaac Newton

'Divinity', 'Chronology', 'Opticks' (1704) and 'Philo. Prin. Math.' (*Philosophia Naturalis Principia Mathematica*, 1686–7). A bas-relief shows boys playing with instruments concerning Newton's mathematical and optical work (including the telescope and prism) and his activity as Master of the Mint. Newton's left hand points to two putti who hold a scroll on which is a mathematical diagram. Above on a globe in low relief are the signs of the Zodiac and of the Constellations; the path of the comet on 24 December 1680 as determined by Newton is also shown. The monument, finished in 1731, is masterly both in its execution by *J. M. Rysbrack* and in the design by *W. Kent*, who even employed mathematics in the crossed diagonals of limbs and folds of drapery. Before the funeral Newton's body lay in state in the Jerusalem Chamber, and his coffin was followed to its grave before the choir screen by most of the Fellows of the Royal Society; the Lord Chancellor, two dukes and three earls bore the pall. On Newton's gravestone are Latin words which may be translated: 'Here lies that which was mortal of Isaac Newton'.

Against the choir screen, to the south of the gates, is a monument also designed by *W. Kent* and executed by *J. M. Rysbrack*. It was erected (1733) in memory of **James (Stanhope), 1st Earl Stanhope**, b. 1673, d. 1721, soldier and statesman, and a distinguished commander in the War of the Spanish Succession. In 1708 he was made commander of the British forces in Catalonia. He took from the Spaniards the port of Mahon (Minorca) in 1708 and further defeated them at Almenara and Saragossa (both in 1710), but he was surprised and captured by the Duc de Vendôme. On his release and return to England he became a leader of the Whig Opposition; Chancellor of the Exchequer (1717) and created Viscount Stanhope of Mahon; Secretary of State (1718) and 1st Earl Stanhope. The monument was intended to match Newton's. Stanhope the general clad in Roman armour reclines on a sarcophagus with a baton in his right hand. Above him is Minerva seated on a military tent in which is Stanhope; the curtain is held back by a putto leaning on the Earl's achievement of arms. On the base are four medallions illustrating respectively the cavalry battle at Almenara, Queen Anne, the capture of Minorca and Sardinia, and lastly Victory laying flags at the Queen's feet after the Battle of Saragossa. Inscriptions to later Stanhopes have been added to the monument. **Lieutenant-Colonel the Hon. George Stanhope**, b. 1717, d. 1754, second son of the 1st Earl; fought the Jacobites at Falkirk and Culloden (both in 1746); took part in the War of the Austrian Succession, being present at Dettingen (1743) but was wounded at Laeffelt (1747). The **2nd–6th Earls Stanhope**. With the death of **James (Stanhope), 7th Earl Stanhope and 13th Earl of Chesterfield, KG**, b. 1880, d. 1967, statesman, both earldoms became extinct. An inscription stating that the last Lord Stanhope gave Chevening House to the nation was unveiled in 1975. All these Stanhopes are buried at Chevening, Kent.

The outer **choir screen** was designed by *E. Blore*, the Abbey Surveyor, and was put up in 1834, but the inner stonework dates from the thirteenth century. The repainting is recent.

In monastic times an altar dedicated to the Holy Cross stood in front of the screen. The present **Nave Altar**, which bears the same dedication, dates from 1968 and replaces an altar put in place after the bombing of the Abbey's east end in

1940. The altar candlesticks and standard candlesticks of gilded oak form part of the memorial to the Captain and crew of HMS *Barham* (see p. 23) and were presented in 1943. Designed by *Sir C. Peers*, executed by *R. Thompson*.

The stalls, kneeling desks, communion rails and other furniture associated with the altar were designed by *S. E. Dykes Bower* and put in place for the Abbey's 900th anniversary service in December 1965. The two kneeling desks were presented respectively by Dean Don (q.v.) in memory of his wife, and by the State of Queensland, Australia.

The lectern, donated by Mr and Mrs E. G. Burgh in memory of Sara Christenberry Davis, was made by *H. Lansdell* to a design of *J. P. Foster* and dedicated in May 1986.

The present **organ** has grown from one built by *Christopher Schrider* in 1727 for the coronation of George II and Queen Caroline, and moved to a position above the choir screen in 1730. This was rebuilt and enlarged by *William Hill and Sons* at various times since, notably in 1849, 1884, and 1909. It was completely rebuilt by *Harrison and Harrison* for the coronation of George VI in 1937. Further restoration and enlargement followed in 1983, 1987 and 1994.

The hanging cases, originally designed for the Hill organ by *J. L. Pearson* and erected in 1899, were restored and richly decorated in 1959. They contain the Great and Choir organs and part of the Pedal organ; the remainder of the Pedal and the Swell and Solo organs are in the south triforium.

Some of the pipework from earlier organs has been preserved and incorporated, after restoration and revoicing, including two stops made for the organ in use in 1694 by the celebrated builder *Bernhard Schmidt* ('Father Smith') – the 8 ft Stopped Diapason and 4 ft Nason on the Choir. The organ has five manuals and pedals; there are a hundred and six speaking stops, twenty-five couplers, and sixty-nine pistons.

A chamber organ by *K. Tickell* for use in the performance of pre-nineteenth-century music was dedicated in 1994.

NORTH-WEST OR BELFRY TOWER

This spot with the monuments of Fox, Tierney, and others was called by Dean Stanley 'the Whigs' Corner'.[1] Since Stanley's time great socialist as well as Liberal statesmen and politicians have been buried or commemorated in the nave near by and in the north aisle.

In the centre is a large monument to **Captain James Montagu**, b. 1752, d. 1794, who was killed while commanding the *Montagu* in the battle off Brest under Admiral Lord Howe. The monument (1798–1804) by *J. Flaxman*, formerly stood in the north aisle in the next bay east.

George (Howe), 3rd Viscount Howe, b. 1725, d. 1758, elder brother of Admiral Richard (Howe), 1st Earl Howe (1726–99). He was killed on the first expedition to Ticonderoga in north America. Wolfe called him 'the noblest Englishman that has appeared in my time, and the best soldier in the British army'. The monument designed by *J. Stuart* and sculpted by *P. Scheemakers* was put up by the Province of Massachusetts. Buried in St Peter's, Albany, New York.

1 A. P. Stanley, *Historical Memorials of Westminster Abbey* (Eighth edition), p. 245.

Sir James Mackintosh, b. 1765, d. 1832, philosopher and jurist. He devoted himself during his parliamentary career to the improvement of the Penal Code. Buried at Hampstead. Monument (1855) with portrait bust by *W. Theed, Jun.*

George Tierney, b. 1761, d. 1830, Whig statesman, notable for his opposition to Pitt, with whom he fought a duel in 1798. A tablet, with portrait bust by *R. Westmacott, Jun.*, put up by his friends.

Above is a mural monument to **Lieutenant-Colonel the Hon. George Augustus Frederick Lake** b. 1781, d. 1808. He fell at the head of his *Grenadiers* storming the heights of Roliça (Portugal) – Wellington's first victory in the Peninsular War. He had fought in India under his father General Viscount Lake, and was wounded at Laswari. Sculptor: *J. Smith.*

Henry (Petty-Fitzmaurice), 3rd Marquess of Lansdowne, b. 1780, d. 1863; Home Secretary (1827), and Leader of the Opposition on Peel's death. He was actively associated with the Whig Party, and took part in all its leading measures, such as the abolition of slavery, and the repeal of the Penal Laws. Portrait bust by *Sir J. E. Boehm.* Buried at Bowood, Dorset.

Henry Vassal (Fox), 3rd Baron Holland, b. 1773, d. 1840, nephew of Charles James Fox. Statesman and writer, the centre of a notable literary circle at Holland House, Kensington. The monument represents the 'Prison House of Death'. Sculptor: *E. H. Baily.* Buried at Millbrook Church, near Ampthill, Beds.

John (Russell), Earl Russell, KG, b. 1792, d. 1878, third son of the 6th Duke of Bedford. Educated at Westminster School; Prime Minister 1842–52, and again on Palmerston's death in 1865; created Earl Russell 1861. In 1866, when his party was defeated on the Reform Bill, Russell resigned, and never again held office. Buried at Chenies, Bucks. Bust by Sir *J. E. Boehm.*

Lieutenant-Colonel Sir Richard Fletcher, b. 1768, d. 1813. Wellington's chief engineer, he constructed from his General's plans the lines at Torres Vedras in 1809 and afterwards directed the siege-works at Badajos. Killed at San Sebastian. The monument was erected by the Corps of Royal Engineers. Sculptor: *E. H. Baily.*

Above Fletcher's monument is one with naval emblems commemorating **Rear-Admiral Sir George Hope, KCB**, b. 1767, d. 1818, erected at the expense of several Captains of the Royal Navy, who served under him as Midshipmen. Admiral Hope is buried in the centre of the nave. Monument executed in 1820 by *P. Turnerelli.*

Joseph Chamberlain, b. 1836, d. 1914, statesman. Colonial Secretary under Lord Salisbury and Balfour. Chamberlain's name is associated with Tariff Reform and with the Imperialist movement, begun in the late nineteenth century under his auspices. Portrait bust by *J. Tweed.*

Zachary Macaulay, b. 1768, d. 1838, merchant; and father of Lord Macaulay. The inscription, by Sir James Stephen, records his work on the abolition of the slave-trade. Portrait bust by *H. Weekes* (1842).

Above a door leading to the tower stairs is commemorated:
Major-General Charles George Gordon, b. 1833, d. 1885. Earlier in his career he was known as 'Chinese Gordon' for his services in China, where he assisted in suppressing the Taiping Rebellion (1863–4), and received the Yellow Jacket and Peacock's Feather, denoting a Mandarin of the First Rank.

Gordon is now chiefly remembered for his service in Africa, where he finally became Governor of Khartoum. Slain there by the Mahdi's forces before the relief expedition arrived. Bronze bust (given in 1892 by the Royal Engineers) by *O. Ford.*

Major James Rennell, b. 1742, d. 1830, geographer, antiquary and author; Surveyor-General of Bengal 1764; FRS 1781; he published the first approximately correct map of India. Buried in the nave. Bust by *T. Hagbolt.*

Major the Hon. Charles Banks Stanhope, b. 1785, d. 1809, son of Charles, 3rd Earl Stanhope, by his second wife. He is commemorated by an inscription on a shield behind which are military emblems. Stanhope was a Major in the 50th Regiment of Foot and was killed at Corunna.

A monument by *P. Scheemakers* commemorates **Captain William Horneck**, b. *c.* 1685, d. 1746, son of Dr Anthony Horneck (q.v.) and military engineer (one of the earliest) and Director of the Royal Engineers; served under Marlborough. Standing figure of Britannia holding back drapery to disclose a portrait bust of Horneck on a medallion. The monument also includes engineering instruments as well as a putto with a model of a military fortification. Buried in the south transept with his father.

Dr Thomas Arnold, b. 1795, d. 1842. The celebrated Head Master of Rugby School (1828–42), classical scholar and writer; Regius Professor of History, Oxford University (1841); father of Matthew Arnold (q.v.). Bust (1896) by *Sir A. Gilbert* subscribed for by his old pupils. Buried at Rugby.

NORTH AISLE

At the western end, across the eastern bay of the belfry tower, now stands the memorial to the **Rt Hon. Charles James Fox**, b. 1749, d. 1806, statesman; younger son of Henry (Fox), 1st Baron Holland; opponent of the American War of Independence and Leader of the Whig Opposition to the Younger Pitt; Foreign Secretary (1806), but died before the passing (1807) of the Act abolishing the slave-trade. The fine monument by *Sir R. Westmacott* was erected by March 1823 and originally stood in the north transept 'against the wainscotting of the Choir, near the great north-east column'.[1] Fox, lying on a mattress is 'expiring in the arms of Liberty'; the likeness to Fox was considered excellent by Lord Holland. At Fox's feet is Peace 'regretting, in pensive resignation' the death of her champion; a Negro, kneeling at his feet, is thanking him for his labour on behalf of the abolition of the slave-trade. Buried in the north transept close to Pitt.

In a case near by is the **Roll of Honour of HMS *Barham*** sunk by a German U-boat off Sollum on the Libyan coast on 25 November 1941. It contains the names of those missing presumed killed and those who died of wounds. Presented to the Dean and Chapter on the fifth anniversary by (Mrs) Constance May Cooke, widow of Captain G. C. Cooke, RN, commander of the *Barham*. The U-boat commander, Hans Dietrich, Freiherr von Tiesenhausen, visited the Abbey in November 1981 to see the **Barham candlesticks** (see p. 22) and to pray at the nave altar.

A small monument in the window, previously standing where the Herries memorial now is, commemorates **Colonel**

---

1 Neale and Brayley, *History . . . of Saint Peter, Westminster,* vol. II, p. 302.

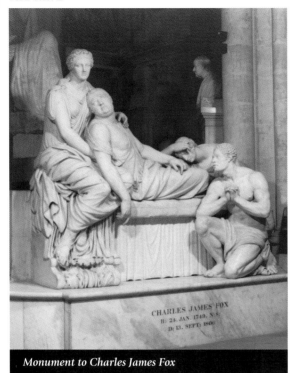

Monument to Charles James Fox

Churchill's wartime coalition (1940–5); after the 1945 general election, won by the Labour Party, he became Prime Minister until defeated in 1951; Leader of the Opposition (1951–5); created Earl (1955); KG (1956).

Sidney James (Webb), 1st Baron Passfield, b. 1859, d. 1947, socialist statesman and writer, President of the Board of Trade (1924) in first Labour Government; Secretary of State for Dominions (1929–30), and for Colonies (1929–31); created Baron (1929); voluminous writer on socialism. Also his wife **Beatrice**, b. 1858, d. 1943, ardent socialist and writer; the daughter of Richard Potter, sometime chairman of the Great Western Railway.

The Rt Hon. Ernest Bevin, PC, b. 1881, d. 1951, statesman; born of poor parents, he rose to become Foreign Secretary (1945–51), and Lord Privy Seal (1951); member of General Council of Trades Union Congress (1925–40); Labour MP (1940); Minister of Labour and National Service (1940–5); in 1946 as Foreign Secretary under Attlee he played an important role in setting up the Federal Republic of Germany.

Nearby stones in the floor commemorate: **The Rt Hon. James Ramsay MacDonald, PC, FRS**, b. 1866, d. 1937, three times Prime Minister, and writer; joined the newly founded Independent Labour Party (1894); Secretary of the Labour Party (1900–12); MP for Leicester (1906–18); Leader of the Parliamentary Party (1911–14); opposed Britain's entry into the First World War, and lost his Leicester seat (1918); MP and Leader of Opposition (1922); first socialist Prime Minister (1924) and again (1929–31); Prime Minister of National Coalition Government (1931–5); Lord President of the Council (1935–7). Buried near Lossiemouth, Scotland. Also **David (Lloyd George), 1st Earl Lloyd George, OM**, b. 1863, d. 1945, statesman and twice Prime Minister; entered Parliament as Liberal (1890); President of the Board of Trade (1905); Chancellor of the Exchequer (1908); First Minister of Munitions (1915); Secretary of State for War (1916); Prime Minister in the wartime Coalition Government (1916–18); Prime Minister again (1918–22) in Liberal-Conservative Coalition; Liberal Leader (1925–31), and (1931–5) leader of Independent Liberals. Buried by the River Dwyfor. Memorial by *J. Jones*, dedicated on 27 July 1970.

On the wall is a monument with an effigy reclining on a sarcophagus to **Anne, Dowager Countess of Clanricarde**, b. *c.* 1686, d. 1733, widow of Michael (Burke), 10th Earl of Clanricarde (d. 1726), and previously of Hugh Parker (d. 1713), and daughter of John Smith (q.v.). Buried in the centre of the nave near her father and young son.

A large mural monument commemorates **(Mrs) Martha Price**, b. 1640, d. 1678, wife of **Gervase Price**, d. 1687, Sergeant Trumpeter to Charles II. Both buried in the nave.

Beneath is a white marble tablet to the **6,873 Officers, Non-Commissioned Officers, and Men of the Royal Army Medical Corps**, who fell in the First World War. Field-Marshal HRH the Duke of Connaught unveiled the memorial on 13 July 1922, and presented a cheque for £10,000 to Dean Ryle for the Abbey Preservation Fund, the balance of the sum raised in memory of the fallen. Tablet designed and executed by *Wilcoxson*. An additional tablet commemorates those who died 1939–45. (For the R.A.M.C. Rolls of Honour, see p. 109 below.)

Dr John Woodward, b. 1665, d. 1728, Professor of Physic at Gresham College (1692); FRS (1693). Founder of the

John Davis, b. *c.* 1663, d. 1725, President of the Council of the island of St Christopher. Buried in the south aisle.

A mural monument commemorates **James Egerton**, b. 1677, d. 1687, the only son by his second wife, Elizabeth, of **Randolph Egerton**, d. 1681, Major-General of Horse to Charles I and Lieutenant-Colonel of the Horse Guards to Charles II. Father and son are buried side by side. A black marble stone to the **Hon. Penelope Egerton**, d. 1670, daughter of Robert, 2nd Viscount Kilmorey, and first wife of Randolph Egerton, is inset in the floor of the north-west tower, having been removed from the position now occupied by the memorial to:

Sir Henry Campbell-Bannerman, b. 1836, d. 1908, Prime Minister (1905–8). During his premiership self-government was granted to South Africa; his policy with regard to the reform of the House of Lords was embodied in the Parliament Act of 1911. Bronze bust under classical portico erected as a memorial by Parliament. Sculptor: *P. R. Montford*. Buried at Meigle, Scotland.

Major-General Stringer Lawrence, b. 1697, d. 1775, was a Marine under Admiral Wager, and afterwards served under General Wade in Flanders and Scotland. Appointed Major-General of the East India Company's forces in 1747, he helped by a brilliant series of campaigns to lay the foundations of the Indian empire. Upon the monument, put up by the Company, is a bas-relief of Trichinopoly, which Lawrence defended against the French from May 1753 to October 1754. Monument with portrait bust by *W. Tyler*. Buried near Exeter.

Stones cover the ashes of four great socialists: **Clement Richard (Attlee), 1st Earl Attlee, KG, OM, CH**, b. 1883, d. 1967, statesman and Prime Minister. Labour MP (1922); Leader of Labour Party (1935); held several offices in

Chair of Geology named after him at Cambridge University, and writer on geology and natural history. He had incessant controversies with Drs Mead and Freind (qq.v.), and is said to have fought a duel with Mead near the College of Physicians. The monument (*c.* 1730), by *P. Scheemakers*, comprises a seated figure holding a medallion on which is a portrait bust. Buried in the nave near Newton.

On the window-ledge in the next bay is the bust, by *W. Theed, Jun.*, of **Sir Charles Lyell**, b. 1797, d. 1875, President of the Geological Society (1835–6, 1849–50), and author of many works on geology. Buried in the nave.

Captain John Harvey, RN, b. 1740, d. 1794, and **Captain John Hutt, RN**, b. 1746, d. 1794, commanders respectively of the *Brunswick* and the *Queen* who fell off Brest in Admiral Howe's great victory of June 1794. This large monument, dated 1804 and by *J. Bacon, Jun.*, formerly stood near by but on the floor of the aisle, as a companion to that to Captain Montagu. By 1823 it had met with the disapproval of the Committee of Taste; it was deprived of its large base, on which was a relief of the battle, and the remainder was placed on the window-ledge. At present the monument consists of portrait busts on an urn, with figures of Fame and Britannia accompanied by a large lion.

Below are memorials to three sons of Sir William Twysden, 3rd Bt, of Roydon Hall, Kent; **Captain Heneage Twysden**, seventh son, d. 1709, Aide-de-Camp to the Duke of Argyll, was killed at Malplaquet (called on the monument by its other name – Blaregnies) in Hainault; **Lieutenant John Twysden, RN**, eighth son, d. 1707, was shipwrecked with Sir Clowdisley Shovell (q.v.); and **Captain Josiah Twysden**, ninth son, d. 1708, an officer in Sir Richard Temple's Regiment of Foot, was killed at the siege of Aigremont in Flanders. Among the Abbey muniments there is a reference to Josiah's death in a letter, dated 10 September 1708, from Charles Battely, Receiver-General of the Abbey. Battely was concerned about his own nephew, Charles Knipe, an Ensign in Temple's Regiment; he had heard from someone who had 'had a Letter from Ostend wch say's ye Regimt. he served in suffer'd much at ye taking ye Counterscarp. yt. Capt. Twisden was kill'd & Coll. Newton kill'd or wounded with several Subaltern's. Mr Twisden was a good friend to poor Charles & if Charles be Living He has Lost his Two best freind's.'

An oval tablet, behind which are emblems of war, commemorates yet another officer killed in the War of the Spanish Succession: **Colonel James Bingfield**,[1] d. 1706, Equerry to Prince George of Denmark and Aide-de-Camp to the Duke of Marlborough. The inscription states that while he was helping the duke to mount a fresh horse he 'had his Head fatally shott by a Cannon Ball, in ye Battell of Ramelies . . . ' Marlborough writing (24 March) to his wife says 'Poor Bingfield, holding my stirrup for me, and lifting me on horseback, was killed. I am told that he leaves his wife and mother in a poor condition.' In a formal dispatch the duke wrote: 'You may depend that Her Majesty will not fail to take care of poor Bingfield's widow.' The widow, Constance, put

up the monument in 1706. Buried at Beauvechain in Brabant.

A plain tablet commemorates **William Levinz**, b. *c.* 1712, d. 1765; MP for Notts (1734–47); a Commissioner for the Customs (1747), and Receiver-General and Cashier of the same (1763). Buried in the aisle. Sculptor: *R. Hayward.*

A monument consisting of an inscription with martial emblems commemorates **Robert Killigrew**, d. 1707, page to Charles II and **Brigadier-General** of the British forces in Spain. Killed at Almanza, where the British were defeated by the Spanish and French forces commanded by the Duke of Berwick, natural son of James II. Executed by *F. Bird*, and cut from a single piece of stone.

Thomas Banks, RA, b. 1735, d. 1805, sculptor. Apprenticed at the age of fifteen to William Barlow, sculptor, who lived near Scheemaker's studio, and there Banks studied after his day's work. This was very highly regarded by great contemporary artists as Reynolds, Westmacott, Flaxman, and others. There are five monuments by Banks in the Abbey, including that to Governor Loten (near by) and that to Sir Eyre Coote. Buried in Paddington churchyard.

A modern paving-stone marks the place of **Ben Jonson's** grave,[1] the ancient stone having been placed against the wall in 1821 to preserve the inscription. The poet was buried standing on his feet. One story says that, dying in great poverty, he begged '18 inches of square ground in Westminster Abbey' from Charles I. Another, that 'one day being railed by the Dean of Westminster about being buried in Poets' Corner, the poet is said to have replied: "I am too poor for that, and no one will lay out funeral charges upon me. No, sir, 6 feet long by 2 feet wide is too much for me: 2 feet by 2 feet will do for all I want." "You shall have it," said the Dean, and thus the conversation ended.'[2]

John Hunter, b. 1728, d. 1793, the celebrated surgeon and anatomist, lies under a brass near Ben Jonson's grave. In 1859 his remains were removed here from St Martin-in-the-Fields, by the Royal College of Surgeons, at the instigation of Frank Buckland (1826–80), son of Dean Buckland (q.v.). The brass consists of an inscription beneath a canopy and includes the symbols of the Evangelists.

General Sir Robert Thomas Wilson, b. 1777, d. 1849, Governor and Commander-in-Chief of Gibraltar; Colonel of the 15th Dragoons. Wilson was not, apparently, knighted in England; having obtained a royal licence to accept the Order of Maria Theresa, he had the rank of Knight Bachelor and the right to the appellation 'Sir'. His brass represents him as a medieval knight in armour. His wife **Dame Jemima** (*née* Belford), b. 1777, d. 1823, also appears on the brass, together with their seven sons and six daughters.

On the window-ledge is the monument executed in 1793 by *T. Banks* to **John Gideon Loten, FRS, FSA**, d. 1789, Governor of Batavia (Djakarta) in Java. It has been considerably reduced in size; in addition to recently repainted shields, the memorial consists of a standing figure of Generosity (attended by a lion) placing a medallion portrait on a column. On the base is incised almost all of Psalm 15 ('Lord, who shall dwell in Thy tabernacle . . . '). Loten died at Utrecht.

---

1 Dean Stanley, *Historical Memorials of Westminster Abbey* (Eighth edition), p. 222, notes that on the monument the name is given as 'Bringfield', but that Marlborough calls him Bingfield'. The quotation from the letter and despatch are both from Stanley.

---

1 His monument is in Poets' Corner, see p. 95.
2 See also Peter Cunningham, *Handbook of London* (1850, reprinted 1978), p. 536.

Adjoining is a tablet surmounted by flags and naval emblems to **Captain John Stewart, RN**, b. *c.* 1775, d. 1811; the son of William Stewart of Castlestewart, Wigtownshire; his principal exploit was in 1808 when, in command of a single ship, the frigate *Sea-Horse* (thirty-eight guns), he defeated a Turkish squadron, and captured the *Badere Zaffre* (fifty-two guns). Buried in the centre of the nave.

Below, a monument signed by *Grinling Gibbons* commemorates **Mary Beaufoy**, d. 1705, daughter of Sir Henry Beaufoy of Guys Cliff, Warwick. It consists of a figure kneeling on a sarcophagus, with weeping putti at each end, and hovering cherubs in the clouds above. On top of the pediment, supported on twisted columns, there was formerly an urn with flowers and foliage, apparently removed when the Loten monument was erected (*c.* 1793). Buried near by in the aisle.

In the aisle floor in front of the Beaufoy monument is commemorated **John Smeaton, FRS**, b. 1724, d. 1792, civil engineer. He designed numerous bridges, mills and steam engines, but is best remembered for the third Eddystone lighthouse (depicted on the stone) completed in 1759. Buried at Whitkirk, near Leeds. Purbeck stone with bronze inlay, designed by *D. Buttress*, executed by *D. Dewey*. Unveiled November 1994.

East of Mary Beaufoy is the oldest surviving monument in the nave; it commemorates (**Mrs**) **Jane Hill**, d. 1631, wife of Dr Othowell Hill, Chancellor of the diocese of Lincoln, and daughter of Thomas Stotevill. The monument consists of a kneeling effigy, a shrouded skeleton, mottoes, and arms on a lozenge and two shields. Next, a double monument on the wall commemorates:

William Morgan, b. *c.* 1666, d. 1684, second son of William Morgan of Tredegar (who first translated the Bible into Welsh), and **Thomas Mansell**, b. *c.* 1648, d. 1684. Monument perhaps by *W. Stanton*.[1]

Near by a gravestone covers the ashes of **Sir John Ninian Comper**, b. 1864, d. 1960, architect. Buried near the series of great stained-glass windows which he designed (see pp. 117 and 118).

In the window on a cartouche is an inscription to **Edward Herbert, Esq.**, b. *c.* 1693, d. 1715; he was of Swansea and late of Fryers, near Cardiff.

On the ledge is: **The Rt Hon. Spencer Perceval**, b. 1762, d. 1812, statesman and Prime Minister; MP (1796); Solicitor-General (1801); Attorney-General (1802–6); Chancellor of the Exchequer (1807); Prime Minister (1809–12). On 11 May 1812 in the lobby of the House of Commons Perceval was shot and mortally wounded by John Bellingham, a bankrupt man with a grievance which had unbalanced his mind. The monument, erected in 1816 by the Prince Regent and Parliament, is by *Sir R. Westmacott* and consists of the dead Prime Minister on a mattress, allegorical figures – Power, sitting mourning at his head, Truth and Temperance, standing at his feet – and a relief of the assassination behind the recumbent effigy. Buried at Charlton, near Greenwich.

Gilbert Thornburgh, d. 1677, Gentleman of the Cellar to Charles II; a baroque cartouche with arms and a Latin inscription recording his burial here. Beneath is a plain monument with arms recording the burial of **Edward**

Mansell, d. 1681, aged fifteen years; the eldest son of Sir Edward Mansell, 3rd Bt, of Margam, Glam. Sculptor: *W. Woodman, Sen.*

A fine mural monument with shields of arms commemorates the burials of two sons of Robert (Cholmondeley), 1st Viscount Cholmondeley: **The Hon. Robert Cholmondeley**, b. 1665, d. 1679, King's Scholar, Westminster School, and **The Hon. Richard Cholmondeley**, d. 1680, aged twelve years.

In 1871 James Townsend Oswald of Dunnikier, Fife, placed a brass to record here the burial of his great-grandfather **James Oswald**, b. 1715, d. 1769, successively Commissioner of the Navy, a Lord of the Treasury, and Vice-Treasurer of Ireland under George II and George III.

West of the doorway which led to the medieval sacristy is a memorial by *F. Bird* to **Vice-Admiral John Baker**, b. 1661, d. 1716; he was second in command to Sir Clowdisley Shovell, and brought the fleet back from the Scillies after Shovell's shipwreck. He commanded the Mediterranean fleet and died Vice-Admiral of the White, at Port Mahon, Minorca, of which island he was Governor; buried there. The somewhat perplexing monument consists of a column made into a naval trophy by the addition of cannon, bows and sterns of ships, with heads of beasts and monsters, and emblems from classical antiquity.

East of the doorway is another monument by *F. Bird* to **Admiral Henry Priestman**, d. 1712. He fought in the second and third Dutch Wars and latterly commanded a squadron; a Commissioner of the Navy, and under William III was a Commissioner for executing the office of Lord High Admiral. The monument comprises a portrait bust, nautical emblems and navigational instruments.

A monument with portrait bust commemorates **Dr Richard Mead**, b. 1673, d. 1754, physician and collector. One of the first-advocates of inoculation for smallpox and the fashionable doctor of his day, he attended Queen Anne, George II, and Newton; author of a work on poisons. Sculptor: *P. Scheemakers*. Buried in the Temple Church.

A stone in the floor covers the graves of **Dr Samuel Smith**, b. *c.* 1732, d. 1808, Prebendary of Westminster (1787–1808); Head Master of Westminster School (1764–88); also his first wife **Anna** (*née* Jackson), b. 1738, d. 1789; his second wife **Susannah** (*née* Pettingall), b. 1749, d. 1792; and son **John**, b. and d. 1792, buried in his mother's grave.

In the splay of the next window is a memorial to **Sir James Stewart Denham, Bt**. d. 1780, aged sixty-seven years; an urn, an inscription, and a shield of arms.

The Hon. Philip Carteret, b. 1692, d. 1711, a son of George (Carteret), 1st Baron Carteret of Haynes, Beds. This monument, by the Burgundian sculptor *the Chevalier Claude David*, is apparently one of the earliest representations of a King's (or Queen's) Scholar of Westminster School. Beneath the bust Time holds a scroll inscribed with Latin verses composed by Dr Robert Freind. Buried in the aisle.

A large monument to a seven-year-old boy **Edward Carteret**, b. 1670, d. 1677, son of Sir Edward Carteret (1620–83), Gentleman-Usher of the Black Rod and first Gentleman-Usher Daily-Waiter in Ordinary to Charles II. Buried in the aisle.

Another with a fine achievement of arms commemorates **Lieutenant-General Thomas (Livingston), 1st Viscount Teviot**, b. 1652?, d. 1711; born at Batavia in the Dutch East

1   The suggestion of Dr John Physick.

Indies; followed his father – a Colonel in the Dutch service – and reached the rank of Colonel in the Scots Brigade of the Dutch Army; under William of Orange he became (1690) Commander-in-Chief, Scotland.

Beneath the Teviot memorial is an inscription which is the remaining fragment of a monument to **Dame Elizabeth Carteret**, b. 1663, d. 1717, widow of Sir Philip Carteret, 2nd Bt (d. 1693), Seigneur of Saint-Ouen, and daughter of Sir Edward Carteret, Gentleman-Usher of the Black Rod. Also commemorated is her only son: **Sir Charles (de) Carteret**, b. 1679, d. 1715, Gentleman of the Privy Chamber to Queen Anne and High Bailiff of Jersey; baptised at St Margaret's, Westminster on 4 June 1679, Charles II and the Duke of Monmouth being his godfathers. At his death was extinguished 'the Eldest branch of the ancient family . . . of Carteret, Seigneurs of Saint Ouen in ye Island of Jersey'. This monument was originally sited where the memorial now is to Lord John Thynne, just inside the north choir aisle. Having become dilapidated it was removed by Lord John, representative of the Carterets, to Haynes, Beds. The inscription, now horizontal, was originally set diagonally across the monument.[1] Dame Elizabeth and Sir Charles (de) Carteret are buried near by.

Near by are buried: **Dr George Stradling**, b. c. 1622, d. 1668, divine; Prebendary of St Paul's (1660); Prebendary of Westminster (1663–88); youngest son of Sir John Stradling, 1st Baronet of St Donat's, Glam.; said to have been a Cornet of Horse but to have left the Army at the Restoration; Precentor (1671) and then Dean of Chichester (1672). Also his wife **Margaret** (*née* Salter), d. 1681.

A memorial to **Howard Walter (Florey), Baron Florey of Adelaide and Marston, OM**, b. 1898, d. 1968, records that he 'made penicillin available to mankind'. The black syenite stone, which came from a quarry at Black Hill, South Australia, was the gift of the government and people of the State of South Australia. Unveiled 2 November 1981. Designed by *J. Peters*, letters cut by *P. Trappe*.

Sir John Frederick William Herschel, 1st Bt, FRS, b. 1792, d. 1871, astronomer and mathematician, 'having explored the heavens, rests here near Newton'; he established the first observatory in the southern hemisphere. Near by a stone in the floor unveiled in 1954 commemorates his father: **Sir William Herschel, FRS**, b. 1738, d. 1822, astronomer and the 'father' of modern stellar astronomy. An immigrant from Hanover and at first an amateur astronomer, he took up telescope-making to further his private study and by making reflecting telescopes of far greater power he discovered (1781) the planet Uranus. For this achievement George III gave him the means to devote all his energies to science. Buried at Upton, near Slough, Berks. Designed by *S. E. Dykes Bower*.

Beside Sir J. F. Herschel is the actual grave of **Charles Darwin**, for whom see page 29.

In February 1983 a memorial containing the **Book of Remembrance of the Queen's Westminsters**, which records those who died in South Africa, 1900–2 and in the world wars of 1914–18 and 1939–45, was unveiled and now stands in this aisle. Memorial designed by *J. P. Foster*.

---

1 See plate in Ackermann, *History of the Abbey Church of St Peter's Westminster*, vol. II. facing p. 241.

NORTH CHOIR AISLE

On the north side a mural monument to **Robert (Constable), 3rd Viscount Dunbar**, b. c. 1651, d. 1714; also his second wife **Dorothy, Dowager Countess of Westmorland**, b. c. 1646, d. 1740, widow also of Charles (Fane), 3rd Earl of Westmorland and daughter of Robert (Brudenell), 2nd Earl of Cardigan. Both buried in the nave near the entrance to the choir.

Next is a monument, executed by *J. Bacon, Jun.*, erected 1815 to **Charles (Agar), 1st Earl of Normanton** and **Archbishop of Dublin**, b. 1736, d. 1809; educated at Westminster School; Bishop of Cloyne (1768–79); Archbishop of Cashel (1779–1801); Archbishop of Dublin (1801–9). This prelate-statesman was created Baron Somerton (1795), Viscount Somerton (1800), and finally Earl of Normanton (1806). The monument is remarkable in that it has a representation of Cashel Cathedral, which the Archbishop erected 'principally at his own expense'. The inscription relates also that under his 'direction and assistance' while he was bishop no fewer than seventeen churches and 'twenty-two glebe houses for the residence of his clergy were built'. The monument also serves as a memorial to **Welbore (Ellis), Baron Mendip**, d. 1802, in whose grave in the north transept the Archbishop was buried. His widow **Jane** (*née* Benson), **Dowager Countess of Normanton**, d. 1826, is also buried there.

A baroque cartouche commemorates **Charles Williams**, d. 1720, aged eighty-seven years; he was of Caerleon, Mon.

Beneath is a plain black marble monument to **Dr Peter Heylyn**, b. 1600, d. 1662, divine and historian, author of a *Life of Archbishop Laud*, whose chaplain he was. Appointed Prebendary of Westminster in 1631. Later became Sub-dean and spoke against Dean Williams from the Abbey pulpit. After Williams's imprisonment he became the supreme authority in the Abbey and superintended the repairs of the fabric. During the Civil War he was stripped of his property and obliged to hide himself; he returned to his post at the Restoration, and died two years afterwards. In accordance with a dream he had before his last sickness, he was buried close to, or beneath, the Sub-dean's stall. In the dream Charles I had stood before him, and said: 'Peter, I will have you buried under your own seat in church, for you are rarely seen but there or at your study.'

A worn stone in the floor covers the grave of **Walter Mortimore**, d. 1684, aged thirty-seven. The arms carved on the stone are those of the medieval baronial family of Mortimer.

A brass on the floor marks the grave of **Howel Holland Edwards**, b. 1762, d. 1846, Canon of Westminster (1803–46), and rector of St John the Evangelist, Westminster (1806–32); Prebendary of St Asaph (1799). Also his wife **Caroline**, b. 1762, d. 1834, daughter of Robert Palmer of Hurst, Berks.

Two of the greatest organists of the Abbey, Purcell and Blow, were buried in this aisle because the organ once stood above it. This has resulted in the burial or commemoration near by of a number of great British musicians.

A plain stone in the floor was unveiled in June 1972 in memory of **Sir Edward Elgar**, OM, b. 1857, d. 1934, musician and composer. Among his best known works are

North and South Choir Aisles and Choir

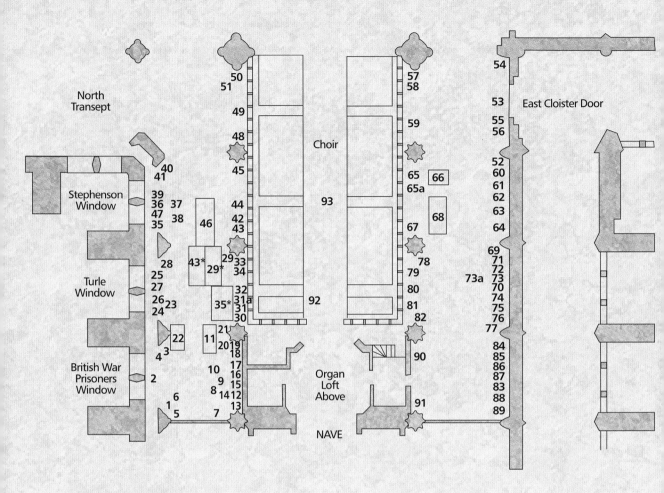

North Transept

Stephenson Window

Turle Window

British War Prisoners Window

Choir

Organ Loft Above

NAVE

East Cloister Door

1 Dunbar	24 Sutton	47 Watt	70 Methuen
2 Normanton and Mendip	25 Staunton	48 James	71 Knipe
	26 Prideaux and Bassett	49 Hesketh	72 Knipe
3 Williams		50 Forster	73 Wesley
4 Heylyn	27 Le Neve	51 Buxton	73a Charles
5 Mortimore	28 West	52 Confessor's Shield	74 Stepney
6 Edwards	29 Purcell	53 Harrison	75 Watts
7 Elgar	30 Plenderleath	54 Annandale and Johnstone	76 Chester
8 Vaughan Williams	31 Wilberforce		77 Lyte
9 Howells	31a Clarkson	55 Wemyss	78 Kendall
10 Stanford	32 Kingsale	56 Dalrymple	79 Paoli
11 Bennett	33 Bryan	57 Bell	80 Owen
12 Thynne	34 Raffles	58 Thynne	81 Tyndale
13 Darwin	35 Croft	59 Richardson	82 Trigge
14 Wallace	36 Blow	60 Blake	83 Churchill
15 Lister	37 Boult	61 Kneller	84 Creed
16 Adams	38 Walton	62 Shovell	85 Bingham
17 Stokes	39 Burney	63 Clive	86 Creed
18 Joule	40 Sausmarez	64 Wragg	87 Folkes
19 Hooker	41 Holy Roman Empire Shield	65 Norton, Freke and Austin	88 Julius
20 Ramsay			89 Strode
21 Duppa	42 Gibbons	65a Dimbleby	90 Thynne
22 Milman	43 Arnold	66 Coward	91 Barnett
23 Britten	44 Chamberlen	67 Gethin	92 Duckworth
	45 Balfe	68 Thorndike	93 Carey
	46 Monk	69 Burney	

The Enigma Variations and the oratorio *The Dream of Gerontius*. Buried at Little Malvern, Worcs.

Small stones near by cover the ashes of **Ralph Vaughan Williams, OM**, b. 1872, d. 1958, musician and composer and **Herbert Norman Howells, CH, CBE, D Mus**., b. 1892, d. 1983, musician and composer.

Beneath gravestones in this aisle also lie: **Sir Charles Villiers Stanford**, b. 1852, d. 1924, musician, Professor of Music at Cambridge University; composer of church music; and **Sir William Sterndale Bennett**, b. 1816, d. 1875, Professor of Music at Cambridge University, Principal of the Royal Academy of Music, London (1866).

On the south side of this aisle at the west end is the monument of white and red veined marble with a white marble effigy of **Lord John Thynne**, b. 1798, d. 1881, third son of the 2nd Marquess of Bath. Canon of Westminster for forty-nine years and Sub-dean for forty-six years. The form of the monument with a recumbent effigy is misleading, for Lord John is buried at Haynes, Beds, Sculptor: *H. H. Armstead*.

Above and to the east of this monument the wall has been covered with medallions commemorating great scientists. At the west end is a bronze head by *Sir J. E. Boehm* (1888) to **Charles Robert Darwin, FRS**, b. 1809, d. 1882, naturalist, famous as the author of *The Origin of Species* (1859), in which the theory of evolution by 'natural selection' was published. Buried in the north aisle of the nave not far from Newton.

Alfred Russel Wallace, OM, FRS, b. 1823, d. 1913, naturalist; independently of Darwin he formulated a theory of evolution by natural selection or 'survival of the fittest', and in 1858 he and Darwin publicly announced it in a joint paper to the Linnean Society. Portrait bust on white marble medallion by *A. Bruce Joy*.

Next to Wallace's memorial is one to **Joseph (Lister), 1st Baron Lister, OM, FRS**, b. 1827, d. 1912, surgeon, the pioneer of antiseptic treatment and particularly of the prevention of death resulting from an operation. Portrait bust on white marble medallion by *Sir T. Brock*. Buried at Hampstead.

Another white marble bust on a medallion next to Lister commemorates **John Couch Adams, FRS**, b. 1819, d. 1892, mathematician and astronomer. Whereas Sir William Herschel had discovered Uranus by telescope, Adams predicted (1845) the existence of another planet (Neptune) by calculations based on the variations in the movement of Uranus. Sculptor: *A. Bruce Joy*.

Sir George Gabriel Stokes, 1st Bt, PRS, b. 1819, d. 1903, mathematician. Stokes (like Newton) was Lucasian Professor of Mathematics, MP for Cambridge (but also like Newton, never spoke in the House), and was PRS (1885–90). Bronze bust by *Sir W. H. Thornycroft*.

Beneath the medallion to Stokes is a square white marble tablet to **James Prescott Joule, FRS**, b. 1818, d. 1889, physicist. He established the Law of Conservation of Energy and determined the mechanical equivalent of heat. Buried at Sale, Ches.

A medallion portrait bust in white marble by *F. Bowcher* commemorates **Sir Joseph Dalton Hooker, OM, GCSI, PRS**, b. 1817, d. 1911, botanist, and close friend of Darwin; Director of Kew Gardens (1865–85); he published the *Flora* of Antarctica, New Zealand, and Tasmania, and spent forty

years studying the botany of British India. Buried at Kew, Surrey.

In 1922 a medallion portrait was placed beneath Hooker's in memory of **Sir William Ramsay, KCB, FRS**, b. 1852, d. 1916, chemist; he discovered, together with Lord Rayleigh (q.v.), the gas argon, and himself isolated helium, neon, krypton, and xenon. Bronze bust by *C. L. Hartwell*.

A monument on a column near by commemorates **Sir Thomas Duppa**, d. 1694, who served Charles II, when Prince of Wales, and was rewarded, after the Restoration, by the post of Gentleman-Usher of the Black Rod. He was probably the son of John Duppa of Eardisley, Hereford, and nephew of Charles's tutor, Bishop Duppa; the inscription says that the bishop first introduced him at court. Buried in this aisle.

A stone in the floor, inlaid with brass letters marks the grave of three young children of Henry Hart **Milman**, Canon of Westminster and rector of St Margaret's (1835–49), Dean of St Paul's (1849–68); **Augusta Frances**, d. 1839, aged nine years; **Louisa Harriet**, d. 1842, aged fourteen years; and **Charles Louis**, d. 1849, aged three years.

Eastward lies a small stone to **Benjamin (Britten), OM, CH, Baron Britten of Aldeburgh**, b. 1913, d. 1976, musician and composer. The first London performance of his *War Requiem* was given in the Abbey in 1962. Buried at Aldeburgh, Suffolk.

On the window-ledge to the north is a monument by *Sir F. Chantrey* to **Evelyn Levett Sutton**, b. 1777, d. 1835, Canon of Westminster, rector of High Halden, and vicar of St Peter's in Thanet. Erected by his widow.

Also on the ledge is another monument (1824) by *Sir F. Chantrey* to **Sir George Leonard Staunton, Bt**, b. 1737, d. 1801, diplomat. One of the commissioners who concluded the treaty with Tippoo Sahib in 1784, and was rewarded with a baronetcy. He went as secretary on the first British embassy to China, and wrote an account of it. Buried in this aisle.

The monument to **Sir Edmund Prideaux, 5th Bt**, b. 1675, d. 1729, of Netherton, Devon, and his widow **Dame Anne**, d. 1741, daughter of Philip Hawkins, was executed by *Sir H. Cheere*. Beneath an oval medallion with portrait busts two weeping putti stand on a sarcophagus on either side of 'an expiring lamp'. Both are buried in the middle aisle, apparently of the nave. The inscription on the sarcophagus states that the monument was erected by their daughter **Anne**, the wife of John Pendarves Bassett of Tehidy, Cornwall. An additional inscription on the base constitutes a memorial to **Anne Bassett**, d. 1762, her husband **John Pendarves Bassett**, d. 1739, and their son **John Prideaux Bassett**, b. 1740, d. 1756, all three being buried at Illogan, Cornwall.

A handsome monument commemorates **Captain Richard le Neve, RN**, b. c. 1646, d. 1673, commander of the frigate *Edgar*, who was killed having 'signaliz'd his valour to admiration in that sharp engagement with the Hollanders' on 11 August 1673. Buried here 'under the organ loft'.

Eastward is the monument, with a fine portrait bust by *J. Wilton*, of **Vice-Admiral Temple West**, b. 1713, d. 1757, Admiral Balchen's son-in-law, who distinguished himself as Captain of Sir Peter Warren's ship in the victory obtained over the French on 3 May 1747, and again as Rear-Admiral in the battle off Minorca, 20 May 1756. Monument erected by his widow in 1761.

Monument to Henry Purcell

On the south side of the aisle against a column is a cartouche with a lamp above and a shield beneath in memory of **Henry Purcell**, b. *c.* 1659, d. 1695, great composer and musician, who is buried here; Organist of Westminster Abbey (1679–95), and at the Chapel Royal (1682–95). He appears to have been the son of Henry Purcell, a lay vicar of the Abbey and Gentleman of the Chapel Royal. Blow, recognising Purcell's greatness, resigned his two posts as organist to the younger man. During his fifteen years as organist at the Abbey Purcell arranged and composed music for or sung at many State ceremonies including the marriage of the future Queen Anne (1683) and the coronations of James II (1685) and of William III and Mary II (1689). He died aged thirty-six and was buried in this aisle beneath the organ loft, and 'dirges' which he had composed for Queen Mary's funeral (1695) were 'played by trumpets and other musick'.[1] His wife **Frances**, d. 1706, was buried near her husband's grave. The epitaph, which used to be ascribed to Dryden may, in fact, have been composed by Lady Elizabeth Dryden, the poet's wife, or by her sister-in-law Dame Annabella Howard, who erected the monument.

A small monument, by *J. Bacon, Jun.*, commemorates **John Plenderleath**, d. 1811, aged twenty-eight, at Coimbra in

---

1   Carpenter (ed.), *A House of Kings*, p. 426; quoting *The Flying Post* (for 26 November 1695).

Portugal of typhus, while serving as a physician in Wellington's army.

William Wilberforce, b. 1759, d. 1833, the philanthropist. He 'removed from England the guilt of the African slave trade and prepared the way for the abolition of slavery in every colony in the Empire'. Carried to his grave in the north transept by the Peers and Commons of England with the Lord Chancellor and the Speaker at their head. A seated figure on a pedestal executed by *S. Joseph* (1840).

A posthumous biography of Wilberforce by his sons failed to give due credit to another anti-slavery campaigner, **Thomas Clarkson**, b. 1760, d. 1864, now commemorated by a stone at the foot of the de Courcy monument. Clarkson adopted the cause while at Cambridge and threw aside a promising career in the Church to become the architect of a national campaign to abolish the slave trade. He enlisted Wilberforce to wage the battle in Parliament and the two men worked closely together for twenty years. In old age Clarkson was revered as the father of anti-slavery throughout the world. Buried at Playford near Ipswich, Suffolk. Memorial executed by the *Kindersley workshop*, Cambridge. Unveiled September 1996.

Almericus (de Courcy), 1st Baron Kingsale, b. 1665, d. 1720, a favourite of Charles II and James II, and commander of a troop of horse under the latter. It was this peer who seems first to have asserted the alleged 'de Courcy privilege' of remaining covered in the presence of royalty. By wearing his hat in the presence of William III he attracted the king's attention, and explained to the king that he was asserting the privilege of his family 'granted to John de Courcy, Earl of Ulster, and his heirs, by John, king of England'. There does not, however, appear to be any basis for this claim.[1] His widow, **Ann**, erected the monument: both buried in this aisle.

A tablet above to a young Guardsman, **Captain George Bryan**, who fell fighting under Wellington at Talavera, Spain on 28 July 1809, and is buried in the garden of the convent of St Jeronimo there. Monument executed by *J. Bacon, Jun.*

Sir Stamford Raffles, b. 1781, d. 1826, Lieutenant-Governor during the period that Java was under British rule (1811–16), and the founder of the colony and city of Singapore on 29 January 1819. He was the first President of the Zoological Society of London. Seated figure by *Sir F. Chantrey* (1832). Buried at St Mary's, Hendon.

William Croft, b. 1677, d. 1727, composer, Organist of the Chapel Royal (1704–27). Blow's pupil and successor as Organist of Westminster Abbey (1708–27). The end of the Latin inscription may be translated as follows: 'He emigrated to the heavenly choir with that concert of angels for which he was better fitted, adding his Hallelujah.' Croft's setting of the Burial Sentences is often sung at Abbey funerals. Monument with fine portrait bust. Buried in the bay eastward near Wilberforce's monument.

Dr John Blow, b. 1649, d. 1708, Organist of Westminster Abbey (1669–79 and 1695–1708). 'His own musical compositions, (especially his church musick) are a far nobler monument to his memory, than any other can be rais'd for him.' In 1679 he resigned his post as organist in favour of his pupil Henry Purcell, but resumed it again on Purcell's death

---

1   See *The Complete Peerage*, vol. VII, p. 287n.

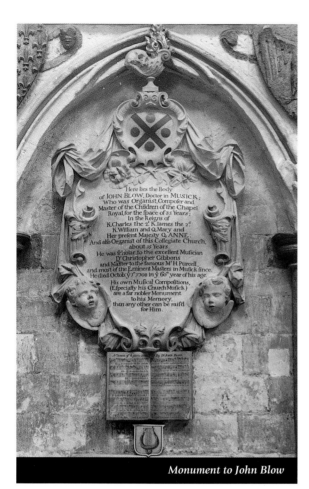

Monument to John Blow

himself alone as Captain of the *Nottingham* and did so again in 1747 under Admiral Anson at the first Battle of Finisterre. The monument includes a portrait bust on a medallion; one putto holds aside drapery to reveal the bust and another, on the right, wipes his weeping face. A bas-relief on the base illustrates a sea-battle, presumably that in which Sausmarez was killed. Buried at Plymouth.

Beneath the level of the window-ledge to the left of the Sausmarez monument is a **carved stone shield** with the arms of *an eagle displayed*. For this (representing the Holy Roman Empire) and the other carved and painted shields in the choir and nave aisles, see south choir aisle below (p. 32).

Dr Orlando Gibbons, b. 1583, d. 1625, composer and musician; Organist of Westminster Abbey (1623–5) and of the Chapel Royal (1604–25). Gibbons comes close to Purcell in distinction as the Abbey's greatest organist. He was commanded by Charles I to compose music to celebrate Henrietta Maria's reception at Canterbury (1625), and while there he died. Buried in Canterbury Cathedral. The black marble bust, a copy of that on his monument at Canterbury, was executed by *A. G. Walker* and presented in 1907 by C. T. D. Crews, on behalf of the Worshipful Company of Musicians, at a service of commemoration in the Abbey.

Above Gibbons's bust is a small tablet of white marble erected in memory of **Dr Samuel Arnold**, b. 1740, d. 1802, by his widow Mary Anne, daughter of Dr Archibald Napier. Arnold was Organist of Westminster Abbey (1793–1802); one of the Children of the Chapel Royal under Bernard Gates (q.v.) and Dr Nares; he became composer to Covent Garden Theatre in his twenty-third year; Organist at the Chapel Royal (1783–1802); sub-director of the commemoration of Handel in 1784; succeeded Benjamin Cooke (q.v.) as Abbey organist in 1793. Buried just north of Purcell.

Eastward is the monument to the physician **Dr Hugh Chamberlen, FRS**, b. 1664, d. 1728. It was erected in 1731 and is a fine joint work executed by *P. Scheemakers* and *L. Delvaux*. The Doctor reclines on a sarcophagus between standing figures representing Health (with serpent) and Longevity, of which Scheemakers carved Chamberlen's figure and probably that of Longevity, while Health is probably by Delvaux. A cherub descends blowing a trumpet and holding a wreath to crown the Doctor. Dean Atterbury composed the long Latin inscription. Edmund (Sheffield), 2nd Duke of Buckingham (q.v.) erected the monument.

To the left of Chamberlen is a small monument to **Michael William Balfe**, b. 1808, d. 1870, composer. His English operas included *The Bohemian Girl* and one based on Scott's *Talisman*. Buried at Kensal Green. Sculptor: *L.-A. Malempré*.

In the floor of the aisle a brass covers the grave of **Dr James Henry Monk**, b. 1784, d. 1856, Bishop of Gloucester and Bristol (1830–56); Canon of Westminster (1830–56); Fellow of Trinity College, Cambridge; Regius Professor of Greek (1808–22); Dean of Peterborough (1822).

On the window-ledge is a bronzed plaster bust of **James Watt**, b. 1736, d. 1819, civil engineer and craftsman; best known as the improver of the steam-engine. Buried at Handsworth near Birmingham. This small bust was given by the Institution of Mechanical Engineers to replace the large white marble monument by *Sir F. Chantrey*, formerly in

in 1695. Blow was Organist of the Chapel Royal, and Composer in Ordinary to James II. Beneath the tablet is a representation of the score of Blow's canon 'Gloria Patri' from his Service in G major.

Charles Burney, b. 1726, d. 1814, author of the celebrated *History of Music*. He was a close friend of Dr Johnson, and contributed many anecdotes of him to Boswell's *Life*. In 1789 he was appointed organist of Chelsea College, and lies in the burial-ground there. His daughter Fanny Burney (Mme D'Arblay) wrote the inscription. Monument by *S. Gahagan* unveiled in 1819.

Small floor-stones commemorate: **Sir William Walton, OM**, b. 1902, d. 1983, composer. His works included music for the Queen's coronation in 1953. Stone cut by *A. Ayres*. Buried in Italy. **Sir Adrian Cedric Boult, CH**, b. 1889, d. 1983, conductor. He was educated at Westminster School which now has a music centre named after him.

At the end of this aisle on the north side is a fine monument, by *Sir H. Cheere*, to **Captain Philip de Sausmarez, RN**, b. 1710, d. 1747. Sausmarez, a son of Matthew de Sausmarez of Guernsey,[1] was killed, fighting under Admiral Hawke, at the second Battle of Finisterre on 14 October 1747. Previously, (1740–44) he had served under Commodore Anson; in 1746 Sausmarez had distinguished

---

St Paul's Chapel. The Chantrey monument was removed in 1960 and is now at Heriot-Watt University, Edinburgh.[1]

Admiral Sir Edward Spragge, d. 1673, was buried 'in the north aisle', perhaps this choir aisle in company with Le Neve (q.v.) since they died in the same 'sharp engagement with the Hollanders' – the Battle of the Texel (11 August 1673). He was the son of Lichfield Spragge, Governor of Roscommon and Captain of Horse in Charles I's army; knighted on board his ship (*Triumph*) after Lowestoft (1665). He had become Admiral of the Blue by the time of the battles of Schooneveld (28 May and 4 June 1673) in both of which he fought. That August in his journal Spragge noted his hope that Cornelis Tromp would 'fall to my share in the Blue Squadron tomorrow'. But it was Spragge in fact who died: when his ship the *Royal Prince* was disabled he shifted his flag to the *St George* only for that ship to lose her main topmast. Spragge was drowned when the boat carrying him to a third ship was hit. His body was recovered eventually and buried in the Abbey on 23 September. Pepys knew Spragge and called him 'a merry man that sang a pleasant song pleasantly'.[2]

East of the Balfe and Chamberlen monuments is a small one with an urn on top and shields on either side to **Dame Mary James**, b. 1623, d. 1677, wife of Sir John James (who claimed descent from the ancient Lords of Haestricht in Holland); she was the daughter of Sir Robert Killigrew, Vice-Chamberlain to Queen Henrietta Maria. Buried near by.

Sir Thomas Hesketh, d. 1605, Attorney of the Court of Wards and Liveries in the reign of Elizabeth I. Monument with reclining figure under a canopy, painted and gilt, erected by **Juliana, Lady Hesketh**, d. 1629. A small figure of her, kneeling at a desk, was formerly in the centre niche at the base of the monument.

William Edward Forster, b. 1818, d. 1886, statesman and Chief Secretary for Ireland. Buried at Burley in Wharfedale. The memorial was unveiled by Lord Knutsford in 1888; Dean Bradley wrote the inscription. Sculptor: *H. R. Pinker*.

Sir Thomas Fowell Buxton, b. 1786, d. 1845, philanthropist, who worked for the abolition of the slave-trade. He also worked for the improvement of prison discipline and the suppression of suttee in India. Buried at Overstrand, Norfolk. Seated figure by *F. Thrupp*.

The **Roll of Honour of the Women's Voluntary Service 1939–45** is usually kept in a case in this aisle.

SOUTH CHOIR AISLE

The most ancient and important pieces of sculpture in this and the north choir aisle are the **painted shields** in the spandrels of the wall-arcade. Originally there were sixteen, eight on each side, and they reached as far west as Henry III's work extended, i.e. one bay west of the choir screen. Those which remain have been ascribed to (on the south side): Edward the Confessor; the King of England; the Count of Provence; Roger de Quincy, Earl of Winchester; Henry de Lacy, Earl of Lincoln; Richard, Earl of Cornwall; an Earl of Ross. On the north side: the Holy Roman Emperor; the King of France; Richard de Clare, Earl of Gloucester; Roger Bigod, Earl of Norfolk; Simon de Montfort, Earl of Leicester; John de

Warenne, Earl of Surrey; William de Forz, Count of Aumale. On the south side the shield of the King of Scots has disappeared and on the north that of the Bohuns, Earls of Hereford. The series was continued in the fourteenth-century nave by simply painting the shields on the walls, but remarkably the arms are those of families or individuals who were prominent in the thirteenth century, and no 'new' fourteenth-century families appear. Starting at the east and going westwards the carved shields can be seen to be arranged in descending order of rank. On the south side: St Edward, followed by two kings and five earls (or counts); on the north side the Emperor, followed by one king and six earls (or counts). The painted shields continued on each side with three earls (or counts), seven barons, and two barons of the Palatinate County of Chester. The surviving painted shields are (on the south): Ferrers, Earl of Derby; Longespée, Earl of Salisbury; Thweng; FitzWarin; Monhaut; Venables. On the north they are: Vere, Earl of Oxford; the Breton Earls of Richmond; Hastings; Mowbray; Ros; Balliol; Talbot. By tradition these shields are those of the men or families who were benefactors to the building in Henry III's reign. The rounded shape of the tops of the shields is an early form as opposed to the 'heater' or flat-iron shape of the later thirteenth century. It is clear that a definite scheme for the shields was drawn up, and, in the main, was adhered to, even when the building of the nave was continued in Abbot Litlyngton's time (1362–86). The presence of most, if not all, of the shields and the absence of others, points to the decade 1245–55 as the most likely time that such a scheme was made and even when the sculptured shields were set up.

An inscription within four quatrefoils above the east cloister door commemorates **Rear-Admiral John Harrison**, b. *c.* 1722, d. 1791; Captain of the *Namur*, under Admiral Pocock, in several battles against the French in the Seven Years War; also under Pocock he went to Havana (1762) and brought the Fleet and treasure home; upon his return he suffered a stroke which paralysed him; superannuated with rank of Rear-Admiral (1779). Buried in the south transept.

East of the door is a monument with achievement of arms to **Sophia, Marchioness of Annandale**, b. 1667, d. 1716, wife of William (Johnstone), 1st Marquess of Annandale, and daughter of John Fairholm of Craigie Hall. Buried in the south transept with her younger son **Lord William Johnstone**, b. *c.* 1697, d. 1721. Her son **James (Johnstone), 2nd Marquess of Annandale**, b. *c.* 1688, d. 1730, who erected the monument (designed by *J. Gibbs*), is buried in the north transept.

West of the cloister door is a tablet to **Anne Wemyss**, b. *c.* 1633, d. 1698, daughter of Dr Ludovick Wemyss (d. 1659), Prebendary of Westminster, by Jane, daughter of John Bargrave of Bifrons, Kent. Buried outside in the east cloister at the foot of the steps.

Beneath is a monument to **William Dalrymple**, Midshipman, RN, d. 1782, aged eighteen years; eldest son of Sir John Dalrymple, Bt, Baron of the Exchequer of Scotland; killed off the Virginian coast in the *Santa Margareta* during the capture of the French ship *Amazone*.

Dr Andrew Bell, b. 1753, d. 1832, Prebendary of Westminster (1819–32), inventor of the Madras scheme or monitorial system in education. Sculptor: *W. Behnes*.

William Thynne, d. 1585, Receiver of the Marches (1546); brother of Sir John Thynne. A monument of marble and

---

1   For more about the memorial and the damage done in erecting it, see p. 64.

2   *Diary*, 11 January 1666.

alabaster with a fine figure in armour, recumbent upon a rush mattress, put up by John Chamberleyn of Prestbury.

Sir Thomas Richardson, b. 1569, d. 1635, Speaker of the House of Commons (1621); Chief Justice of the Common Pleas (1626); refused to allow John Felton, Buckingham's assassin, to be put on the rack to induce him to confess, a decision which marks an epoch in criminal jurisprudence (1628); Chief Justice of the King's Bench (1631). He was known as 'the Jeering Judge'; when he condemned Prynne, Richardson is said to have remarked that 'he might have the *Book of Martyrs* to amuse him in prison'. Black marble monument with fine bronze bust of the judge by *H. Le Sueur* (1635).

A monument which formerly stood here is now in the triforium: **Sir John Burland**, b. 1724, d. 1776, Baron of the Exchequer. Buried in the aisle.

In 1945 a memorial, executed by *G. Ledward* was placed here to **Robert Blake**, b. 1599, d. 1657. **Admiral and General-at-Sea**. He was originally buried in Henry VII's Chapel but was exhumed pursuant to a Royal Warrant dated 9 September 1661 and buried in the churchyard north of the Abbey. Arguably the greatest naval commander of his age and one to whom Nelson considered himself inferior. A younger son of Humphrey Blake, gentleman, of Bridgwater, Somerset, died of fever on 17 August 1657 as his ship (*George*) was entering Plymouth harbour on return from Santa Cruz; MP for Bridgwater (1640; 1645); defended Bristol and Lyme Regis for Parliament; Lieutenant-Colonel in the Parliamentary Army; captured Taunton and was made Governor there; Admiral and General-at-Sea (1649); unsuccessfully blockaded Prince Rupert (q.v.) at Kinsale (1649), and pursued him to Portugal (1650), subsequently destroying many of the Prince's ships; reduced the Scillies and Jersey, both held by Royalists (1651). He was engaged (1652–3) in the first Dutch War, when he defeated Admirals Marten Tromp, De Witt, and De Ruyter. Blake destroyed the Tunisian corsair squadron at Porto Farina (1655) and the Spanish plate fleet from the West Indies at Santa Cruz in the Canaries (20 April 1657).

Beneath the window: **Sir Godfrey Kneller**, b. at Lübeck *c*. 1648, d. 1723, the great Court portrait-painter. Kneller chose a place in Twickenham church for his monument and designed it himself, but the spot selected was occupied by Alexander Pope's tablet to his father. Afterwards Kneller gave money and directions for the putting up of the monument by *J. M. Rysbrack* in the Abbey. It was erected at the west end of the north aisle of the nave – the place now occupied by Fox's monument. The verses are by Pope, who confessed them to be 'the worst thing he ever wrote in his life'. Buried at Twickenham. Kneller declared to Pope: 'By God, I will not be buried in Westminster . . . They do bury fools there.'

Beneath is the large monument by *Grinling Gibbons* to **Admiral Sir Clowdisley Shovell**, b. 1650, d. 1707, Rear-Admiral of England (1704) and Admiral of the Fleet (1705). Son of John Shovell, gentleman, of Cockthorpe, Norfolk. Shovell went to sea in 1664 with Admiral Sir Christopher Myngs (d. 1666), probably a relative, and then served with another probable kinsman Admiral Sir John Narbrough, whose widow he married (1691). Tradition has it that as a boy (in the second Dutch War) he carried dispatches in his mouth swimming under enemy fire. Captain of the *Sapphire* (1677); cruised against Barbary corsairs until 1686. Shovell

was knighted after Bantry Bay (1689); he distinguished himself as Rear-Admiral of the Red at Barfleur (1692) against the French; and assisted Rooke in the capture of Gibraltar and commanded the van at Malaga (1704); joint Commander-in-Chief of the Fleet with Peterborough (1705), and assisted him in the capture of Barcelona. Returning to England in 1707 Shovell's flagship struck the rocks off the Scilly Isles and broke up. The Admiral, still living, was thrown on shore in Porthellick Cove, where a woman, seeing his emerald finger-ring, killed him for it.[1] His body was later found, embalmed, and buried in this aisle on 22 December 1707.

Robert (Clive), 1st Baron Clive of Plassey, b. 1725, d. 1774, twice Governor of Bengal, one of the most famous of the East India Company's men. During his three visits to India, Clive helped to lay the foundations of the British Empire in India. Although a civilian and a clerk by training he got a commission in the Army and served under his friend Stringer Lawrence (q.v.) in the south of India and established his own reputation as a military commander on the expedition against Arcot. Six years later (1757) at Plassey in conjunction with Admiral Watson (q.v.) Clive defeated the Nawab of Bengal, and was made the first Governor of the province of Bengal. He returned to England in 1760 and was afterwards given an Irish peerage and made a KB (1764). In 1765 he became Governor of Bengal for the second time, but after a brief tenure of the office ill-health obliged him to come back to England. His conduct was severely criticized and, although he cleared himself, his mind became unbalanced and he committed suicide in 1774. The memorial was erected in 1919 by public subscription. Sculptor: *J. Tweed.*

Beneath Clive's memorial is one by *R. Hayward* (1779) to **William Wragg, Esq.**, d. 1777, of South Carolina, who out of loyalty felt compelled to leave his family and fortune and return to England. He was drowned when his ship was wrecked on the Dutch coast. Monument put up by his surviving sister.

On the north side of the aisle is a monument which **Dame Frances Norton**, d. 1731, widow successively of Sir George Norton (d. 1715) of Abbotts Leigh, Som., of the latter's cousin Colonel Ambrose Norton (d. 1723), and of William Jones, Esq., erected to her two sisters: **(Mrs) Elizabeth Freke**, b. *c*. 1650, d. 1714, wife of her kinsman Percy Freke, Esq., of West Bilney, Norfolk; and **(Mrs) Judith Austin**, d. 1716, widow of Robert Austin (or Austen), Esq., of Tenterden, Kent. The three sisters, who are all buried in the nave, were daughters of Ralph Freke, Esq., of Hannington, Wilts., and of Cecily, his wife, daughter of Sir Thomas Colepeper of Hollingbourne, Kent. Next is a monument to Lady Norton's daughter **Dame Grace Gethin**, d. 1697, aged twenty, wife of Sir Richard Gethin, 2nd Bt. After Dame Grace's death a book of devotions was published, purporting to be reflections noted down by her 'with a pencil at spare hours, or as she was dressing'; it was prefaced by a poem written in her honour by Congreve. The work, in fact, is a compilation from Bacon and others. An anniversary sermon is preached in her memory in the Abbey every Ash Wednesday. Buried at Hollingbourne, where there is a similar monument.

---

1   For details about the woman's deathbed confession of his murder and the fate of the ring, see *The Dictionary of National Biography.*

At low level is commemorated **Richard Dimbleby, CBE**, b. 1913, d. 1965, journalist and broadcaster. He provided memorable television commentaries for the coronation of HM The Queen in 1953 and for the funeral of Sir Winston Churchill (at St Paul's Cathedral) in 1965. Buried at Lynchmere, Sussex. Memorial designed by *D. Buttress*, bronze relief sculpted by *N. Dimbleby*. Unveiled November 1990.

A gravestone with inscription, executed by *A. Ayres*, covers the ashes of **Dame Sybil Thorndike, CH**, b. 1882, d. 1976, actress, and widow of Sir Lewis Casson, b. 1875, d. 1969. The inscription is based on the lines which J. B. Priestley composed in honour of Dame Sybil for her eightieth birthday. Specially adapted for her epitaph these appear to be the first verses so written and placed on an Abbey monument or grave since Tennyson's lines on Lord Stratford de Redcliffe (q.v.).

An adjacent floor-stone, unveiled 28 March 1984, commemorates **Sir Noel Coward**, b. 1899, d. 1973, actor and playwright. Buried in Jamaica. Stone cut by *R. Beyer*.

In the window is a tablet, executed by *S. Gahagan* with portrait bust (said to have been made from a 'likeness' by *Nollekens*) to **Dr Charles Burney, LLD, FRS**, b. 1757, d. 1817, Classical scholar and lexicographer; son of Dr Charles Burney (q.v.); Prebendary of Lincoln (1817); rector of St Paul's, Deptford, and of Cliffe, Kent. Buried at Deptford.

Near by is the monument, by *J. M. Rysbrack*, to **The Rt Hon. John Methuen**, b. *c.* 1650, d. 1706, diplomat; Lord Chancellor of Ireland (1697–1703); Master in Chancery (1685); MP for Devizes (1690); Envoy to Portugal (1691; 1702); as Ambassador Extraordinary to Portugal (1703) he concluded the 'Methuen (or Port Wine) Treaty'; died at Lisbon on 13 July 1706. His body was brought to England and buried in this aisle on 17 September 1708. Also his son: **The Rt Hon. Sir Paul Methuen, KB**, b. 1672, d. 1757, diplomat; Envoy to Portugal (1697–1705); Minister at Turin (1705); Ambassador to Portugal (1706–8); MP for Devizes (1708–10); MP for Brackley (1713–47); PC (1716); Ambassador to Spain and Morocco (1714); Lord of the Admiralty (1714–17); Comptroller of the Household (1720); an original Knight Companion of the Order of the Bath invested 27 May and installed 17 June 1725. Buried in this aisle.

Dr Thomas Knipe, b. *c.* 1639, d. 1711; Prebendary of Westminster (1707–11) and Head Master of Westminster School, in succession to Dr Busby (1695–1711). Captain of the King's Scholars (1656); Usher (1661) then Under Master of Westminster (1663–95). Also his two wives **Anne**, d. 1685, daughter of Devereux Wolseley of Ravenstone, Staffs., and **Alice**, d. 1723. All buried in the north cloister.

Also a memorial to two brothers apparently members of the same family: **Captain John Knipe**, d. 1798, aged twenty-one; a Captain in the 90th Regiment of Foot, he was killed at Gibraltar where, at the garrison, his brother officers erected a memorial; and **Captain Robert Knipe**, d. 1811, aged thirty-two, of the 14th Light Dragoons; mortally wounded at the Battle of Fuentes de Mora on 5 May 1811 in Portugal.

A tablet commemorates the brothers: **John Wesley**, b. 1703, d. 1791, and **Charles Wesley**, b. 1707, d. 1788. The elder, John, is the greatest member of that branch of the distinguished family, and the leader and founder of the Wesleyan Methodists. John Wesley is buried at the City Road Chapel-Yard. Charles Wesley was associated with his elder brother in the foundation of Methodism, but is celebrated in his own right as a hymn-writer. 'Jesu, lover of my soul',

'Rejoice, the Lord is King', 'Christ, the Lord, is risen today', 'Lo! He comes with clouds descending' are some of Charles Wesley's best-known hymns, and 'Hark! the herald-angels sing', perhaps the most familiar of all, is an adaptation from Charles's original 'Hark, how all the welkin rings'. Buried in Old Marylebone churchyard. Monument by *J. Adams-Acton*, put up by private subscription in 1876.

Beneath the Wesley memorial a tablet commemorates **Sebastian Charles**, b. 1932, d. 1989. Canon of Westminster (1978–89). Buried in this aisle. Tablet designed by *D. Buttress*, executed by *T. Metcalfe*, 1992.

George Stepney, b. 1663, d. 1707, diplomat and minor poet; educated at Westminster School and Trinity College, Cambridge. In the course of his diplomatic career he was an envoy to the courts of the Emperor (Vienna), the King of Poland, most of the Electoral Princes of Germany, the Frankfurt Congress (1696–7), the Landgrave of Hesse, and the States of Holland. Buried in this aisle.

Dr Isaac Watts, b. 1674, d. 1748, hymn-writer and Nonconformist divine. Dr Johnson called him 'one of the first authors that taught the Dissenters to court attention by the grace of language'. Among Watts's best-known hymns are: 'When I survey the wondrous Cross', 'Jesus shall reign where e'er the sun' and 'O God, our help in ages past'. Buried in Bunhill Fields. The monument, executed in 1779, by *T. Banks*, incorporates a figure of Dr Watts being inspired to write by a flying Muse.

Colonel Joseph Lemuel Chester, LLD, b. 1821, d. 1882, the distinguished American genealogist, who transcribed and edited with exhaustive notes *The Registers of Westminster Abbey.*[1] Tablet erected by the Dean and Chapter. Buried at Nunhead cemetery.

A tablet commemorates in this aisle yet another great hymn-writer: **Henry Francis Lyte**, b. 1793, d. 1847, with the first line of his best-known hymn: 'Abide with me: fast falls the eventide'. Unveiled 1947. Buried at the English cemetery, Nice.

On the north side is a monument to **James Kendall**, b. *c.* 1646, d. 1708; Governor of Barbados and a Commissioner of the Admiralty. Buried near by close to the grave of Sir Clowdisley Shovell.

Pasquale de Paoli, b. 1725, d. 1807, the champion of Corsican independence. Took refuge in England, where he died; buried in Corsica. Bust by *J. Flaxman*.

A large Elizabethan monument commemorates **Thomas Owen**, d. 1598, Justice of the Court of Common Pleas (1594–8); MP for Shrewsbury (1584–5).

In 1938 a memorial tablet was placed here to **William Tyndale**, b. 1494, d. 1536. He was executed at Vilvorde, Netherlands, for heresy, but his translation of the Bible into English, though incomplete, greatly influenced the translators of the 1611 Authorized Version for its substantial accuracy and fine literary style.

A monument by *J. Bacon, Jun.*, commemorates **General Sir Thomas Trigge, KB**, d. 1814, aged seventy-one; Lieutenant-General of the Ordnance. He began his military career as an Ensign in the 12th Regiment of Foot and was present at several battles in the Seven Years War: Colonel of the 44th Regiment; Lieutenant-Governor of Gibraltar. As Commander-in-Chief, West Indies he captured Surinam and

---

1　Harleian Society Publications, vol. X (1876) for 1875.

Murder of Thomas Thynne

various islands, and gained the KB.

Against the south wall is a monument by *Grinling Gibbons* to **Admiral George Churchill**, b. 1654, d. 1710, younger son of Sir Winston Churchill and brother of Marlborough; Lieutenant, RN (1672–4); joined the Prince of Orange; fought at Beachy Head (1690) and Barfleur (1692); Commissioner of the Admiralty (1699–1702); Rear-Admiral (1701); Admiral of the Blue (1702); MP (1700–8). Buried near by.

A tablet by *J. Thomas* commemorates **Lieutenant Richard Creed**, d. 1841, aged twenty-seven; an officer in the Bombay Artillery killed leading a party of volunteers in an assault on the Fort of Kujjuck in Upper Sinde. His fellow officers 'to whom his generous nature, amiable deportment and Christian virtues' had 'in no common degree endeared his memory' erected the memorial.

A plain tablet commemorates a distinguished Elizabethan commander: **Sir Richard Bingham**, b. 1528, d. 1599; Governor of Connaught; Marshal of Ireland; General of Leinster; present at the Battle of Lepanto, and fought not only in Ireland and Scotland but in France and elsewhere. Erected by Sir John Bingley, formerly his servant. Buried near by.

A memorial to **Major Richard Creed**, d. 1704, killed at Blenheim in one of the cavalry charges which began the battle. He was the eldest son of John Creed (the acquaintance of Pepys) by Elizabeth, only daughter of Sir Gilbert Pickering, Bt, of Tichmarsh. Elizabeth was a niece of Lord Sandwich, Pepys's cousin and patron, and she erected the monument near that to Harbord and Cottrell, because her son used to look upon it with pleasure for the worthy mention on it of Sandwich 'to whom he had ye honour to be related, and whose heroic virtues he was ambitious to imitate'. Creed's monument was later moved to this choir aisle. His brother took his body off the battlefield and buried it apparently near Blenheim, now known as Blindheim.

Martin Folkes, PRS, FSA, b. 1690, d. 1754, numismatist. The monument, which was designed by *W. Tyler*, and executed by *R. Ashton*, was erected in 1788. Buried at Hillington, Norfolk.

Captain William Julius, RN, b. *c.* 1645, d. 1698, commander of the *Colchester* and previously the *Chester*, is commemorated by a tablet. Buried in this aisle.

Near by is a monument to **Lieutenant-General William Strode**, b. *c.* 1697, d. 1776; Colonel of the 62nd Regiment of Foot. Buried in the centre of the nave. Sculptor: *R. Hayward*.

On the north side of the aisle is the well-known monument, by *A. Quellin*, to the rich squire of Longleat, **Thomas Thynn(e)**, b. 1648, d. 1682. Known as 'Tom of Ten Thousand' and a favourite at Charles II's Court. Thynne had married the Percy heiress, Lady Elizabeth, already the widow of Henry (Cavendish), Earl of Ogle. The Swedish adventurer, Count Karl von Königsmarck, hoping to marry the heiress himself, hired three killers, who shot Thynne in his coach at the Pall Mall end of the Haymarket. Lord Cavendish, a friend of Thynne's, saw to it that the principals were brought to justice, but the Count was acquitted and fled abroad before Cavendish could challenge him to a duel. The relief in front of the pedestal, on which is Thynne's figure 'in a languid position', shows two of the thugs stopping the coach while the third fires at Thynne. Buried near by.

Above the door to the organ loft is a monument put up by his widow to the memory of **Samuel Barnett**, b. 1844, d. 1913, social reformer, vicar of St Jude's, Whitechapel (1872–94); founder and first Warden of the Toynbee Hall University Settlement (1884); Canon of Bristol (1894–1906), and Canon of Westminster (1906–13); buried at Brampton. Also **Dame Henrietta Barnett, DBE**, his wife, b. 1851, d. 1936. Described by Asquith as 'the unofficial custodian of the children of the State', she campaigned to improve the education of London's children and instigated the building of Hampstead Garden Suburb. Sculptor: *Sir G. Frampton*.

Sanctuary and Confessor's Chapel, North and South Ambulatories

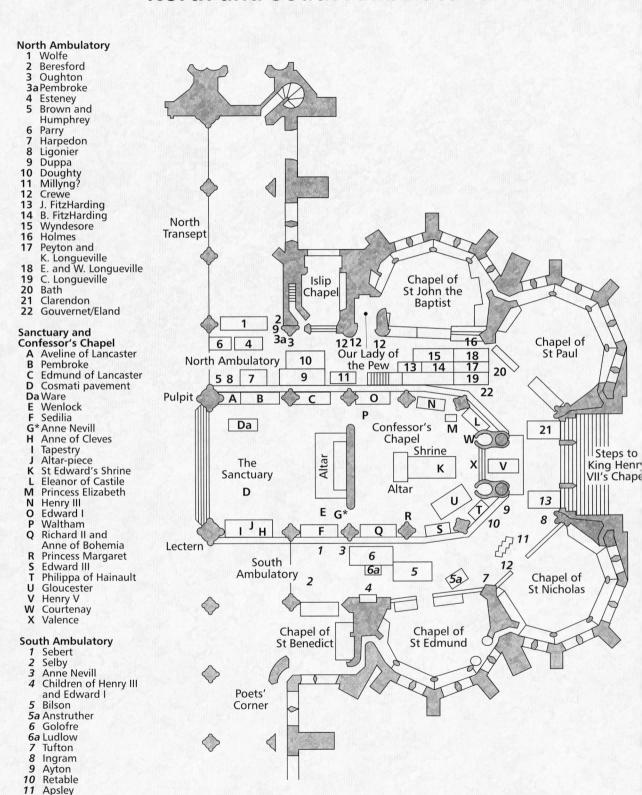

North Ambulatory
1. Wolfe
2. Beresford
3. Oughton
3a. Pembroke
4. Esteney
5. Brown and Humphrey
6. Parry
7. Harpedon
8. Ligonier
9. Duppa
10. Doughty
11. Millyng?
12. Crewe
13. J. FitzHarding
14. B. FitzHarding
15. Wyndesore
16. Holmes
17. Peyton and K. Longueville
18. E. and W. Longueville
19. C. Longueville
20. Bath
21. Clarendon
22. Gouvernet/Eland

Sanctuary and Confessor's Chapel
A. Aveline of Lancaster
B. Pembroke
C. Edmund of Lancaster
D. Cosmati pavement
Da. Ware
E. Wenlock
F. Sedilia
G*. Anne Nevill
H. Anne of Cleves
I. Tapestry
J. Altar-piece
K. St Edward's Shrine
L. Eleanor of Castile
M. Princess Elizabeth
N. Henry III
O. Edward I
P. Waltham
Q. Richard II and Anne of Bohemia
R. Princess Margaret
S. Edward III
T. Philippa of Hainault
U. Gloucester
V. Henry V
W. Courtenay
X. Valence

South Ambulatory
1. Sebert
2. Selby
3. Anne Nevill
4. Children of Henry III and Edward I
5. Bilson
5a. Anstruther
6. Golofre
6a. Ludlow
7. Tufton
8. Ingram
9. Ayton
10. Retable
11. Apsley
12. Spelman
13. Harweden

The Choir & Sanctuary

See plans, pages 28 and 36

• •

The choir was formerly separated from the transepts by wooden partitions; these were replaced by iron gates, which were removed in the nineteenth century. The greater part of the present stalls and pews were set up in 1848, and designed by *E. Blore*, then Surveyor of the Fabric. Above the Dean's stall at the west end of the choir is the shield of arms of the Collegiate Church. Other stalls are allotted to the Abbey clergy, lay officers, Head Master of Westminster School, the Under Master and Master of the Queen's (or King's) Scholars, the Lord Mayor of Westminster, and the High Commissioners for the Commonwealth countries.

Beneath the pavement close to their own stall are buried two Sub-deans, **Dr Peter Heylyn** (see page 27) and **Dr Robinson Duckworth, CVO**, b. 1834, d. 1911, Canon of Westminster from 1875. As a young don at Christ Church, Oxford, he rowed the boat in which the original story of *Alice's Adventures in Wonderland* was told by 'Lewis Carroll' to Alice Liddell (daughter of Dr H. G. Liddell, Head Master of Westminster School (1846–55), Dean of Christ Church, Oxford (1855–91)).

In the centre of the pavement a Latin inscription marks the grave of **Dame Anne Carey**, d. 1660, daughter of Sir Nicholas Hyde (d. 1631), Chief Justice of England, and widow of Sir Ross Carey, Bt.

The present seventeenth-century oak **pulpit** was replaced in its original position in 1935. It had been removed in 1775, at the same time that *H. Keene* the Abbey Surveyor destroyed the thirteenth-century choir stalls. Dean Ryle placed it in the nave but it was again stored away after the coronation of Edward VII. The pulpit has now been repainted and gilded, and put upon a modern pedestal.

The carved English walnut **lectern**, inscribed to the memory of **William Carey** (1761–1834), missionary in India and translator of the Bible, was presented to the Abbey in 1949 by the Baptist Missionary Society. Designed by *Sir A. E. Richardson*.

The **lantern roof**, destroyed by bombing in 1941, was restored and painted to a design by *S.E. Dykes Bower* in 1958.

The **sanctuary** or presbytery – often called the 'sacrarium' – was formerly hung round with cloth of arras, adorned with legends of the Confessor. This was replaced in Queen Anne's reign by wooden wainscoting which concealed the fine sanctuary tombs. The wainscoting was removed in 1820. The three easternmost **chandeliers** are thought to date from the refurnishing of the Abbey at the Restoration. The other two are later copies.

The **ceremony of coronation** takes place before the High Altar, and is now always performed by the Archbishop of Canterbury, who on that occasion only can claim a place in the Abbey by right. The sovereign afterwards ascends a raised throne erected under the lantern and receives the homage of the Peers. The first coronation here was possibly that of Harold, the last of the Saxon kings in January 1066. Less than twelve months afterwards, on Christmas Day 1066, William the Conqueror was crowned by Aldred, Archbishop of York. Since that time all the sovereigns (except Edward V and Edward VIII) have been crowned in the Abbey.

The stone **altar screen** dates from 1440–1, but only on the eastern side can the medieval work be seen (see p. 47). Prior to its erection the Confessor's Shrine would have been clearly visible beyond the sanctuary. The present **High Altar** and reredos were erected between 1867 and 1873 after Sir G. Scott's design. The sculptured figures of the reredos (Moses, St Peter, St Paul, King David) were executed by *H. H. Armstead*, the mosaic, representing the Last Supper, was designed by *J. R. Clayton* (of Clayton and Bell's) and carried out by *A. Salviati*.

Coronation setting 1953, looking south

The thirteenth-century pavement is Cosmati work and is composed of various kinds of mosaic and porphyry set in squares and circles. The design represents the probable duration of the world according to the Ptolemaic system. The inscription, of which only a few brass letters remain, incorporated the date (1268), the name of the reigning king (Henry III), and the city (Rome) whence the materials came. It has been suggested by Lethaby that the materials for the pavement may have been presented by the Pope.[1]

Underneath the pavement on each side of the altar are the bases of pillars which formed part of the Confessor's church.

Three fine tombs occupy the north side of the sanctuary. They are somewhat similar in design and two of them, Edmund's and Aveline's, may, perhaps, be attributed either to *Master Alexander of Abingdon* or to *Master Michael of Canterbury*. Aymer's tomb is later, and may be by *Master Richard of Reading*, but the exact dates of their erection are unknown.

The westernmost tomb, farthest from the altar, is that of **Aveline, Countess of Lancaster**, d. 1274, daughter of William de Forz, (titular) Count of Aumale in Normandy, Lord of Holderness in Yorkshire, and of much land elsewhere in the north of England. On her mother's side she was heiress presumptive to the Earldom of Devon and Lordship of the Isle of Wight. She was married by Henry III to his younger

---

1   *Westminster Abbey Re-examined* (1925), p. 224.

The 13th-century Cosmati pavement

Choir (looking west) with nave and great west window (beyond)

son Edmund 'Crouchback' in April 1269, apparently the first royal wedding in the new building. However, Aveline died childless and Crouchback did not get her lands. The recumbent figure of Aveline, her head supported by two angels, lies on crossed pillows upon an altar tomb, and may be by the sculptor who made her husband's effigy. She is dressed in a long mantle, and wears a close coif and wimple. In front of the base are six figures (now headless or defaced) standing in arched niches. The pointed canopy has been greatly injured. The whole was once richly coloured, and traces of painted vine leaves can still be seen in the vaulting of the trefoiled arch.

Aymer de Valence, Earl of Pembroke, b. *c.* 1270, d. 1324, son of William de Valence (q.v.) and cousin to Edward I. He was much employed in the wars with Scotland, where in 1306 he defeated King Robert I and captured his brother Nigel Bruce. In 1312 Pembroke's honour was seriously impugned by the other earls' killing of Piers de Gaveston, who had been placed in Aymer's custody. Aymer was trusted by his cousin Edward II to whom he remained loyal in the war with their cousin Thomas of Lancaster (son of Crouchback). In 1322, after the Battle of Boroughbridge, Pembroke was one of the earls present when Lancaster was judged guilty of treason. By inheritance and by marriage Aymer was the lord of many estates in France as well as those in England, Wales, and Ireland, and this fact together with his integrity and diplomatic skill frequently involved him as an envoy to France. In 1324 he died suddenly in France while on an embassy to Charles IV. Aymer's first wife Beatrice, daughter and co-heir of Raoul de Clermont, Sire de Néelle

High Altar in festal array

the three; a triple canopy richly decorated (perhaps by *Master Alexander of Abingdon*) rises over the fine sculptured effigy of the Earl; he is in mail armour (the links modelled in putty) and wears a surcoat of his arms. On both sides of the tomb are ten arched niches in which stand 'weepers' alternately male and female. Above each figure are two shields with the arms once finely modelled in putty and coloured, but the arms do not appear to relate to the individual figures. The canopy, which has suffered much from the preparations for coronations, is richly decorated and, like Aveline's, an elaborate leaf-pattern is painted on the underside of the vault. Earl Edmund appears again, on either side of the canopy at the top, in a trefoil-shaped recess, but unlike Aymer he has dropped the reins of his horse and his hands are together in prayer. On the ambulatory side of the monument painted on the basement may still be seen ten figures in mail with armorial surcoats, and each man holding a banner. Possibly these were the Earl's household knights. This frieze of knights and the whole monument was seriously damaged by fire in 1968; and has since been restored.

and Constable of France, died in 1320. He married secondly Mary, daughter of Guy de Châtillon, Comte de Saint-Pol; she, who was the foundress of Pembroke College, Cambridge, died in 1377. The arms of that college today are those of Valence dimidiating Châtillon/Saint-Pol. The little figures of weepers (mourners) on the lower part of the Earl's tomb, though now mutilated, and Aymer's effigy in armour are very fine. His surcoat is painted with the variant of the Lusignan arms which his father William assumed, and on the latter's shield is shown so splendidly in enamels (see p. 82). His feet rest on a lion; his shield has disappeared. Above on the richly carved canopy he is again represented, fully armed, and galloping in the manner usual on seals of great lords. This magnificent tomb was in danger of being removed to make way for the memorial to General Wolfe. Horace Walpole protested against the idea, and intended, if his remonstrance proved ineffectual, to have Aymer's monument set up in his garden at Strawberry Hill. Dean Zachary Pearce, on hearing that Aymer was not, as he had supposed, one of the Knights Templars, 'a very wicked set of people',[1] allowed it to remain.

Edmund, Earl of Lancaster, b. 1245, d. 1296, surnamed 'Crouchback', son of Henry III and younger brother of Edward I. He became Earl of Lancaster in 1267, and married Aveline de Forz (see p. 37) in 1269. After her death he married Blanche, widow of Henry, King of Navarre, and daughter of Robert, Count of Artois. Crouchback was employed actively in England, Wales (where in 1282 he captured and beheaded Llewellyn ap Gruffyd), and France. He died at Bayonne in 1296 during the siege of Bordeaux. Crouchback's monument is the largest and most elaborate of

1 Toynbee (ed.), *Walpole's Letters*, vol. V, p. 95 and *Supplement*, vol. II, p. 120.

Detail of monument to Edmund Crouchback, Earl of Lancaster

The grave of **Richard de Ware**, d. 1283, abbot of Westminster from 1258, is on the north side of the presbytery, beneath the pavement which was laid down under his superintendence. During his abbacy the *Customary* (rules for the daily life of the monastery) was compiled.

His successor **Walter de Wenlock**, d. 1307, lies on the south side of the altar; the little head wearing a mitre on the sedilia above may represent him. He was at first high in royal favour and Treasurer of England, but fell under a cloud after the robbery of the royal treasure, which had been placed in the monastic treasury during Edward I's absence in Scotland. In his time also occurred the great fire which consumed many of the monastic buildings.

Two **oak chairs** for the Dean and Sub-dean were placed on the north side of the presbytery in 1922. About thirty shields appear on the Dean's chair, which was designed by *S. Jack* and made by *Messrs Armitage*. Now removed to the triforium.

The ancient **sedilia** rest on Sebert's tomb, and used to be mistaken for part of it. They were erected under Edward I in the time of Abbot Wenlock, and are richly decorated; the paintings have been recently cleaned. On the north (the sanctuary) side two of the panels are painted with full-length figures of kings between whom is an ecclesiastic, probably a saint (?St Peter) almost entirely defaced. A fourth figure has completely disappeared. On the ambulatory side restoration has uncovered the figure of the Confessor holding the ring out to the pilgrim, of whose figure no traces remain, and also part of a fourteenth-century painting of the Annunciation, of which only the lower portion is intact.

Near the door in the screen leading into the Confessor's Chapel in an unmarked grave, lies buried Queen **Anne Nevill**, d. 1485, wife of Richard III. For a tablet to her memory, see p. 85.

On the south side of the presbytery, west of the sedilia, is the tomb, attributed to *Theodore Haveus* from Cleves, of **Anne of Cleves**, b. 1516, d. 1557, daughter of Duke John III of Cleves, and fourth queen of Henry VIII. She lived quietly in England for sixteen years after her divorce from the king, and, dying a Roman Catholic (at Chelsea), was buried here by the monks. The marble slab over the tomb dates only from 1606 and cost £7.

Above the tomb of Anne of Cleves hangs a sixteenth-century piece of tapestry, which traditionally formed part of the scenery used in the annual performance of the Latin play at Westminster School.

In front of the tapestry stands a **fifteenth-century altar-piece** painted on panel by *Bicci di Lorenzo* (1375–1452) and bequeathed to the Abbey by Viscount Lee of Fareham (d. 1947). It represents the Madonna and Child enthroned in the centre; with St Antony Abbot and St Giovanni Gualberto on her right, and St John Baptist and St Catherine of Egypt on her left. At one time it appears to have been in the Capella San Giovanni Gualberto in Sta Trinità at Florence, belonging to the Campagni family.

In 1949 the two **chairs and faldstools** were given by the Canada Club in memory of those Canadians who fell in the Second World War. They are made of Canadian birch to the design of *S. Comper*, and the decoration includes the maple leaf of Canada as well as the arms of King George VI and Queen Elizabeth, for whose use they were made, and the arms of the Dominion of Canada.

Sedilia painting of a king: Edward I (?)

The **processional crosses** are four in number:

A cross of ivory and silver gilt, adorned with a series of panels of beaten gold and sapphires. This cross and its staff of silver gilt were given at Christmas 1922 by Rodman Wanamaker, Hon. CVO.

The silver-gilt 'Abyssinian Cross', presented, together with its ebony staff, by Raz Makunan, envoy of the King of Abyssinia to the coronation of King Edward VII and Queen Alexandra, at the time of King Edward's sudden illness (1902).

A cross of Abyssinian ivory decorated with shields, made from a tusk presented by Emperor Haile Sellasie in 1924. The cost of fashioning the cross was borne by Mrs E. B. Wright. Dedicated 1940.

A cross of English wood painted red with gilt decorations, the gift of the Brotherhood of St Edward in 1933, is used during Lent.

Shrine of Edward the Confessor

Chapel of St Edward the Confessor

See plan, page 36

• •

In many of the great churches of the Middle Ages immediately behind the High Altar there is a 'shrine' containing the relics of the patron saint, or of a great benefactor to the church. In Westminster Abbey this shrine encloses the body of Edward the Confessor whose great benefactions to the Abbey were so largely responsible for the pre-eminent position it subsequently occupied. St Edward's shrine and the five kings and four queens whose bodies lie near it make this chapel the most sacred part of the Abbey. In the centre of the chapel is the Confessor's tomb; at the east end is the chantry chapel of Henry V. Where this chantry now stands the relics were originally kept, but after its erection they were moved to a chest placed between the tomb of Henry III and the shrine, and there remained until the dissolution of the monastery. The most precious among them were: the Virgin Mary's girdle, presented by Edward the Confessor; a stone marked with the print of Christ's foot at the Ascension; His blood in a crystal vase; a piece of the Cross, set in jewels, brought from Wales, and given by Edward I; the head of St Benedict, brought from France and presented by Edward III.

Several of these great royal tombs retain their original Latin or French inscriptions in Lombardic lettering. Wooden tablets, upon which were Latin verses with English translations, used to hang near each of the royal tombs. These epitaphs were long supposed to have been the work of John Skelton, who certainly wrote those affixed to the tombs of Henry VII and his mother, but all the early ones have been found in a chronicle written by a Westminster monk late in the fourteenth century. They appear to have survived into the eighteenth century.

Edward the Confessor, b. between 1002 and 1005 at Islip, Oxfordshire, reigned 1042–66. Driven from England by the Danes, and spending his exile in Normandy, the story goes that Edward vowed that if he should return safely to his kingdom, he would make a pilgrimage to St Peter's, Rome. But once on the throne he found it impossible to leave his subjects, and the Pope released him from his vow on condition that he should found or restore a monastery to St Peter. This led to the building of a new church in the Norman style to replace the Saxon church at Westminster.

The work took fifteen years, and the church was consecrated on Holy Innocents' Day, 28 December 1065, but the king was ill and probably not present at the service. He died 5 January 1066, and was buried before the High Altar in his own new church. After his death many miracles were said to have been worked at his grave. Wulfstan II, the Saxon Bishop of Worcester, when required to resign his see at the Conquest, appealed for help to the dead king, and struck his staff into the tomb, where it remained upright, and could be displaced by no one but Wulfstan himself. On hearing of this miracle William the Conqueror allowed Wulfstan to retain his bishopric and raised a costly stone tomb, sparkling with gold and jewels, over the Confessor's remains. In 1102 the tomb was opened by Abbot Gilbert in the presence of Henry I and a Norman chronicle relates how the body was found entire, the joints as flexible as if it were 'a body asleep'. Gundulf, Bishop of Rochester, 'who is very bold, strokes the yellow beard whence he wishes to draw an hair, but he cannot draw it from the beard'. Two attempts were made to canonize Edward. The first (in 1140) failed but the second was successful; Pope Alexander III issued the bull of canonization in February 1161. On 13 October 1163, the saint's body was transferred to the shrine prepared for it by Henry II, in the presence of the king and of Thomas Becket, Archbishop of Canterbury. The robes in which the body was wrapped were made into three copes, and Abbot Laurence drew St John's famous ring off the finger and deposited it among the relics. After that the corpse remained undisturbed for nearly a hundred years until Henry III pulled down that part of the church and removed the old shrine containing the saint's body to another part of the church, while a new tomb was prepared for it. Abbot Ware brought the workmen and porphyries for the pavement from Italy, and the ancient inscription gives the name of the chief artist, *Peter the Roman* (alias *Pietro di Oderisio*). Only the base now remains of Henry's magnificent fabric; the material is Purbeck marble, decorated with mosaic. Above this marble and mosaic base was the golden shrine enclosing the Confessor's coffin. The shrine was decorated with eleven small gold images of kings and saints; among them were St Edmund with the church in one hand, St Peter trampling on Nero, and a king, probably Henry III himself, holding a model of the shrine; besides these were many great jewels. At the sides, upon two pillars, were golden statues of St Edward and St John the Evangelist; at the west end was an altar, which was destroyed at the dissolution and used to be replaced at coronations by a table called St Edward's Altar. A permanent altar was placed here at the coronation of King Edward VII in 1902. For the ornaments of this altar see p. 116. The hanging lamp to the east of the shrine was presented by the Revd Ivan Young in 1971.

In the lower part of the shrine are the recesses in which sick persons knelt. Round the verge was an inscription formed by blue glass set in gold mosaic. Traces of letters can be seen in places under the plaster. On 13 October 1269, the chest which contained the Confessor's body was brought in solemn procession to its new resting-place; Henry III, his brother (Richard, Earl of Cornwall and King of Germany) and his two sons, bore the coffin on their shoulders. This day, 13 October, the date of the two translations, was kept yearly with great ceremony in the Abbey; processions resorted to the shrine from many of the religious houses in London and the steps are worn away by the knees of the pilgrims. But in 1540 came the dissolution of the monastery; the shrine was despoiled of its relics and the gold images and jewels carried off, and the body of the saint was removed and buried in some obscure place. Under Mary I the coffin was restored to its place, and the shrine was rebuilt by Abbot Feckenham in 1557. The queen presented fresh jewels and images to replace the stolen ones. Later on the shrine again suffered, losing its new images and jewels, but was not destroyed. Soon after James II's coronation (1685) a golden cross and chain were

Effigy of Eleanor of Castile

Effigy of Henry III

taken out of the Confessor's coffin by Charles Taylour, 'one of the singing men, who, as the scaffolds were taken down after his Majesty's coronation, espying a hole in the tomb and something glisten, put his hand in and brought it to the Deane, and he to the King',[1] receiving a bounty of £50. Through the hole Taylour saw the saint's head, 'sound and firm, the upper and lower jaws full of teeth, a list [i.e. a band] of gold round the temples', and 'all his bones and much dust in his coffin'. King James had the old coffin enclosed in one strongly clamped with iron, where it has remained undisturbed until this day. St Edward's Day continues to be observed at the Abbey as a major festival.

Edith, d. 1075, queen of Edward the Confessor and daughter of Earl Godwin, was buried near her husband's tomb, in the old church, before the High Altar. There do not seem to be any strictly contemporary references to the removal of her coffin in 1163 or in 1269 when Edward was translated, but the late medieval tomb-lists state that her grave was on the left side of the shrine. Estranged from her husband and immured in a nunnery after his quarrel with her father (1052), she returned to court after their reconciliation.

Near the Confessor lay his great-great-niece **Maud** (first called '**Edith**') d. 1118, the first queen of Henry I. She was the daughter of Malcolm III, King of Scots, by St Margaret, who was daughter of Edward 'the Exile' (d. 1057), son of King Edmund 'Ironside', the Confessor's half-brother. As in the case of Edith, only the late medievel tomb-lists state that her grave was on the right side of the shrine. Her marriage with Henry I in 1100 united the Saxon and Norman lines.

The heart of **Henry of Almayne** (son of Richard, Earl of Cornwall, King of Germany, and so nephew of Henry III), was preserved in a golden heart shrine near the Confessor's shrine. He was murdered by his cousin Guy (son of Simon) de Montfort during Mass in the church of San Silvestro at Viterbo in 1271. Dante mentions the fact of the preservation of the heart 'on the banks of the Thames'.[2]

Eleanor, b. c. 1244, d. 1290. Edward I's first wife, and daughter of Ferdinand III, King of Castile and Leon. She was Edward's constant companion during the thirty-six years of their marriage and accompanied him on crusade. On their return they were crowned together in the Abbey (1274). She died at Harby, Nottinghamshire, in November 1290. Her body was embalmed and Edward brought it in state to Westminster, erecting memorial crosses at the places where the procession rested from Lincoln to Charing Cross.

Three monuments were raised over Eleanor's remains: one containing her entrails was at Lincoln Cathedral but was destroyed in the Civil Wars; another over her heart was put up at the Blackfriars (or Friars Preachers), London, but was lost when that house was dissolved. The third, containing her embalmed body, remains here in the Abbey. It was erected about the time that the tomb of Henry III was approaching completion. *Master William Torel*, goldsmith of London, cast the effigy of Eleanor in 1291.

---

1   See L. E. Tanner, 'The Quest for the Cross of St Edward the Confessor', *Journal of the British Archaeological Association*, XVII (1954), pp. 1–10.

2   *Inferno*, Canto XII, lines 119–20. See P. Brieger, 'A Statue of Henry of Almain' in *Essays in Medieval History Presented to Bertie Wilkinson*, ed T. A. Sandquist and M. R. Powicke (Toronto, 1969), pp. 133–8.

Tomb of Henry III from the ambulatory

A story has come down to us that when Edward was in the Holy Land a would-be assassin stabbed him with a poisoned dagger and that Eleanor saved her husband's life by sucking the poison from the wound. A more reliable tradition names another as Edward's rescuer. Traces of him still remain in a painting, perhaps by *Master Walter of Durham*, on the ambulatory side of the tomb. This shows an armed knight identifiable by his armorial surcoat as Sir Otes de Grandison (b. c. 1238, d. 1328), kneeling before the Virgin and Child, and four pilgrims praying before the Holy Sepulchre. Sir Otes was a close friend of Edward I and accompanied him to the Holy Land. After Edward's death he returned to his native land; his castle at Grandson still stands on Lake Neuchâtel. He died at an immense age and his tomb is in Lausanne Cathedral. Above the painting is the tomb itself of Purbeck marble, designed very probably by *Master Richard of Crundale*; the sides are divided into panels in which are sculptured shields hung on branches of trees bearing the arms of England, Castile quartering Leon, and Ponthieu. Above is Torel's fine effigy, which is an idealised likeness of the queen, made of gilt bronze. Her right hand once held a sceptre; the left is closed over the string of the cloak. The gilt-bronze tomb-top and the crossed pillows beneath Eleanor's head are covered all over with the castle of Castile and the lion of Leon. Round the queen's head is a gilt-bronze gablet. William Sprot and John de Ware furnished the bronze, and gold florins for the gilding were brought from Lucca. *Master Thomas de Hokyntone* did the woodwork, which included a canopy painted by *Master Walter of Durham*, but this original canopy has gone and the present one is Perpendicular. On the ambulatory side is a curved iron grille of exquisite workmanship by an English smith *Master Thomas of Leighton Buzzard*. Round the edge of the tomb-top on which lies the effigy there is a Norman-French inscription, partly hidden from sight by Henry V's Chantry: ICI GIST ALIANOR IADIS REYNE DE ENGLETERE FEMME AL REY EDEWARD FIZ LEREY HENRY EFYLLE AL REY DE ESPAYGNE ECONTASSE DE PVNTIV DEL ALME DELI DEV PVR SA PITE EYT MERCI AMEN (Here lies Eleanor, sometime Queen of England, wife to King Edward, son of King Henry, and daughter of the King of Spain and Countess of Ponthieu, on whose soul God in His pity have mercy. Amen.)

The small tomb to the east of Henry III's is that of **Princess Elizabeth Tudor**, b. 1492, d. 1495, daughter of Henry VII. She died at Eltham aged three years and two months. The gilt effigy and inscriptions have disappeared.

Henry III, b. 1207, d. 1272. Succeeding his father King John in 1216, as a boy he was hastily crowned first at Gloucester Abbey and then in 1220 at Westminster.

It is to Henry III that we owe the rebuilding of the Abbey, and almost all of the church west of King Henry VII's Chapel, as far as one bay of the nave west of the organ, dates from his reign. In 1220 he laid the foundation-stone of the old Lady Chapel – the forerunner of Henry VII's Chapel. Henry III had a special devotion to the Confessor and named his eldest son after the saint. He determined to build a church to emulate the great churches being built in the Ile-de-France and to transfer St Edward's body to a new shrine close to which he would himself be buried. Craftsmen of the Cosmati school were brought from Rome to construct the two great mosaic pavements (the one before the High Altar, the other in the Confessor's Chapel) and the base of the new shrine itself. The king was recklessly extravagant in the money spent on his new Abbey, its decoration, and the jewels with which he enriched St Edward's shrine. Contemporary chronicles tell us that Henry's work was started in 1245, and the Public Records fill in many of the details, in which Henry took the greatest personal interest. He survived to see the Confessor's translation to the shrine but died himself at Westminster Palace on 16 November 1272. The funeral on St Edmund's day was a magnificent ceremony. Henry's body was temporarily laid before the High Altar in the grave which had been the Confessor's, and nineteen years later was placed in the splendid tomb prepared for it by his son, Edward I. Henry's heart was in the same year (1291) according to his wish, delivered to the Abbess of Fontevrault, the Angevins' foundation and burial-place.

The king's tomb consists of a Purbeck marble base built in two stages. Into the sides are set slabs of Italian porphyry and the tomb was inlaid with mosaic gilded and brightly coloured with tesserae made of red and green porphyry, marble, and glass, like the other Cosmati work. Much of the mosaic has been robbed, but from the north ambulatory it is still possible to form an impression of the tomb's original splendour. On the side of the tomb nearest the Confessor's shrine there are arched recesses which may have contained relics of saints. High up on the tomb lies the superb effigy cast in bronze and gilt by the same *Master William Torel*, who made Eleanor's effigy. It appears to be an idealised portrait of the king, because the account for payment refers to it as made 'in the likeness of King Henry'. The king's head rests on

crossed pillows decorated with the lions of England, and these also cover the tomb-top. The gablet, presumably once similar to Eleanor's, is missing. An iron grille, by *Master Henry of Lewes*, formerly protected the tomb, and the plain wooden canopy was once gilt and painted. The original Norman-French inscription cast in Lombardic letters round the chamfered edge remains: ICI GIST HENRI IADIS REY DE ENGLETERE SEYGNVR DE HIRLAVNDE EDVC DE AQVITAYNE LEFIZ LIREY IOHAN IADIS REY DE ENGLETERE AKIDEV FACE MERCI AMEN (Here lies Henry, sometime King of England, Lord of Ireland and Duke of Aquitaine, the son of King John, sometime King of England: on whom may God have mercy. Amen.)

Edward I, nicknamed 'Longshanks', b. 1239, d. 1307. He succeeded his father Henry III in 1272, and was the first *king* crowned in Henry III's new church; and he and Eleanor were the first king and queen who were *jointly* crowned in it. Here he raised splendid tombs to his father and his own first wife; here he deposited the Stone of Scone and the Scottish regalia; and it was before the shrine that his young son Alphonso hung the golden coronet of Llewellyn, Prince of Wales, and, dying shortly after, was buried by his father's wish close by the saint. Edward died on 7 July 1307, at Burgh-on-the-Sands in Cumberland, on his way to Scotland. His body was carried with great pomp to Waltham Abbey, where it lay for about fifteen weeks. Parliament, which met next in August, ordered its removal to Westminster Abbey. In October the king's body was taken to London, and after resting for three nights successively in the churches of Holy Trinity, St Paul's, and the Friars Minors, was brought to the Abbey on 27 October where it was interred the next day. He lies in a very plain tomb-chest composed simply of grey marble upon a freestone base. Over it was a wooden canopy broken down in a riot at a funeral. The tomb was protected from the ambulatory by an iron grille. On the north side the words *Edwardus Primus Scotorum Malleus* ('the hammer of the Scots') and *Pactum Serva* ('keep troth') were probably painted on the tomb in Abbot Feckenham's time. In 1774 the tomb was opened; within was a Purbeck marble coffin. The king's body was wrapped in a large waxed linen cloth, the head covered with a face-cloth of crimson sarsenet. Beneath this were the royal robes, a tunic of red silk damask with gold tissue, and a mantle of crimson velvet; a piece of rich cloth of gold laid loosely over them. In the right hand was a sceptre, in the left a rod surmounted by a dove and oak leaves in white and green enamel; a gilt crown was upon the head. The corpse was found almost entire, the innermost cover being another waxed cloth fitting closely to the face and limbs; the length of the body was six feet two inches.[1]

South of Edward I's tomb is a large grey slab with an imperfect brass to **John de Waltham**, Bishop of Salisbury, d. 1395. Richard II made him Master of the Rolls (1381–6), Keeper of the Great Seal (1382, 1383), and finally Lord Treasurer (1391–5). So great was Richard's affection for him that he caused him to be buried in the chapel of the kings. There was great indignation at such an intrusion into the royal chapel, but the Abbey was compensated by the present of two splendid copes and a large sum of money from the king and the bishop's executors. The brass represents the bishop in Mass vestments, with his pastoral staff; within the

---

1   See account in *Archaeologia*, vol. III, by Sir Joseph Ayloffe.

crook and down the front of the chasuble are representations of the Virgin and Child.

The **Coronation Chair** was made on the orders of Edward I to contain the Stone of Scone (now at Edinburgh Castle) which he had brought from Scotland in 1296. *Master Walter* decorated the chair with patterns of birds, foliage and animals on a gilt ground, and the figure of a king (the Confessor or Edward I) was painted on the back. The gilt lions date from 1727. At coronations the chair is moved into the Sanctuary, and since 1308 all the sovereigns of England have been crowned in it with three exceptions[1]. The chair was taken out of the Abbey to Westminster Hall for the installation of Oliver Cromwell as Lord Protector in 1657.

The ancient **stone screen** which closes the west side of this chapel seems to date from the middle of the fifteenth century. Upon the frieze are carved the principal events, real and legendary, of Edward the Confessor's life.

The subjects are (beginning on the left):

1. The nobles swearing fealty to Queen Emma in the name of her unborn son.

2. The birth of Edward the Confessor.

3. His coronation in 1043. On either side of the king are the Archbishops of Canterbury and York.

4. King Edward is alarmed by the appearance of the Devil dancing on the casks which contained the Danegeld. The Danegeld was a tax imposed by his father Ethelred on the people to induce the Danes to leave the country, but it was remitted by Edward after this vision. The figure of the demon has been broken off.

5. Edward warns a servant, who is stealing his treasure, to escape with his booty before the return of Hugolin, the king's chamberlain. The king is represented in bed, the thief kneeling at the chest.

6. Christ appears to Edward when at Mass.

7. Edward sees in a vision the shipwreck of the King of Denmark, who was drowned on his way to invade England. In front is a small boat, and an armed figure falling into the sea; behind is a ship and at the top are falling towers, supposed to represent the failure of the expedition.

8. The quarrel between Harold and Tostig, Earl Godwin's sons, from which the king prophesies their future feuds and unhappy fate. The sons are in the foreground; at the back, Edward, Edith, and Godwin sit at a table. Earl Tostig was killed at Stamford Bridge, and King Harold at Hastings, within a few days of each other in 1066.

9. Edward's vision of the Seven Sleepers of Ephesus, who had taken refuge in a cave from their heathen persecutors about AD 250. He sees them turn from their right sides to their left – a portent of misfortune during the seventy years in which the Sleepers were to lie in their new position. The king's messengers are represented arriving at the cave and verifying the vision.

10. St John the Evangelist in the guise of a pilgrim asks alms of the king, who, finding his purse empty, gives him a valuable ring off his finger.

11. Blind men restored to sight by washing in the water used by Edward. The king is in the foreground, washing his hands; at the side an attendant presents the water to the blind men.

12. St John the Evangelist restoring Edward's ring to two pilgrims in Palestine, bidding them announce to the king his approaching end.

13. The pilgrims giving the ring and message to the king shortly before his death. This is the famous ring which was kept among the relics.

14. The subject is uncertain but is generally said to be the dedication of the Abbey church on 28 December 1065.

Richard II, b. 1367, d. 1400, reigned 1377–99, called 'of Bordeaux', the place of his birth, son of Edward the Black Prince and of Joan, the 'Fair Maid of Kent'. Also his first wife, **Anne of Bohemia**, b. 1366, d. 1394, daughter of the Emperor Charles IV, and sister of King Wenceslas IV of Bohemia (Emperor Wenceslas I). The king and queen were married in the Abbey in January 1382. Anne was crowned two days later by Archbishop Courtenay. Richard was devoted to Westminster; his coronation at the Abbey is said to have been more splendid than any that had gone before. He partly rebuilt Westminster Hall, and also the great northern entrance of the Abbey, as well as some bays of the nave; his badge, the white hart, used to be in the glass of the window near the west cloister door. The white hart was painted in the Muniment Room and traces of it can be seen on the roof of the Chapel of Our Lady of the Pew. Richard had a special veneration for the Confessor; he impaled the arms assigned to the Confessor with his own. Richard, though in many ways an accomplished and enlightened prince, was an unsuccessful ruler. Eventually, in 1399, he was deposed by his cousin Henry, Duke of Lancaster, and was murdered or starved to death at Pontefract Castle. A body, purporting to be his, was taken to St Paul's where it lay exposed to public view for three days and was then buried at Langley in Hertfordshire. In 1413 the body was disinterred by Henry V's orders, and removed to Westminster Abbey, the king and his nobility following. There Richard was buried in the tomb which he had himself raised over the remains of his beloved first wife, **Anne**. She died at the Palace of Sheen, and the king loved her so passionately that he not only abandoned and cursed the place where she died, but pulled down the building. Richard's tomb is similar to Edward III's, and fills up the whole large end bay. The names of the master masons, *Henry Yevele* and *Stephen Lote*,[1] and the coppersmiths, *Nicholas Broker* and *Godfrey Prest*, all citizens of London, have been preserved; by the contracts the tomb was to be completed in 1397;[2] it cost £670, £279 being for the marble work only. The effigies are of gilt bronze and are undoubtedly portraits. By the king's own wish he was represented holding the queen's right hand in his. He is attired in coronation robes, his hair curls, and he wears a pointed beard. The cape to his mantle is bordered with the broompod badge of the Plantagenets. The effigies are stamped all over with intricate badges and patterns, among them the white hart, and the sun-burst, besides the two-headed imperial eagle and the lion of Bohemia. The queen's bodice was set with precious stones; the table beneath the figures is fretted with fleurs-de-lis, lions, and eagles. There used to be twelve gilt images of saints and eight angels round the tomb, besides enamelled coats of arms. Upon the inside

---

1 Edward V, Edward VIII and, seemingly, Mary I.

1 John Harvey, *English Medieval Architects* (rev. 1984), pp. 187–9, 358–66.

2 Final payments for it appear on the *Exchequer Issue Rolls* early in 1399.

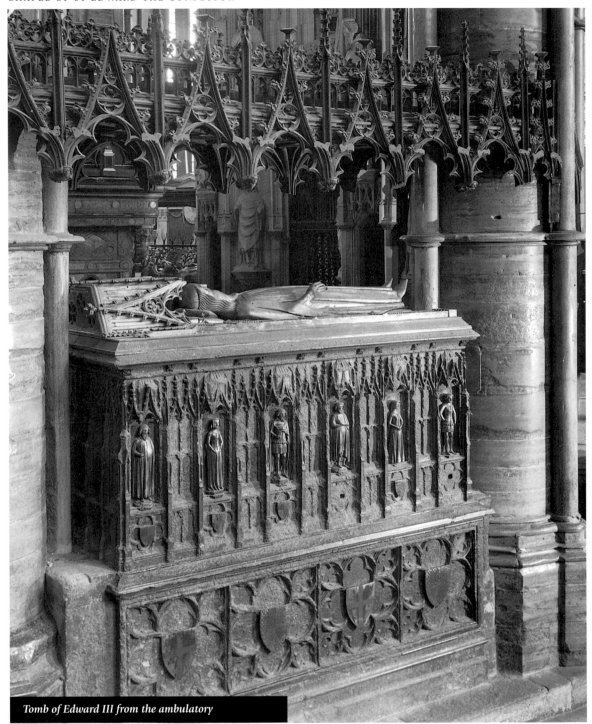

Tomb of Edward III from the ambulatory

of the wooden canopy over the tomb are painted a representation of Christ in Majesty and the coronation of the Virgin, and Queen Anne's armorial bearings. The painter was one *John Hardy*. Round the edge of the wooden canopy is a Latin rhyming inscription. Through a hole in the wooden case visitors to the Abbey used to insert their hands, and in 1766 a Westminster schoolboy removed the king's jawbone, which was restored by his descendants in 1906.

Princess Margaret, d. 1472, sixth daughter of Edward IV, who died at the age of nine months. A little tomb of grey marble probably moved here from somewhere else. The brass effigy and inscriptions have been torn off.

Edward III, b. 1312, reigned 1327–77, son of Edward II

and Isabel, daughter of King Philip the Fair, and through her King Edward III laid claim to the crown of France. Edward was crowned in the Abbey on his father's deposition, and the shield and sword of State, now displayed in the Undercroft Museum, were then first carried before the sovereign. The early part of his reign was taken up with achievements in France and Scotland. But the end was in gloomy contrast to the beginning. After Philippa's death his fortunes went into a decline, and the death in 1376 of the Black Prince was a great blow. He died, deserted, it is said, and robbed even to the rings off his fingers, by his favourites and servants, at his Palace of Sheen on 21 June 1377, attended only by one poor priest. His body, with the face uncovered, carried by four of his sons, and followed by his surviving children, was deposited either in Philippa's tomb, or where now stands the monument erected to him by his grandson, Richard II. It consists of an altar tomb of Purbeck marble; round the sides are niches in which were once little bronze images of twelve of the fourteen children of Edward and Philippa.[1] Only six – those on the south side – remain. These are from left to right: the Black Prince; Joan of the Tower; Lionel, Duke of Clarence; Edmund, Duke of York, the founder of the House of York; Mary of Brittany; and William of Hatfield. Their arms were on little enamelled shields at the feet, only four of which are left. On the basement of the ambulatory side are four large enamelled shields with the arms of England and St George. The king's effigy, of gilt bronze, lies on the tomb. Round the verge runs a Latin rhyming inscription. It is thought that the face was modelled from a cast taken after death, and, although the hair and beard are conventionalized, the features no doubt resembled the king. The elaborate wooden canopy over the tomb is perhaps by *Master Hugh Herland*.

Philippa, b. 1314, d. 1369, Edward III's queen and daughter of William, Count of Hainault. She was married in 1327, and crowned with Edward at Westminster in the same year. She sometimes accompanied her husband on his foreign expeditions, as on the occasion of the well-known anecdote of her intercession for the lives of the burgesses of Calais. At other times, in his absence, she defended the kingdom against the Scots.

Throughout their long union of forty-two years Philippa had great influence over the king, and the scene at her deathbed, as described by Froissart, is most touching. Holding the king's right hand in hers, she told him her last wishes; and, above all, entreated that 'when it should please God to call you hence you will not choose any other sepulchre than mine, and that you will lie beside me in the cloister at Westminster'. She was the reputed foundress of Queen's College, Oxford, which was really founded by her chaplain in her honour. The tomb is an altar tomb of black marble and the king spent immense sums – about £3,000 – on its erection; the name of the artist is *Hennequin de Liège*. Round the sides were once many niches containing weepers. None of these appeared to have remained and the tomb was quite bare until Sir Gilbert Scott discovered some of the alabaster tabernacle work in a museum in 1857, and replaced it on the south side of the monument. He also found two of the figures and niches which had been built into the chantry

chapel, but scarcely had he replaced them when one of them, an angel with gilt wings, was stolen. The other figure, a lady holding a monkey, is now protected by a grille. From the coat of arms it would appear that she is Blanche, Duchess of Lancaster. The effigy is alabaster, enriched with paint and gilding; the features are undoubtedly a portrait. It was finished in 1369. The queen held the string of her cloak in one hand, but the sceptre has gone and the hands are broken; the columns at the sides enclosed little figures, and the holes were filled up with glass mosaic. A wooden canopy covers the tomb, and it formerly was protected by an iron railing, bought by the king for £600 from the Custodian of St Paul's, where it had covered the tomb of Michael, Bishop of London. It appears from the contracts that seventy figures in all were included in this tomb, 'divers images in the likeness of angels' being made by *John Orchard*, bronze-worker, of London, who also put up and repaired the grate.[1]

Close by his mother is **Thomas, Duke of Gloucester**, b. 1355, d. 1397, called 'of Woodstock' from the place of his birth. He was the youngest son of Edward III and Philippa of Hainault to attain manhood, and the only one of her children present at Philippa's deathbed. It is recorded that the famous relic, the girdle of the Blessed Virgin, was sent for on two occasions when the queen was expecting the birth of her children, the last time when her son, Thomas, was born. He married Eleanor, one of the co-heiresses of Humphrey de Bohun, Earl of Hereford and Constable of England. Richard II summoned him to Parliament by the title of 'the King's dearest uncle', and created him Duke of Gloucester (1385). But Thomas presumed 'on the old maxim Patruus est in loco parentis ("an uncle is in the place of a father"). He observed the King too nearly and checked him too sharply.' He was accused of conspiring against the Crown. The king went himself and arrested the duke at his castle of Pleshy and had him conveyed to Calais; there the duke was smothered under a feather bed. The duke was first buried in St Edmund's Chapel but his body was afterwards removed by Henry IV to its present position, and placed beneath a fine brass with figures of himself and his relatives upon it. Unfortunately, the brass has entirely disappeared, except for some rivets.

Henry V, b. 1387, d. 1422, surnamed 'of Monmouth', the place of his birth. He was the eldest son of Henry IV, by Mary de Bohun, and succeeded his father in 1413. His life and reign, especially his conquests in France, including the great victory at Agincourt, are matters of general history. He married Catherine de Valois, daughter of Charles VI, and was actually Regent of France and heir to the French King after the Treaty of Troyes (1420). A *Te Deum* for the victory of Agincourt, fought on St Crispin's Day, 25 October 1415, was sung before the shrine, and the king contributed 1,000 marks yearly towards the rebuilding of the nave, besides other gifts of money; he also restored a ruby ring, originally given by Richard II, to St Edward's shrine. He died at Vincennes, in his thirty-fourth year (August 1422), and his body was embalmed and deposited for a time in Rouen Cathedral. Detailed accounts survive of his funeral procession and burial in the Abbey. At Dover the great bishops and ecclesiastics met the procession and accompanied it to London, where the body was placed in state in St Paul's Cathedral. Thence it was taken in procession to the Abbey on

---

[1] Two, whose statues were among these – William of Windsor and Blanche of the Tower – have a little tomb in St Edmund's Chapel, p. 83.

[1] John Harvey, *English Medieval Architects* (1954), p. 199.

View of chantry chapel of Henry V from west

7 November 1422, and interred with much pomp, James I, the captive King of Scots, attending as chief mourner. Behind the effigy of the king his three chargers were led up to the altar and his banners were borne by great nobles. Henry's will directed that a high chantry chapel should be raised over his body, and the eastern end of St Edward's Chapel was accordingly cleared out in order to carry out his wishes. This structure, which was supervised by John Thirske, encroaches on the ambulatory and on the tombs of Eleanor and Philippa. The tomb, which was not finished until about 1431, is beneath the arch, and the **chantry chapel**, with the Altar of the Annunciation, where prayers were said for the king's soul, is over it. Above this altar is an Annunciation and the patron saints of England and France, St George and St Denis, and two kings, the Confessor and St Edmund, on either side. The centre niche, which probably contained a representation of the Trinity, is vacant. In the niches are smaller statues. At one time displayed on the bar above the chantry were a shield and saddle, purchased for the funeral, and also a contemporary tournament helm. All these have now for better preservation been placed in the Undercroft Museum. On the ambulatory sides, north and south, are representations of the homage and crowning at Henry V's coronation – on the north is his figure on horseback leaping a stream with the tents of his soldiers behind. Among the

devices on the frieze and cornice are heraldic badges of a cresset, a collared antelope, and a swan also collared, chained to a beacon. The Purbeck marble tomb has lost its ancient splendour; the figure is now a block of oak; the head, sceptre, and other regalia, all of silver, and the plates of silver gilt which covered the body, were stolen in 1546. A new head modelled in polyester resin by *Louisa Bolt*, following a contemporary description of the king and the earliest portrait of him, was added in 1971, together with new hands. The gates, by a London smith, *Roger Johnson*, put up in the ninth year of Henry VI (1430–31), still remain. **Catherine de Valois**, b. 1401, d. 1437, Henry V's queen, daughter of Charles VI of France. After Henry's death she married Owen Tudor, a Welsh squire. Edmund, Earl of Richmond, the father of Henry VII, was one of Catherine's sons by this marriage and she thus became the ancestress of the Tudor line. Catherine died in the monastery at Bermondsey. Her body was apparently embalmed before her burial on 10 February 1437. The painted funeral wooden effigy (now in the Undercroft Museum) was 'fully robed in a satin mantle, surcote, and tunic, all furred with ermine; crown, sceptre, and rings silver gilt' and was carried on a magnificent hearse. Her son, Henry VI, and his queen attended the funeral in the Lady Chapel. When Henry VII pulled down the old chapel he removed his grandmother's body and it was placed above ground in an open coffin of loose boards near Henry V's tomb. There it remained for over 200 years. Samuel Kiechel of Ulm saw her body in 1585 and noted that it was like an Egyptian mummy.[1] Pepys, writing in 1669, notes that he saw, 'by perticular favour, the body of Queen Katherine of Valois, and had her upper part of her body in my hands. And I did kiss her mouth, reflecting upon it that I did kiss a Queen, and that this was my birthday thirty-six years old that I did first kiss a Queen.'[2] In the eighteenth century the bones were still 'firmly united, and thinly cloth'd with flesh, like scrapings of tann'd leather'. In 1778 the queen's body was at last hidden from sight beneath the Villiers monument in the Chapel of St Nicholas. It was removed in 1878 by Dean Stanley and placed beneath the ancient altar slab in the chantry chapel of Henry V.

In an unmarked grave immediately in front of the north turret of Henry V's Chantry Chapel is buried **Richard Courtenay**, Bishop of Norwich, who accompanied Henry V to France and died at the siege of Harfleur in 1415. He was buried here by the express command of the king.

Partly covered by the step up from the Confessor's Chapel to the tomb of Henry V and wholly concealed from view by the present wooden ramp are the fragmentary brasses to **Margaret de Valence**, d. 1276, and her brother **John de Valence**, d. 1277, young children of William de Valence (q.v.). When complete the two slabs had cross brasses and were inlaid with separate single Lombardic letters. One of the slabs has its centre lined up on the axis of the chapel and is, therefore, probably the first of the two to be laid down (and so probably Margaret's). This slab is inlaid with mosaic like the other Cosmati works.

1   *Bibliothek des Litterarischen Vereins in Stuttgart*, vol. LXXVI, p. 23.
2   *Diary*, 23 February 1669.

The North Ambulatory & its Chapels

See plan, page 36

CHAPELS OF ST JOHN THE EVANGELIST, ST MICHAEL, AND ST ANDREW

Commonly now – at the Abbey – called 'Nightingale', from *Roubiliac's* spectacular monument, what is structurally the eastern aisle of the north transept was once three chapels dedicated to these saints.

CHAPEL OF ST JOHN THE EVANGELIST

Queen Maud alias Edith, first wife of Henry I and great-great-niece of the Confessor, gave to the monastery various relics of St John. A fifteenth-century screen given by Abbot Esteney, stood until about 1772 between this chapel, the north transept, and the north ambulatory. Part, including the doorway, remains on the transept side. Set in the doorway is the memorial to **Sir John Franklin, KCH**, b. 1786, d. 1847, Arctic explorer, lost with all his crew when completing the discovery of the North-West Passage. Actual evidence of Franklin's death was not found until 1859. Portrait bust by *M. Noble* erected in 1875. The monument has appropriate words from the *Benedicite* and a quatrain specially written by Tennyson.

Beneath the Franklin memorial is a small tablet to **Admiral Sir Francis Leopold McClintock, KCB**, b. 1819, d. 1907, Arctic explorer; he discovered evidence of the fate of the expedition of Franklin, McClintock's former chief.

The middle of the chapel is occupied by the monument and tomb of **Sir Francis Vere**, b. 1560, d. 1609, military commander and man of letters. Sir Francis was the son of Geoffrey Vere, brother of John (de Vere), 16th Earl of Oxford, and was one of the greatest of Queen Elizabeth's soldiers. He commanded the English forces in the Low Countries and distinguished himself particularly at the Battle of Nieuport (1600) and during his five-month-long defence of Ostend against the Spanish. Although there is a slight resemblance between Vere's tomb and that of the 1st Lord Salisbury at Hatfield, there seems to be little doubt that the Abbey tomb was inspired directly by the tomb of Count Engelbert II of Nassau-Dillenburg (d. 1504), Stadtholder of the Netherlands under Maximilian I, and of his wife Limburga von Baden, in the Hervormde Kerk at Breda. This tomb is somewhat later than the date of Count Engelbert's death – perhaps about 1530 – but it is reasonable to suppose that Sir Francis had seen the Breda tomb and wished his own to resemble it. The figures of the deceased on the Breda tomb are carved in alabaster and above is a slab supported on the shoulders by four classical worthies – Julius Caesar, Regulus, Hannibal, and Philip of Macedon. Laid out on the slab is a complete suit of armour. On Vere's tomb Sir Francis is represented recumbent in civil dress carved in alabaster, and four men in armour, kneeling each upon one knee, support on their shoulders a slab of marble on which is laid out a complete contemporary armour in alabaster with, in the centre, an achievement of the arms of Vere with its quarterings.

In the grave beside his brother, Sir Francis, lies also **Horace (de Vere), 1st Baron Vere of Tilbury**, b. 1565, d. 1635, who succeeded his brother as Commander-in-Chief of the English forces in the Low Countries. **Aubrey (de Vere), 20th** and last **(Vere) Earl of Oxford**, b. 1627, d. 1703, lies in a grave to the north of the two brothers.

South of the Vere monument and fixed to the back of General Wolfe's monument in the ambulatory is one executed by *J. Bacon, Jun.*, in memory of **Captain Edward Cooke, RN**, b. 1772, d. 1799, mortally wounded commanding the *Sybille* while capturing a French frigate (*La Forte*) in the Bay of Bengal. This event was of such importance to British trade in India that the East India Company erected this monument in 1806.

Clement Saunders, d. 1695, Carver in Ordinary to Charles I, James II, and William III. His monument was formerly in the central aisle of the north transept above that to Admiral Warren. Buried in the Abbey by his own desire having left several bequests solely on that condition.

East of the Vere tomb formerly stood an altar dedicated to St John the Evangelist, above which was erected *c.* 1520 a roundel of the head of Christ by *P. Torrigiano* which is depicted in the Islip Roll (p. 58). The roundel (now in the Wallace Collection) was probably taken down when John (Holles), 1st Earl of Clare commissioned a monument to his brother **Sir George Holles**, d. 1626. Buried in this chapel, Holles was nephew of Sir Francis Vere, whom he served

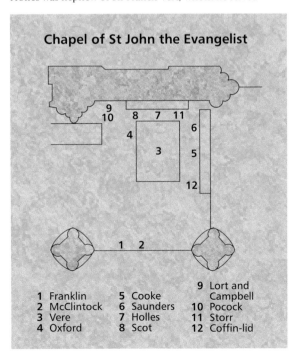

Chapel of St John the Evangelist

1 Franklin	5 Cooke	9 Lort and Campbell
2 McClintock	6 Saunders	10 Pocock
3 Vere	7 Holles	11 Storr
4 Oxford	8 Scot	12 Coffin-lid

under in the Low Countries as Major General, and is represented as a standing figure in Roman armour. Beneath is a bas-relief of the Battle of Nieuport at which like his uncle he distinguished himself. Monument by *N. Stone*.

On the east wall of the chapel and above the Holles monument is a small tablet to (**Mrs**) **Grace Scot**, b. 1622, d. 1646; she was the wife of Colonel Thomas Scot (d. 1660) and the daughter of Sir Thomas Mauleverer, 1st Bt (d. 1655) of Allerton Mauleverer. Both Sir Thomas and his son-in-law Colonel Scot were regicides; the former, dying before the Restoration, was fortunate, but Scot was hanged and quartered at Charing Cross in October 1660. Mrs Scot was buried near the then door into the chapel, and her monument was formerly in the central aisle of the north transept high up above Admiral Warren's monument.

The monument to **Sir Gilbert Lort, 3rd Bt**, b. *c.* 1671, d. 1698, of Stackpoole, Pemb., was also outside in the central aisle directly to the south of Admiral Warren's memorial. He was the son of Sir John Lort, 2nd Bt, by Lady Susanna Holles, the daughter of John (Holles), 2nd Earl of Clare. Buried in the north transept. Sir Gilbert's sister, **Dame Elizabeth Campbell**, b. *c.* 1666, d. 1714, who erected the monument to him, is also commemorated by a tablet. She was the widow of Sir Alexander Campbell of Calder and is also buried in the north transept.

Beneath the Scot, Lort, and Campbell monuments is one by *J. Bacon* to **Admiral Sir George Pocock, KB**, b. 1706, d. 1792. It consists of a figure of Britannia seated, holding a thunderbolt in her right hand and resting her left upon an oval medallion with a portrait bust of Pocock. His father was a naval chaplain and a Fellow of the Royal Society, and his mother was a sister both of Captain Streynsham Master, RN (1682–1724) and of Margaret, Viscountess Torrington, the wife of Admiral George (Byng), 1st Viscount Torrington (1663–1733). Pocock entered the Navy under the auspices of Torrington, and first seems to have seen action on board Captain Master's ship, the *Superbe*, in 1718. He subsequently fought many actions against the French and served in the East Indies. In 1758 he became Commander of the East India Station. He was sent in 1762 to reduce Havana and afterwards returned home with £122,697 in prize-money. He 'spent the remainder of his life in dignified ease and splendour'. The monument erected by his son was executed in 1796. Buried at Twickenham, Middx.

Another monument now on the east wall but formerly in the central aisle of the north transept is that by *W. Tyler*, consisting of a portrait bust and inscription in memory of **Rear-Admiral John Storr**, b. 1709, d. 1783; he was of Hilston, Yorks.; Captain (1748); Rear-Admiral of the White (1779); and of the Red (1780). Buried in the north transept.

Beneath the floor north of the Vere tomb is a medieval stone coffin containing a skeleton and a chalice and paten of pewter. The **coffin-lid with a floriated cross** now stands upright immediately west of Captain Cooke's monument. Possibly these are the remains of **Richard de Crokesley**,[1] d. 1258; Abbot of Westminster (1246–58). He died at Winchester during the Parliament held there; it was said that his death was due to poison. At first Crokesley was buried in a chapel built by him and dedicated to St Edmund of

Canterbury; his chapel was demolished when the new work on the nave was continued and his body we are told was transferred to the Chapel of St Nicholas.

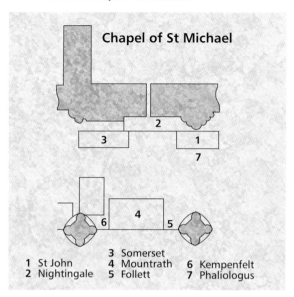

Chapel of St Michael

1	St John	3 Somerset
2	Nightingale	4 Mountrath
		5 Follett

3 Somerset 4 Mountrath 6 Kempenfelt
1 St John 5 Follett 7 Phaliologus
2 Nightingale

CHAPEL OF ST MICHAEL

On the east side of this chapel part of the site of the altar of St Michael was occupied by the monument to the Duchess of Somerset and part is now taken up by the Nightingale one. The ancient **stone altar** was found in the floor of the north transept in 1872 and replaced in the chapel in 1876. The northern part of the late medieval **reredos** also survives. In Keepe's time the chapel, with part of those on either side of it, and the monuments within were covered by the scaffolds which were placed there for the use of the Lower House of Convocation.[1] The western screen was apparently still in place, but the Cavendish/Newcastle monument in the transept had been erected against it. It would seem to have been destroyed when the Mountrath monument was put up in 1771, just as the St John monument was displaced by the Nightingale memorial about 1761.

The monument to **Catherine, Baroness St John of Bletso**, d. 1615, is shown in Ackermann[2] in the Chapel of St Nicholas on top of the indent of Bishop Dudley's brass. It was restored to the Chapel of St Michael by Dean Stanley, who placed it on a new base. Lady St John, represented by a stiff effigy resting on one elbow, was the widow of John (St John), 2nd Lord St John (d. 1596)) and daughter of Sir William Dormer. Buried in this chapel.

Against the east wall is the celebrated monument, executed by *L. F. Roubiliac* (signed and dated 1761) with the assistance of *N. Read*, to **Lady Elizabeth Nightingale**, b. 1704, d. 1731, and her husband **Joseph Gascoigne Nightingale** (*né* Gascoigne), b. 1695, d. 1752, of Mamhead, Devon, the heir of Sir Robert Nightingale, 5th Bt. Lady Elizabeth, the date of whose death is incorrectly given as 1734 on the monument,

---

1 H. F. Westlake, *Antiquaries Journal* (January 1921), pp. 56–7 suggests Abbot Thomas Millyng, d. 1474.

1 The Upper House sat in Henry VII's Chapel.
2 *History of the Abbey Church of St Peter's Westminster*, vol. II. Plate 32, facing p. 121.

Monument to Lady Elizabeth Nightingale

was the eldest daughter and co-heir of Washington (Shirley), 2nd Earl Ferrers, and died in childbed. The design of the monument is essentially simple and the allegory easily understood – the horror-struck husband attempting to defend his wife from Death. Brayley, embarrassed that his admiration for it and the artist borders on 'enthusiasm', writes of Death ('the gristly King of Terrors'), the skeleton 'in shroudlike habiliments bursting hideous from his darksome cavern' aiming his dart at Lady Elizabeth whose husband 'fondly clasps to his breast the dying female, whose languid helplessness beautifully contrasts with the muscular exertion . . . of her affectionate partner', and of 'the genius . . . and the talents' of Roubiliac, who has contrived 'to express the severe pangs of conjugal affection . . . to portray the last expiring struggle of female imbecility . . . '.[1] The monument was

erected under the will of their only surviving son Washington Gascoigne Nightingale. Husband and wife are buried in a vault in the north ambulatory near Queen Eleanor's tomb.

North of this is the monument of **Sarah, Duchess of Somerset**, d. 1692, married successively to George Grimston (d. 1655), John (Seymour), 4th Duke of Somerset (d. 1675), and Henry, 2nd Lord Coleraine; the duchess was the daughter of Sir Edward Alston, MD (d. 1669), President of the Royal College of Physicians (1635–66), and left much of her fortune to charities in Westminster, Oxford, Cambridge, and Wiltshire. Buried close by in St Andrew's Chapel.

The west side of the chapel is mostly taken up by the now mutilated monument, executed by *J. Wilton*, to **Algernon (Coote), 6th Earl of Mountrath**, b. 1689, d. 1744. The design by *Sir W. Chambers* has been made obscure by the removal of the upper part of the monument, where there was originally a representation of the earl 'seated in glory, with a vacant chair for his Lady'. What now remains shows

1   Neale and Brayley, *History and Antiquities of the Abbey Church of Saint Peter, Westminster*, vol. II, pp. 196–7.

Lady Mountrath (**Lady Diana Newport**, the daughter of Richard, 2nd Earl of Bradford) being assisted from her tomb by an angel, pointing upwards to 'the realms of bliss'[1] where her husband should be awaiting her arrival. The monument was put up when the Countess died in 1766. Mountrath was first buried in a vault in Henry VII's Chapel, but his body was transferred to a newly constructed vault in the Chapel of St John the Evangelist at the time of his wife's burial.

On a pedestal south of the Mountrath monument is a statue, executed in 1850 by *W. Behnes*, formerly in the central aisle of the transept, of **Sir William Webb Follett, KC, MP**, b. 1798, d. 1845; Solicitor-General (1834–5 and 1841); Attorney-General (1844).

North of the Mountrath monument is one executed by *J. Bacon*, Jun. pursuant to the will of Gustavus Adolphus Kempenfelt, Esq. (d. 1808) of Hurley, Berks., in memory of the latter's brother **Rear-Admiral Richard Kempenfelt** b. 1718, d. 1782; well known from Cowper's poem 'The Wreck of the *Royal George*':

> His sword was in its sheath,
> His fingers held the pen:
> When Kempenfelt went down,
> With twice four hundred men.

He became Rear-Admiral of the Blue in 1780. In 1781, off Ushant, Kempenfelt, with only twelve of the line, succeeded in taking fifteen valuable French prizes bound for the West Indies, despite their being escorted by a squadron of nineteen under Admiral de Guichen. The following year on 29 August while at Spithead the *Royal George* 'overset and sunk . . . by which fatal event about nine hundred persons were launched into eternity'. The monument has representations of the ship submerged but with her masts above water, Kempenfelt's soul on its way heavenwards, and a descending winged Victory with crown and palm branch. Buried at Alverstoke, Hants.

Also buried in this chapel is **Theodore Phaliologus**, d. 1644. He was almost certainly the eldest son of Theodore Paleologus (d. 1636) on whose monument in the church at Landulph, Cornwall, is set out in full his claim to be directly descended from the brother of Constantine Paleologus the 'last Christian Emperor of Greece'. The son, Theodore, served as Lieutenant in the Parliamentary regiment commanded by Oliver, 1st Earl of Bolingbroke.

CHAPEL OF ST ANDREW

King Athelstan and King Edward the Confessor are said to have given relics of St Andrew to the Abbey and also part of the cross on which by tradition he met his death.

Abbot Kyrton when he was sacrist either built or, at least, enriched the screen of this chapel with heraldry and other devices. This seems to have been destroyed at the time of the erection of the Holles Newcastle monument, the back of which now forms the west wall of St Andrew's Chapel. On this are three monuments which were formerly in the Chapel of St John the Evangelist.

A memorial, executed in 1803 by *J. Bacon, Jun.*, to two brothers: **Lieutenant Benjamin John Forbes**, d. 1791, aged

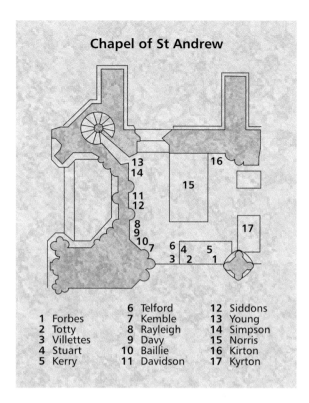

Chapel of St Andrew

1	Forbes	6	Telford
2	Totty	7	Kemble
3	Villettes	8	Rayleigh
4	Stuart	9	Davy
5	Kerry	10	Baillie
		11	Davidson
12	Siddons		
13	Young		
14	Simpson		
15	Norris		
16	Kirton		
17	Kyrton		

nineteen, of the 74th Foot and killed at the assault on Kistnagherry in the East Indies; and **Lieutenant Richard Gordon Forbes**, d. 1799, aged twenty; of the 1st Foot Guards and killed near Alkmaar in North Holland. They were both sons of Lieutenant-General Gordon Forbes, Colonel of the 29th Foot. A seated figure of Affection represented by a mourning female is beside two urns overshadowed by a weeping willow.

Near by is a monument by *J. Nollekens* comprising a portrait bust on a medallion to **General the Hon. Sir Charles Stuart, KB**, b. 1753, d. 1801. He was a younger son of John, Earl of Bute, and fought in Corsica and Minorca, which latter place he captured from the Spanish in 1798.

Above to the right of the latter is a monument by *Sir R. Westmacott*, to **Lieutenant-General William Anne Villettes**, b. 1754, d. 1808; Governor and Commander-in-Chief of the forces in Jamaica. Buried at Kingston, Jamaica.

Immediately above Stuart is another monument by *J. Bacon, Jun.*, erected by William Totty to the memory of his brother **Rear-Admiral Thomas Totty**, b. *c.* 1746, d. 1802; he was Commander-in-Chief of the Leeward Island Station (1801), and at Martinique contracted fever of which he died. Buried in the Garrison Chapel at Portsmouth.

Beneath is the tomb of **Anastasia, Countess of Kerry**, d. 1799, wife of **Francis Thomas (FitzMaurice), 3rd Earl of Kerry**, b. 1740, d. 1818, and daughter of Peter Daly of Quansbury, Co. Galway. The fulsome epitaph expressing Lord Kerry's devotion to her during thirty-one years of their married life and his distress upon her death is corroborated by Ackermann in the following words in a footnote: 'At the north end of the tomb, a large kneeling cushion appeared for a long succession of time after the lady's death, on which her lamenting lord, at stated and very frequent periods, used to

---

1   Neale and Brayley, *History and Antiquities of the Abbey Church of Saint Peter, Westminster*, vol. II, p. 196.

pour forth his devout and afflicted spirit.'[1] Lord Kerry himself is also buried near by.

Close by is the monument by *E. H. Baily* (1839), to **Thomas Telford**, b. 1757, d. 1834, celebrated in his time as the first engineer in Europe. He was one of the founders, in 1818, of the society which became the Institution of Civil Engineers. He was its first President and in 1828 procured for it a charter of incorporation. The Menai Bridge, the Caledonian Canal, and the inland navigation of Sweden are among his best-known works. Buried in the nave.

Near by the celebrated actor **John Philip Kemble**, b. 1757, d. 1823, is commemorated, represented as Cato, by a statue executed by *J. Flaxman* (d. 1826), and finished after Flaxman's death by *J. E. Hinchliffe*. Until 1865 it stood in the north transept. Buried at Lausanne.

On the north wall is a memorial with a medallion portrait bust by *D. Wood* to **John William (Strutt), 3rd Baron Rayleigh, OM, PRS**, b. 1842, d. 1919, physicist and mathematician, Cavendish Professor of Experimental Physics at Cambridge in succession to Clerk Maxwell and Chancellor of the University (1908–10); the aspects of physics which he studied were electrodynamics, electromagnetism, optics, and colour vision; his publications included works on the theory of sound, on photography and the density of gases. With Sir William Ramsay he discovered argon for which they were jointly awarded the Nobel Prize.

A memorial tablet to **Sir Humphry Davy, Bt, PRS**, b. 1778, d. 1829, the inventor of the famous safety-lamp is by *Sir F. Chantrey*. He was a chemist, physicist, traveller, poet, and, in addition, author of a book on fly-fishing. Buried at Geneva.

Beneath Davy's memorial is another by *Chantrey*, to **Matthew Baillie**, b. 1761, d. 1823, physician and anatomist. A nephew of John Hunter (q.v.), he was Physician Extra-Ordinary to King George III (1810–20) and Physician in Ordinary to Princess Charlotte (1816–17). Buried at Duntisburne Abbots, Glos.

To the east is a tablet by *R. Hayward* to **Susannah Jane Davidson**, d. 1767, aged twenty.

The famous actress (**Mrs**) **Sarah Siddons**, b. 1755, d. 1831, is commemorated close to her brother J. P. Kemble by a statue executed by *T. Campbell* (1845). Buried in Paddington Cemetery.

A medallion bust by *Sir F. Chantrey* commemorates **Dr Thomas Young**, b. 1773, d. 1829, physician, physicist, Coptic scholar, and decipherer of Egyptian hieroglyphs; Professor of Physics at the Royal Institution; Foreign Secretary of the Royal Society. He has left his name also in the study of mechanics in 'Young's modulus' of elasticity. In the study of human vision he discovered astigmatism, and he also worked on the wave-theory of light. Buried at Farnborough, Kent.

Sir James Young Simpson, Bt, b. 1811, d. 1870, physician. His name may be linked with Dr Chamberlen (q.v.), who improved the use of forceps in midwifery, because Simpson discovered the use of chloroform as an anaesthetic for women in childbirth (1847) and when in 1853 Queen Victoria consented to have chloroform at the birth of her seventh child, her example overcame the hitherto prevalent prejudice against the use of an anaesthetic for this purpose. Sculptor: *W. Brodie*. Buried at Edinburgh.

The large and fine **Norris memorial** is by *I. James*: **Henry (Norris), 1st Baron Norris of Rycote**, b. 1525?, d. 1601, and his wife **Margaret**, d. 1599, daughter of John (Williams), 1st Baron Williams of Thame (d. 1559). Lord Norris was the son of Henry Norris (d. 1536), Henry VIII's courtier, executed on the charge of being a lover of Queen Anne Boleyn, although he was probably innocent. Norris, allegedly so great a favourite of the king that he was offered a pardon if he would confess to adultery, maintained Anne's innocence, and so lost his life. Henry Norris, the son, and his wife were shown exceptional favour by Elizabeth I, partly for his father's sacrificing his life for the honour of Elizabeth's mother and partly because of Lady Norris's father's kindness to Elizabeth when in Lord Williams's custody in Queen Mary's reign. Queen Elizabeth knighted Norris in 1566 and made him Ambassador to France; he was recalled in 1570, and in 1572 was raised to the peerage. Round the monument to Lord and Lady Norris are kneeling figures of their six sons, all in armour. William, the eldest, was Marshal of Berwick and died in his father's lifetime; the second son, Sir John Norris, b. 1547?, d. 1597, military commander, and Lord President of Munster (1584), is said to have died of disappointment at not being made Lord Deputy of Ireland. The third son and the only one to outlive his father, Sir Edward Norris, d. 1603, Governor of Ostend (1590–9), alone is represented looking upwards as if alive, in contrast to his brothers all with bowed heads and praying hands. The fourth and sixth sons Henry and Maximilian were soldiers, and so was the fifth son Sir Thomas Norris, b. 1556, President of Munster (1597–9), mortally wounded in 1599. None of those commemorated by the monument is buried in Westminster Abbey.

A tablet commemorates (**Mrs**) **Anne Kirton**, d. 1603, wife of James Kirton of Castle Cary, Somerset.

On the floor in the south-west corner of the chapel is the indent of the lost brass of **Edmund Kyrton**, d. 1466, Abbot of Westminster from 1440 until his resignation in 1462. From 1421 until about 1427 he was prior of Gloucester Hall, now Worcester College, Oxford, a place set aside for Benedictine monks to study. Kyrton belonged to a family of Lincolnshire gentry called Coppledike, and probably took his name of religion from one of the two places in Lincolnshire called Kirton. His family arms appeared among others on the screen which he erected in St Andrew's Chapel; the abbot's brass was originally raised up on an altar tomb, perhaps on the south side of the chapel. The brass survived into the eighteenth century and there exists an engraving of it.

NORTH AMBULATORY

Major-General James Wolfe. b. 1727, d. 1759. He entered the Army when only fourteen, and, after a brilliant career, was killed at the age of thirty-two. His last and greatest exploit, the capture of Quebec, the capital of French Canada, established the English ascendancy in that province. At the head of his troops he scaled the Heights of Abraham, above Quebec, and was mortally wounded in the moment of victory. He was buried at Greenwich.

The colossal monument, erected by the king and Parliament in 1772, at the cost of £3,000, was the first public

1 *History of the Abbey Church of St Peter's Westminster* (1812) vol. II, p. 189.

work of *J. Wilton*. Esteney's and Harpedon's tombs were moved to make way for it. On the bronze bas-relief, by *Capizoldi*,[1] is the scene of the landing of the British troops, and their ascent of the Heights of Abraham. During the First World War a number of Canadian regiments deposited their Colours in the keeping of the Dean and Chapter, and they were grouped upon Wolfe's monument. After the Armistice, the different regiments fetched their colours, but the Canadian Government ordered two flags to be placed on the monument as a perpetual reminder of Canada's help to the mother country in her need.

John Theophilus Beresford, d. 1812, a Lieutenant in the 10th Foot, who was mortally wounded by the explosion of a powder-magazine during Wellington's siege of Ciudad Rodrigo. Buried at Almeida. Memorial by *H. Westmacott*.

Near by is a memorial tablet by *R. Hayward* to **Lieutenant-General Sir James Adolphus Dickenson Oughton, KB**, b. 1720, d. 1780, Commander-in-Chief in north Britain. He was described by Samuel Johnson as 'a man of boundless curiosity and unusual diligence'.

On the pillar between St John the Evangelist's Chapel and the Islip Chapel a small tablet of slate and stone, dedicated in March 1992, commemorates **Mary de St Pol, Countess of Pembroke**, b. 1304, d. 1377. Wife of Aymer de Valence who lies close by. Foundress of Pembroke College, Cambridge and of Denny Abbey, her benefactions to Westminster included an alabaster statue of the Virgin Mary. Designed by *D. Buttress*, executed by *D. Reid*.

John Esteney, d. 1498, Abbot of Westminster from 1474 until his death. He was Millyng's successor, and like him had the guardianship of Elizabeth Woodville, when she and her daughters took sanctuary for the second time (1483). The obligation for each new abbot to go to Rome to be confirmed by the Pope was remitted in Esteney's time. Esteney was Caxton's patron, and it was he who enabled Caxton to set up his press within the precincts in 1476. Esteney continued Millyng's work on the building of the church, the nave was completely roofed, the vaulting of all but three bays of the west end was completed and the great window set up. Esteney's screen was destroyed and his tomb moved and mutilated in the eighteenth century. The brass effigy represents an abbot in Mass vestments under a triple canopy, one hand raised in blessing, the other holding the crosier. A label proceeds from the mouth with the words: *Exultabo in Deo Jhesu Meo* (I shall rejoice in Jesus my God). The tomb was once surmounted by an iron railing; it also had a canopy, through the arch of which St John's altar could be seen. It has been twice opened, in 1706 and again in 1772. In 1706 the abbot's body was found entire, 'lying in a chest quilted with yellow satin, he had on a gown of crimson silk girded to him with a black girdle; on his legs were white silk stockings, and on his face, which was black, a clean napkin doubled up and laid cornerwise'.[2]

In the floor are two slabs, once containing brasses. Two monks of the Abbey – **Thomas Brown** (d. *c*. 1513–14) and **Robert Humphrey** (d. 1509) – lie beneath one. The other was originally raised on a grey marble tomb, but is now level with the floor. Beneath it lies **Sir Thomas Parry**, d. 1560,

Treasurer of the Household and Master of the Courts of Wards and Liveries to Queen Elizabeth. All that remains are four shields reused from earlier brasses, which for better preservation are fixed to the base of a neighbouring Purbeck marble column. The Parry tomb was formerly inside the Chapel of St John the Evangelist and north of Sir John Harpedon's tomb.

In the ambulatory are buried three men killed in the Anglo-Dutch Wars:

Captain James (Ley), 3rd Earl of Marlborough, b. 1618. He commanded the *Old James* and had a distinguished career in the Navy. **Charles (MacCarty), Viscount Muskerry**, the son and heir apparent to the Earl of Clancarty, was a volunteer on the *Royal Charles* (see Charles, Earl of Falmouth, p. 63). Both these sailors were killed at the Battle of Lowestoft on 3 June 1665.

Vice-Admiral Sir William Berkeley, was killed on 1 June 1666, on his ship the *Swiftsure*. The Dutch boarded the ship, embalmed Berkeley's body, and placed it in the cathedral at The Hague. It was later brought back to England and buried here.

Sir John Harpedon, d. 1438, fifth and last husband of the Kentish heiress Joan de la Pole, Lady Cobham. Her fourth husband was Sir John Oldcastle, the Lollard, who was executed in 1417. Lady Cobham died in 1434, and lies in Cobham Church, Kent. His tomb was once raised from the floor, and stood to the west of Esteney's in St John's Chapel, but was removed to make way for Wolfe's monument. The brass represents a knight; his feet rest on a lion, his head on a helmet with the crest of a hind's head issuing from a coronet.

Close by is a monument to **Field-Marshal John Louis (Ligonier), 1st Earl Ligonier, KB**, b. 1680, d. 1770. He was the son of Louis de Ligonnier, Seigneur de Monteuquet in Languedoc, where he was born. He distinguished himself in the Army, fighting under Marlborough in all his battles and later at Dettingen. His long military career was crowned with the Battle of Val (1747), where he checked the advance of the French. He was taken prisoner and led before Louis XV, who complimented him on his brilliant charge. Later he became General of the Ordnance. Medallion heads of the four British sovereigns whom he served and the names of the chief battles in which he took part are on the monument. Sculptor: *J. F. Moore*. Buried at Cobham, Surrey. See also the tablet to his brother, Colonel F. Ligonier (p. 106).

THE ISLIP CHANTRY CHAPEL

This chapel was fitted up by Abbot Islip as a Jesus Chapel and his name and rebus – an eye within a slip or branch of a tree grasped by a hand, and a man slipping from the branch 'I-slip' – are repeated many times with slight variations in the elaborate carving both on the frieze and inside the chapel, and were also painted on the window. Horace Walpole says he saw two panes of glass purloined from Islip's Chapel in the Bishop of Rochester's Palace (1752). It is separated from the ambulatory by a stone screen, part of which was cut away to form a new doorway when the old door inside the chapel was walled up. Two Jesus altars, where Masses were said for the abbot's soul, formerly stood here, one in the chantry chapel above, and one in the chapel below. At the back of each was a representation of the Crucifixion; the red and white damask frontals bore the abbot's arms.

1   M. Whinney, *Sculpture in Britain 1530–1830* (1988), p. 265, suggests that the sculptor was G. B. Capezzuoli.

2   Dart, *Westmonasterium*, vol. II, p. xxxiii.

*Islip Roll: upper and lower chapels showing destroyed Jesus Altar and Tomb of Islip with (left)
destroyed tomb of Abbot Esteney and altar of St John the Evangelist*

The Lower Islip Chapel today

The remains of Islip's tomb are now in the upper chantry chapel; it was originally in the centre of the lower chapel, and consisted of two slabs of black marble; the upper one, supported by brass pilasters, formed a canopy to the lower one, upon which was a figure of the abbot in his vestments. **John Islip**, elected abbot in 1500, was born on 10 June 1464 seemingly at Islip, Oxfordshire, the Confessor's birthplace. He was a favourite with two kings, Henry VII and Henry VIII, and a Privy Councillor. Under his rule Henry VII's Chapel was built, the abbot laying the foundation-stone with his own hands (1503). In his time the nave was completed, the great west window set up by Esteney was glazed, and the abbot himself superintended the erection of the west towers as far as the roof, filling the niches outside with statues of kings who had been benefactors. He also added the Jericho Parlour and the rooms above as well as the 'Abbot's Pew'. Lastly, he planned to build a lofty central tower and lantern, with a chime of bells. Islip died on 12 May 1532, eight years before the dissolution of the monastery, at his manor house of Neyte, whence his body was brought with much ceremony to his own little chapel. It is illustrated in the Islip Roll, a brief announcing his death and intended to be sent round to the other chief monasteries. The Roll was never completed, probably on account of the dissolution. It consists of pen drawings attributed to *Gerard Hornebolt*, which represent: the abbot on his deathbed; the hearse standing before the High Altar; and Islip's Chapel, showing mural paintings including a large Crucifixion and a figure of the abbot praying beneath it.

The altar has been restored. Until 1940 its site was occupied by the monument of **Sir Christopher Hatton, KB**, d. 1619, and Alice, his wife, daughter of Thomas Fanshaw. Buried at the entrance to the Chapel of Our Lady of the Pew. The monument was moved to the triforium in 1940.

In vaults beneath the lower chapel are buried:

Stephen Jack Marriott, b. 1886, d. 1964, Canon of Westminster (1937–63), Archdeacon (1946–51 and 1959–63), Sub-dean (1951–9). Also his wife **Emilia**, d. 1954.

Harold Costley-White, b. 1878, d. 1966, Head Master of Westminster School, (1919–37), Canon of Westminster (1936–8), Dean of Gloucester (1938–53) and **Hope** (*née* **Ranger**), d. 1977, his wife.

Christopher (**Hatton**), **1st Baron Hatton of Kirby**, d. 1670, Comptroller of the King's Household from December 1643 to 1646; Governor of Guernsey 1662. His wife **Elizabeth** (*née* **Montagu**), d. 1672, and their daughter-in-law, **Cecilia** (*née* **Tufton**), **Lady Hatton**, d. 1672. Both the ladies were killed in an explosion of the powder-magazine at Castle Cornet in Guernsey, which was struck by lightning in December 1672.

Sir Charles Reed Peers, CBE, b. 1868, d. 1952, Surveyor of the Fabric (1935–51).

Anna Hassall, d. 1750. In her will she was described as 'late of Jamaica'.

William Barnard, Bishop of Derry, b. 1697, d. 1768, Prebendary of Westminster (1732–43), Dean of Rochester (1743), Bishop of Raphoe (1744), and Bishop of Derry from 1747 until his death.

William Thompson Elliott, b. 1880, d. 1940, Canon of Westminster (1938–40).

Frederic Lewis Donaldson, b. 1860, d. 1953, Canon of Westminster (1924–53), Sub-dean (1944–51). Also his wife **Sarah Louise**, d. 1950.

Cyril Theodore Henry Dams, b. 1906, d. 1973, Precentor of Westminster Abbey (1951–63).

John Dudley Carleton, b. 1908, d. 1974, Head Master of Westminster School (see also p. 112).

Lawrence Edward Tanner, CVO, b. 1890, d. 1979, younger son of Ralph Tanner, Senior Assistant Master, Westminster School. A great authority on Westminster, he was Keeper of the Muniments (1926–66), Librarian (1956–72), and Librarian Emeritus (1972–9). He wrote a number of books and pamphlets on both Westminster School and Abbey. As Secretary to the Royal Almonry (1921–64), he was instrumental in getting the Royal Maundy ceremony once more attended personally by the sovereign. Buried with his wife, **Joan Doreen Tanner, FSA**, b. 1898, d. 1971, eldest daughter of the Hon. Assheton Nathaniel Curzon.

Robert P. Howgrave Graham, b. c. 1880, d. 1959. Assistant Keeper of the Muniments. He restored the early funeral effigies (now in the Undercroft Museum) after war damage.

Edward Wiggett Thompson, d. 1969. Head Master of Westminster Abbey Choir School (1946–65). Also his wife Peggy, d. 1954.

Stephen Ernest Dykes Bower, b. 1903, d. 1994. Surveyor of the Fabric (1951–73). Under his surveyorship began the restoration of the Abbey completed in 1995. He restored many of the monuments and coloured the choir screen and organ cases.

Admiral Sir Charles Saunders, b. 1713?, d. 1775; First Lord of the Admiralty. As Commander-in-Chief of the Fleet he assisted Wolfe in the capture of Quebec.

Also several members of the **Pulteney family** to whom there is a fine heraldic ledger-stone.

On the south wall a tablet in memory of three generations of the Wilberforce family; **William Wilberforce** (1759–1833); **Samuel Wilberforce** (1805–73), Dean of Westminster and Bishop of Oxford; **Basil Wilberforce** (1841–1916), Canon and Archdeacon of Westminster (whose kinsmen helped to restore this chapel in 1940).

A window, by *Hugh Easton*, was presented in 1948 by the then Dean, Dr Alan Don (q.v.), as a thank-offering for the deliverance of Westminster Abbey and St Margaret's Church from the Second World War and in memory of Abbot Islip and Dean de Labilliere.

THE ISLIP UPPER CHANTRY CHAPEL, now the Nurses' Memorial Chapel

A flight of steps leads to the upper chantry chapel of Abbot Islip which in 1950 was furnished as a memorial chapel containing a Roll of Honour with the names of those of the nursing and midwifery professions who died during the Second World War. For this purpose Abbot Islip's tomb-slab on its original gilt-bronze colonnettes was removed from the lower chapel and re-erected against the east wall and on it has been placed the Roll of Honour and two gilded bronze candlesticks presented by HM Queen Elizabeth the Queen Mother in 1950. Above on the wall is a crucifix in bronze, a duplicate of the original by Giovanni da Bologna (1524–1608) in the Church of SS Annunziata at Florence. The memorial window was designed by *Hugh Easton*, the remainder of the memorial by *S. Comper*. From the original decorations there remain two large canopied figures of kings painted in monochrome on either side of a recess in the east wall.

Also in the chapel is a lamp which, since 1973, has been carried in procession at the Florence Nightingale commemoration service. The gift of Sir Dan Mason, in memory of his mother, Kathleen Dampien-Bennett.

Outside in the ambulatory lies **Brian Duppa**, b. 1588, d. 1662, Dean of Christ Church, Oxford, successively Bishop of Chichester, Salisbury, and Winchester and tutor to Charles II. He was a generous benefactor to Christ Church and to All Souls College, Oxford; he also founded a hospital at Greenwich, his birthplace. A Latin inscription records his love for Richmond, where 'he lay concealed in the troublesome times, and afterwards breathed forth his pious soul'. Tablet now on the wall near Wolfe's monument. Sculptor: *B. Burman*.

Near Duppa are buried **Dr John Doughty**, b. 1597, d. 1672; Prebendary of Westminster (1660–72). His widow **Catherine**, d. 1694, married secondly, Sir Thomas Heath (d. 1680) of Stoke, near Guildford, and thirdly Henry Croone (d. 1689). As 'Lady Heath' she desired to be buried near Dr Doughty. **Henry Croone** was buried in the west cloister.

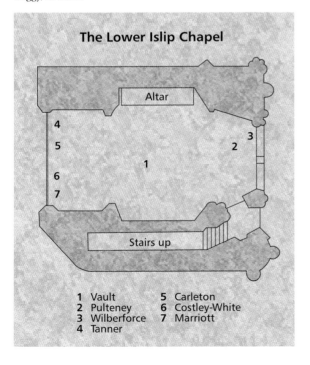

The Lower Islip Chapel

Altar

4
5
6
7

3
2
1

Stairs up

1 Vault
2 Pulteney
3 Wilberforce
4 Tanner
5 Carleton
6 Costley-White
7 Marriott

Thomas Millyng, Bishop of Hereford, d. 1492; Abbot of Westminster (1469–74). In Millyng's time Elizabeth Woodville first took sanctuary, and her eldest son, Edward V, was born and baptised in the abbot's house, the abbot and prior standing as godfathers. In 1468, when prior, Millyng had started a continuation of the nave, the work on which had ceased under Henry VI. He now roofed in another bay of the nave with £520 which King Edward IV, his queen, and the young prince gave him. Edward rewarded Millyng for his protection of the queen with the bishopric of Hereford in 1474. He died at Hereford, but was buried in the centre of St John the Baptist's Chapel. A stone coffin, said to be that of Millyng, was formerly there but is now in the ambulatory. It is an earlier, possibly thirteenth-century, coffin reused. A wooden crosier-head, possibly Millyng's, is in the Undercroft Museum.

CHAPEL OF OUR LADY OF THE PEW

The Chapel of St John the Baptist is now entered through a double vestibule. But in its original form the outer of these vestibules was a self-contained rectangular recess about five feet square, believed to be the Chapel of Our Lady of the Pew (i.e., a small enclosure).[1] The painted vaulting of this recess with its carved boss of the Assumption dates from the second half of the fourteenth century and in the back wall of the recess, facing the ambulatory, was a shallow niche with a bracket on which stood an image. The walls of the recess were elaborately painted and are studded with hooks evidently for votive offerings. The outer doorway with its painted wooden half-gates and iron bracket for an alms-box are also original. In this form the chapel remained until about 1502, when it was enlarged to contain an altar dedicated to St Erasmus. At the same time the bracket with its image was moved back a few feet and placed in the new north wall of the enlarged chapel. The hooks which secured the image still remain, and the painted background still shows a shadow outline of the figure. The present entrance to St John the Baptist's Chapel was made when the tomb of Bishop Ruthall (1524) blocked the original way in from the ambulatory. In May 1971 an alabaster image of Our Lady and Child, carved by *Sister Concordia Scott, OSB*, of Minster Abbey in Thanet, was dedicated and placed on the bracket. The design was inspired by a fifteenth-century English alabaster Madonna at Westminster Cathedral.

On the wall just outside this chapel two tablets commemorate **Juliana Crewe**, d. 1621, daughter of Sir Ranulph Crewe and her sister-in-law **Jane**, d. 1639, daughter of Sir John Pulteney and wife of Sir Clipesby Crewe. She is depicted on her deathbed with her family round her. Sculptor: *Epiphanius Evesham*.

CHAPEL OF ST JOHN THE BAPTIST

A wooden screen with a doorway in the centre originally divided this chapel from the ambulatory until it was displaced by the stone tombs, first of Abbot Fascet, then, in 1524, of Bishop Ruthall. The aumbries, where the sacramental plate was kept, still remain in the north-east wall, but Lord Hunsdon's monument takes the place of

Entrance to Chapel of Our Lady of the Pew

the altar, and only an elevation in the pavement marks the altar step.

A monument with a kneeling figure to **Mrs Mary Kendall**, b. 1677, d. 1709, whose many virtues 'render'd her every way worthy of that close union & friendship, in which she liv'd, with The Lady Catherine Jones.'

George Fascet, Abbot of Westminster (1498–1500). An altar tomb and canopy of freestone with a Purbeck slab; in the panels at the sides are the arms of Fascet and of the Abbey; on the frieze, his monogram.

Thomas Ruthall, Bishop of Durham, d. 1523, Private Secretary to Henry VII, and Privy Councillor to Henry VIII. He is said to have died of grief from having sent an inventory of his own wealth, instead of a volume of State papers, to Henry VIII. Wolsey is said to have discovered the mistake, but, having a grudge against the Bishop, gave the book to the king with the remark that 'he knew now where a man of money was in case he needed it'. The tomb and effigy are of freestone, much decayed; only a few fragments of the canopy remain.

William de Colchester, d. 1420, succeeded Litlyngton as Abbot of Westminster in 1386. The work on the rebuilding of the nave, which had commenced under his predecessor, continued to progress during Colchester's abbacy, with the

---

1   An alternative derivation is from Notre-Dame-du-Puy.

help of gifts of money from Richard II, and from Henry V. The abbot was concerned in a plot to restore Richard II, and committed to the Tower for a short period in 1400 after the accession of Henry IV. Colchester lived for twenty years after the conspiracy, was restored to the favour of Henry V, and was sent on various important embassies during his reign, notably to the Council of Constance in 1414. An altar tomb and portrait effigy of freestone, the canopy of which has long disappeared; the whole has been painted and renovation has restored the brilliant colours of such paint as remains.

Above is a tablet to **Lieutenant-Colonel Charles Macleod**, who fell at the siege of Badajos (1812). Sculptor: *J. Nollekens.*

Near by is a monument to **Elizabeth, Countess of Mexborough**, d. 1821, aged fifty-nine, wife of John (Saville), 2nd Earl of Mexborough, d. 1830, and daughter of Henry Stephenson of East Burnham, Bucks.

Henry (Carey), 1st Baron Hunsdon, b. *c.* 1525, d. 1596, cousin and Lord Chamberlain to Queen Elizabeth. He was Governor of Berwick and suppressed the Northern Rebellion in 1569. During the alarm of the Spanish Armada he had charge of a bodyguard enrolled expressly to guard the queen. Hunsdon died at Somerset House, the use of which the queen had granted him.

The monument was erected by his son against the east wall, where the altar formerly stood, and is thirty-six feet high, the highest in the Abbey. Buried in Hunsdon's vault are his wife, **Anne** (d. 1606/7) and his daughter-in-law

Elizabeth, wife of George, 2nd Baron Hunsdon, who married after her first husband's death Ralph, 3rd Lord Eure and died in 1618. Spenser dedicated his poem *Muiopotmos* to her; and **Alice, Countess of Carbery**, d. 1689 (daughter of John (Egerton), 1st Earl of Bridgwater).

Thomas Carey, d. 1649, son of Robert, 1st Earl of Monmouth. He was Gentleman of the Bedchamber to Charles I, and is said to have died of grief at his master's fate. He lies in Lord Hunsdon's vault.

Colonel Edward Popham, b. 1610?, d. 1651, and **Anne** his wife (daughter of William Carr, Groom of the Bedchamber to James I). He was buried in the north ambulatory, on the evening of the day (24 October) of thanksgiving for the Royalist defeat at Worcester (3 September), and Cromwell and many of the Parliamentarians attended his funeral. His body was disinterred at the Restoration; but, instead of being flung into the pit with the rest, his friends were allowed to carry it away; and the monument was suffered to remain on condition that the inscription was erased. Keepe says that by the intervention of Anne Popham's relations, the Carrs, 'who had eminently served his Majesty, the stone was only turned whereon the inscription was insculpt'.

Sir Thomas Vaughan, d. 1483. Private Treasurer to Edward IV, and Chamberlain to his son, Edward, Prince of Wales. Vaughan was beheaded soon after Edward IV's death at Pontefract Castle by order of the Duke of Gloucester. Shakespeare mentions his arrest and death without a trial in *Richard III*. The tomb has possibly been removed from some other place but nothing authentic is known either of its original position or of the date when it was placed here. The tomb is of grey Purbeck; on the slab is the brass figure of a knight in plate armour; under his head is a helmet, the crest a unicorn's head; the feet and brass shields are gone.

Thomas Cecil, b. 1542, d. 1623, and his first wife, **Dorothy Nevill**, d. 1609. He was the eldest son of William, 1st Baron Burghley, and was created **Earl of Exeter** by James I. He took an active part in the suppression of the Northern Rebellion of 1569, and distinguished himself in the Low Countries. Elizabeth made him Governor of Hull as a reward for his services. He founded a hospital at Liddington, Rutland, and was a benefactor to Clare College, Cambridge. The inscription erroneously states that his second wife, Frances Brydges, for whose effigy a vacant space was left, is buried here; but she died forty years after her husband, and lies in Winchester Cathedral. An altar tomb of black and white marble, with recumbent effigies, in the centre of the chapel; round the sides are shields of arms enclosed in laurel wreaths.

Robert (Devereux), Earl of Essex, b. 1591, d. 1646, son of Queen Elizabeth I's favourite. He did good service for Charles I, but in 1642 sided with Parliament, and became General-in-Chief of the Parliamentarian Army. The Independents gave him a magnificent funeral, but that same night 'some rude vindictive fellows' broke into the Abbey and mutilated the Earl's hearse, which was standing near the Communion table, and at that time damaged Camden's monument. The original intention had been to remove the General's remains to Henry VII's Chapel, and raise a monument over him; but the enthusiasm of the moment passed away, and his body was left here. Dean Stanley placed the present inscription over the vault.

Chapels of Our Lady of the Pew and St John the Baptist

1	Kendall	9	Carey
2	Fascet	10	Popham
3	Ruthall	11	Vaughan
4	Colchester	12	Exeter
5	Macleod	13	Essex
6	Mexborough	14	Bohun
7	Hunsdon	15	Falmouth
8	Carbery		

Hunsdon Monument

Near the wall is the small tomb of **Hugh**, d. 1304, and **Mary de Bohun**, d. 1305, children of Humphrey de Bohun, Earl of Hereford and Constable of England, by Elizabeth, fourth daughter of Edward I. This tomb was originally in St Nicholas's Chapel but was moved to St John the Baptist's Chapel at some date between 1532 and 1600. The material is grey Purbeck marble, and, perhaps, was once coloured; round the sides runs a trefoiled arcade; the tomb resembles that of Archbishop Theobald in Canterbury Cathedral.[1]

Dryden's brother-in-law the dramatist, **Sir Robert Howard**, b. 1626, d. 1698, is buried in this chapel.

Charles (Berkeley), 1st Earl of Falmouth and 1st Viscount FitzHardinge, d. 1665, is also buried here. He died at the Battle of Lowestoft on board the *Royal Charles*; standing beside James, Duke of York. A single chain-shot killed Falmouth, Lord Muskerry, and the Hon. Richard Boyle, but missed the future James II. Samuel Pepys heard that the duke was knocked down by Boyle's head striking him. James's narrow escape and Falmouth's death provoked Andrew Marvell's cruel epigram:

> His shatter'd head the fearless Duke distains
> And gave the last first proof that he had Brains

Also buried here are **Sir James Berners** and **Sir John Salisbury**. These knights of Richard II were both condemned in the Merciless Parliament and executed in 1388.[2]

Outside in the ambulatory: **John (Berkeley), 4th Viscount FitzHarding**, b. 1650, d. 1712; Treasurer of the Chamber and a Teller of the Exchequer; and his wife **Barbara, Viscountess FitzHarding**, b. *c.* 1657, d. 1708, the daughter of Sir Edward Villiers (d. 1689) and governess to Prince William, Duke of Gloucester, son of Queen Anne.

Sir John Wyndesore, d. 1414, nephew to William, Lord Wyndesore, who was a famous man in the reign of Edward III, and Lord-Lieutenant of Ireland. All that remains is the Latin verse inscription. The body of **John Pym**, b. 1584, d. 1643, the leader of the popular party in the Long Parliament, was laid with great pomp and ceremony under Sir John Wyndesore's gravestone on 15 December 1643, both Houses of Parliament following him to the grave. The Royalists nicknamed him 'King Pym', for 'he seemed to all men to have the greatest influence upon the House of Commons of any man, and in truth I think he was at that time [1640], and some months after, the most popular man, and the most able to do hurt, that hath lived in any time.'[3] Pym's body was disinterred in 1661, and flung, with those of other Parliamentarians, into a pit outside the Abbey walls.

Close by rested, until it shared the same fate, the body of **William Strode**, d. 1645, the 'Parliament Driver', one of the five Members demanded by Charles I when he made his memorable entry into the House of Commons with an armed force in 1642.

Rear-Admiral Charles Holmes, d. 1761; Commander-in-Chief of the Fleet at Jamaica. One of the last monuments in the Abbey in which an English seaman was dressed as a Roman soldier. Sculptor: *J. Wilton*.

In the ambulatory outside St Paul's Chapel ledger-stones in the floor mark the graves of: **Sir Thomas Peyton, 2nd Bt**, b. *c.* 1613, d. 1684, of Knowlton, Kent; **Dame Katherine Longueville**, b. 1641, d. 1715, Peyton's second daughter, second wife of Sir Thomas Longueville, 2nd Bt (d. 1685), of Wolverton, Bucks; **(Mrs) Elizabeth Longueville**, b. *c.* 1647, d. 1716, Peyton's third daughter, wife of William Longueville, Esq., b. *c.* 1639, d. 1721, an eminent barrister-at-law, patron, and literary executor of Samuel Butler, author of *Hudibras*. **Charles Longueville, Esq.**, d. 1750, eldest son of William Longueville by Elizabeth Peyton, MP for East Looe, Cornwall, and Auditor to Queen Caroline of Anspach, was also buried in the vault.

William (Pulteney), 1st Earl of Bath, b. 1684, d. 1764, popularly called 'Patriot Pulteney', was an orator and statesman of considerable note. For many years a staunch Whig, in 1721 he quarrelled with his party, and went over to the Tory Opposition and became the chief opponent of Walpole who said he 'feared Pulteney's tongue more than other men's swords'. After his elevation to the peerage his political career practically ceased, and, in Pope's words, he 'foams a Patriot to subside a Peer'. Buried in the Islip Chapel. The funeral took place at night, and, as often happened on the occasions of any ceremonial in the Abbey, the mob outside broke into the building, and, mixing with the mourners, a scene of indescribable confusion ensued. In the tumult the wooden canopy over Edward I's tomb was destroyed, for some of the gentlemen took their stand upon the top of the steps leading into the Confessor's shrine, and defended themselves against the pressure of the crowd with their drawn swords and the broken rafters. Sculptor: *J. Wilton*.

At the foot of the steps leading to Henry VII's Chapel: **Edward (Hyde), 1st Earl of Clarendon**, b. 1609, d. 1674, statesman and historian of the Civil Wars and Restoration. For two hundred years he lay beneath a nameless stone, until, in 1867, the present inscription was cut. Clarendon was created Lord Chancellor by Charles II at Bruges in 1658, and scarcely ten years after, was removed from his post, impeached, and banished. He died in exile at Rouen, and his body was brought over to England and buried on 4 January 1675, in the Abbey, where twenty of his relatives and descendants, among them his royal granddaughters, Queen Mary and Queen Anne, now lie. His mother, **Mrs Mary Hyde**, d. 1661, and his mother-in-law, **Lady Aylesbury**, d. 1661, her daughter **Frances**, his second wife, d. 1667, and three young sons are buried in this vault.

Three Protestant refugees from France are buried in a vault between the Chapel of St Paul and the Confessor's Chapel. **Mme Hester Hervart**, d. 1697, widow of a German-born Parisian banker, Bartholomew Hervart (d. 1676), Comptroller-General of the Finances of France, probably came to England with her daughter **Esther, Marquise de Gouvernet**, b. *c.* 1636, d. 1722, widow of Charles de La Tour, Marquis de Gouvernet. Mme Hervart's husband and his brother (also a banker), in return for lending large sums of money to Louis XIII, were granted various estates, but these were confiscated when the Edict of Nantes was revoked. In 1685 Mme de Gouvernet was allowed to come to England to join her daughter **Esther, Lady Eland**, b. 1666, d. 1694, wife of Henry (Saville), Lord Eland (d. 1688), son and heir

---

1 For an account of the opening of this tomb in 1937 see Sir Charles Peers and L. E. Tanner, 'On some recent discoveries in Westminster Abbey', *Archaeologia*, vol. XCIII, 1949.

2 See Barbara Harvey, *Westminster Abbey and its estates in the Middle Ages*, p. 377.

3 Clarendon, *History of the Rebellion*, vol. VI, p. 438.

apparent of George, 1st Marquess of Halifax (q.v.) Mme de Gouvernet lived for many years in a house in St James's Square and was a well-known figure in English society. In 1704 she had erected, against Queen Eleanor's tomb, a monument by the Huguenot sculptor *Nadauld* in memory of Lady Eland. Last century the monument was divided, the inscription placed above the door inside St John the Baptist's Chapel, and the sculptured figure of Lady Eland removed. Both the figure and the inscription are now in the triforium.

CHAPEL OF ST PAUL

This, the easternmost of the northern apsidal chapels, corresponds to St Nicholas's on the south side; the place of the altar is taken up by the tomb of the Countess of Sussex, and the wall arcading has been either destroyed or hidden by monuments. Dedicated to St Paul, it contained, among other relics, the cloth in which it was alleged St Paul's head was wrapped after execution. This relic was given by Edward the Confessor. When the Chantrey monument to James Watt (now removed and replaced by a bronzed plaster bust in the north choir aisle) was put into the chapel much damage was done. The pedestal divided into three was dragged over the Robessart tomb destroying, it is said, the ancient coffin-lid or (more likely) the top of the tomb-chest. The statue was taken in through the gates, but it was so heavy that the vault in the chapel was broken into and rows of gilded coffins disclosed.

The monument on the right of the gate lavishly painted with shields of arms (renovated in 1967–8) is to **Sir Lewis (de) Robessart, Lord Bourgchier, KG**, d. 1430, and **Elizabeth**, his widow, *suo jure* **Baroness Bourgchier**, d. 1433. Sir Lewis[1] was a son of Sir Thierry de Robessart, who figures in Froissart's *Chronicles* and derived his name from a small village in Hainault. Lewis was an Esquire to Henry V and earlier when the latter was Prince of Wales. He was first knighted and in 1421 nominated KG. Sir Lewis was made the King's Standard-Bearer and also appointed Captain of St Sauveur-le-Vicomte (Manche). He was a favourite and trusted knight of Henry V, an executor of the king's will, and after the king's death a Privy Councillor and Chamberlain to Henry VI. Following his marriage to Elizabeth, the Bourgchier heiress and widow of Sir Hugh Stafford, KG, Robessart was summoned to Parliament by virtue of her barony. In 1430 he fell in a skirmish with the French at Conty near Amiens. A contemporary Burgundian relates that Sir Lewis, saying a Knight of the Garter could not retreat, was killed.

Francis (Cottington), 1st Baron Cottington, of Hanworth b. 1578, d. 1652. He was twice ambassador to Spain. His career there began as a young man, when he was sent by Robert Cecil as English Agent. Later he accompanied the future Charles I and Buckingham as the Prince's secretary to Madrid on their journey to negotiate the Spanish match. By using his influence with James I against the project he incurred Buckingham's enmity,[2] he was disgraced at court, and was not restored to favour until after the duke's murder. He openly opposed Laud at the Council, but retained the

---

1   His elder brother Sir John Robessart, KG, was the ancestor of Amy Robsart, first wife of Robert Dudley, Earl of Leicester, favourite of Queen Elizabeth I.
2   Clarendon, *History of the Rebellion*, vol. I, pp. 30, 58.

confidence of Charles I, and was made Lord Treasurer at Oxford, where he joined him in 1643. For his adherence to the Royalist cause he was ruined and obliged to flee abroad; he soon joined Prince Charles, and was sent by him as ambassador to Madrid in 1649, in company with Hyde (afterwards Lord Clarendon). His mission was a failure, and he finally returned to Spain, and died at Valladolid, having become a Roman Catholic. His remains were brought to England in 1679 by his nephew, who raised this monument by *F. Fanelli*. The upper part, to his wife **Anne**, d. 1634, daughter of William Meredith, was put up by Lord Cottington himself; the bust is by *H. Le Sueur*.

Frances (*née* Sidney), Countess of Sussex, d. 1589, aunt to Sir Philip Sidney; second wife of Thomas Ratcliffe, Earl of Sussex and Lord Deputy of Ireland. She founded the College of Sidney Sussex, Cambridge, which restored her monument in the nineteenth century. Her epitaph describes her as 'A woeman whyle she lyved adorned with many and most rare guifts both of mynde and bodye. Towards God trulie and zelouslie religious: To her frends and kinesfoulke most liberall: to the poore, to prisoners, and to the ministers of the worde of god, allwaies most charitable.' *Simons*, the architect of the college, may also have designed the tomb, though *R. Stevens* has also been suggested.[1]

Dudley (Carleton), 1st Viscount Dorchester, b. 1574, d. 1632; Secretary of State to Charles I. He was the last English Deputy who sat on the States-General of the Netherlands (1615–26). He seems to have understood all that related to foreign affairs, 'but was utterly unacquainted with the government, laws, and customs of his own country, and the nature of the people'.[1] Carleton and his first wife

---

1   M. Whinney, *Sculpture in Britain, 1530–1830*, p. 236.

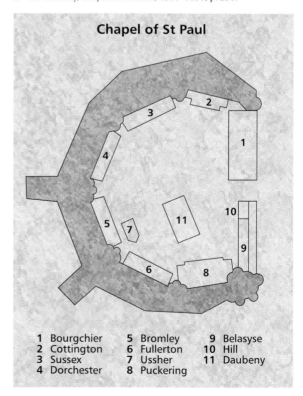

Chapel of St Paul

1 Bourgchier	5 Bromley	9 Belasyse
2 Cottington	6 Fullerton	10 Hill
3 Sussex	7 Ussher	11 Daubeny
4 Dorchester	8 Puckering	

A bedesman from the Daubeny tomb

His wife's effigy is here, but there is no record of her burial in the registers, and the space for her inscription on the monument is left vacant. The effigies are of alabaster, recumbent on a marble altar tomb. Fastened to the lady's girdle is a miniature of her husband.

Close to the tomb of Fullerton lies the Irish Archbishop, **James Ussher**, b. 1581, d. 1656. He lived at Westminster during the troubles in Ireland, and for a time, while Dean Williams was in the Tower, had the use of the Deanery. Ussher was honoured by both parties. He attended Charles I at Oxford, and later on won his way into Cromwell's favour. He was buried here by the Protector's orders, and at his expense. Ussher's funeral is thought to have been the only occasion on which the Anglican funeral service was read in the Abbey during the Commonwealth. The inscribed stone was laid above his grave by desire of Dr Salmon, then Provost of Trinity College, Dublin, in 1904; the inscription is mainly from the pen of Dr Gwynn, who was Regius Professor of Divinity at that time.

Sir John Puckering, b. 1544, d. 1596, Lord Keeper of the Great Seal and twice Speaker of the House of Commons; he took part in the trial of Mary Queen of Scots, and by Queen Elizabeth's wish, prosecuted his secretary Davison for obtaining the queen's signature to Queen Mary's death-warrant. The tomb of different kinds of marble was erected by Puckering's widow; the effigies and the children's statues are alabaster. Above are figures of a Purse- and a Mace-Bearer. An important fragment of sculpture can be seen behind Puckering's tomb (from the ambulatory) being part of the ancient wall arcading, with a figure, probably of St Anne.

Sir Henry Belasyse, d. 1717, of Brancepeth is buried in this chapel, together with six other members of his family. He was Lieutenant-General of William III's forces in Flanders. Sculptor: *P. Scheemakers*.

Sir Rowland Hill, b. 1795, d. 1879, the inventor of penny postage, buried close by. Bust by *W. D. Keyworth, Jun.*

Giles (Daubeny), 1st Baron Daubeny, KG, b. 1452, d. 1508, and his widow **Elizabeth**, daughter of Sir John Arundelle. He was Lord-Lieutenant of Calais and Lord Chamberlain to King Henry VII. He was raised to the peerage in 1486 as a reward for his help to Henry VII in assuming the throne. An altar tomb of Purbeck marble surmounted by alabaster effigies. Daubeny is in plate armour, and wears the mantle and insignia of the Order of the Garter; at his feet are crouching bedesmen with rosaries in their hands. The whole tomb was restored in 1889, and a modern grille replaces the ancient one, which had long disappeared.

Also buried here are **Ezekiel, Baron of Spanheim**, d. 1710; Ambassador Extraordinary from the King of Prussia to Queen Anne, and his wife, **Anna-Elizabeth Kolb, Baroness of Spanheim**, d. 1708.

A new vault was created in the chapel for the **Rt Hon. Susanna** (*née* **Robinson**), **Lady Delaval**, d. 1783, who married first John Potter (d. 1749), Under-Secretary of State, and was subsequently first wife to the **Rt Hon. John (Hussey), Lord Delaval**, b. 1728, d. 1808. He is buried with her; also their youngest daughter, the **Rt Hon. Sarah (Hussey), Countess of Tyrconnel**, d. 1800, second wife of George (Carpenter), 2nd Earl of Tyrconnel.

Anne, daughter of Sir Henry Savile (d. 1627), are buried here in the same grave. The monument was erected about 1635. *Nicholas Stone*, the sculptor, says he received £200 in money for it, and also an 'old monument that stood in the same place sett up for his lady some eight years before'.[2]

Sir Thomas Bromley, b. 1530, d. 1587, succeeded Sir Nicholas Bacon as Lord Keeper. He presided at the trial of Mary Queen of Scots, and died two months after her execution. Dart translates the Latin inscription, which is now illegible: 'When he had for eight years delivered equity with singular integrity and temper of mind, being snatch'd hastily away to the grief of all good men, was here buried.' His son erected the monument of Lydian marble and alabaster. The effigy represents the Lord Keeper in his robes; in front kneel his eight children; at the back is the official purse for the Great Seal, supported by putti; above in spandrels are the figures of Fame and Immortality bearing trumpets.

Sir James Fullerton, d. 1631; First Gentleman of the Bedchamber to Charles I. 'A firme Pillar to ye Cōmon Wealth, a faithful Patron to ye Catholiq Church; a faire Patterne to ye British Court: He Lived To ye welfare of his Country: To ye Honour of his Prince; To ye Glory of His God: He dyed Fuller of Faith then of Feares: Fuller of Resolucōn, then of Paienes; Fuller of Honour then of Dayes.'[1] Buried in the ambulatory.

1   Clarendon, *History of the Rebellion*, vol. I. p. 114.
2   H. Walpole, *Anecdotes of Painting*.

1   Epitaph.

Henry VII's Chapel

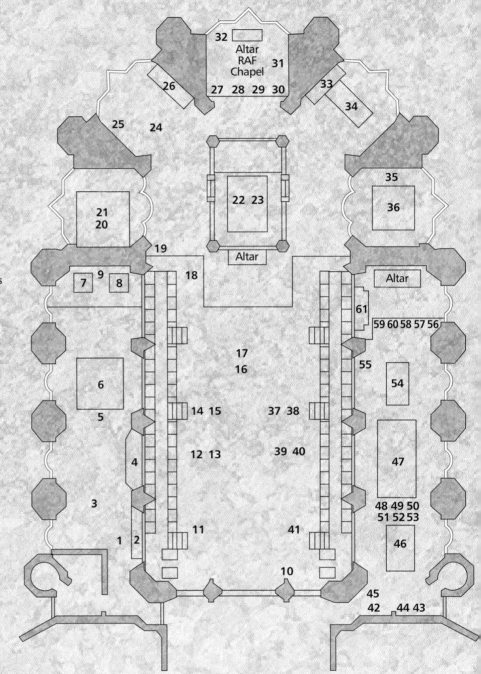

1 Addison and Craggs
2 Halifax
3 Monck vault: Sandwich
4 Halifax
5 Reformation martyrs
6 Elizabeth I and Mary I
7 Princess Sophia
8 Princess Mary
9 Sarcophagus
10 George VI's sword
11 Cumberland
12 Princess Elizabeth
13 Prince Frederick William
14 Augusta, Princess of Wales
15 Frederick, Prince of Wales
16 George II and Caroline
17 Edward VI
18 Claypole
19 Killigrew
20 Villiers
21 Buckingham
22 Henry VII and
   Elizabeth of York
23 James I
24 Anne of Denmark
25 Anne (Mowbray),
   Duchess of York
26 Buckingham
27 Ormond vault
28 Doncaster, Cleveland
   and Plymouth
29 Portland
30 Schomberg
31 Trenchard
32 Dowding
33 Montpensier
34 Stanley
35 Richmond and Lennox
36 Richmond and Lennox
37 Princess Louisa
38 York
39 Princess Caroline
40 Princess Amelia
41 Cumberland
42 Cromer
43 Milner
44 Rhodes
45 Curzon
46 Lennox
47 Mary Queen of Scots
48 Stuart vault
49 Henry, Prince of Wales
50 Elizabeth of Bohemia
51 Prince Rupert
52 Anne, Duchess of York
53 Children of James II
   and of Anne

54 Lady Margaret
   Beaufort
55 Walpole
56 Charles II
57 Mary II
58 William III
59 Anne
60 George of Denmark
61 Albemarle

Chapel of Henry VII

See plan, page 66

• •

This magnificent chapel was built by Henry VII in place of the old Lady Chapel, which was pulled down to make way for this *orbis miraculum* or 'wonder of the world', as it was called by Leland. From the foundations which remain it is believed that the old Lady Chapel was approximately the size of the present chapel, less its aisles and eastern chapels. Besides the original Lady Chapel of Henry III, the small Chapel of St Erasmus, built by Queen Elizabeth Woodville, was demolished. The tenement leased to the poet Chaucer also stood near by.

When Henry VII was firmly established upon the throne he appears to have suffered from an uneasy conscience, and to have determined to try and make his peace with Heaven by founding a splendid chapel to the Virgin, 'in whom', he says in his will, 'hath ever been my most singulier trust and confidence . . . and by whom I have hitherto in al myne adversities ev'r had my special comforte and relief'. The king richly endowed this chapel, in order to make provision for the celebration of Masses and the distribution of alms for the welfare of his soul, 'perpetually for ever while the world shall endure', as he reiterates, little foreseeing how quickly his own son was to sweep away a great part of his work. He also desired to give lustre to the new dynasty, of which he was the founder, by providing a magnificent place of burial for himself and his family. In order to give prominence to his claim, as a descendant of John of Gaunt, to be a member of the House of Lancaster and a relation of Henry VI, by this time popularly revered as a saint, Henry VII originally intended to build in the easternmost part of the chapel a chantry tomb in which the 'bodie and reliquies of our uncle of blessed Memorie King Henry VI' might repose, and for whose canonisation he applied to Pope Julius II.

To the west of this was to be the principal altar (dedicated to Our Lady) and in the centre of the nave, considerably west of its present position, Henry VII's own tomb. This original scheme was never executed, for the Court of Rome demanded a bigger sum in return for Henry VI's canonisation than the king was prepared to pay, so the matter was dropped, and the connection of Henry VI with the new chapel gradually faded away. One of its altars may have been dedicated to his memory, but his body was never brought here from Windsor. A licence, however, for its removal was obtained from the Pope, and a large sum paid to the king by the Abbey for the expenses of its transit.

'On the 24th daie of January [1503], a quarter of an hour afore three of the clocke at after noone of the same daie, the first stone of our Ladie Chapell within the monasterie of Westminster was laid, on behalf of the king, by the hands of John Islip, Abbot of the same monasterie . . . and diverse other.' It has been suggested that the designer of this chapel may have been one of Henry's three master masons, Robert Vertue, whose brother, William Vertue, vaulted St George's Chapel, Windsor, about 1505. The king's will and numerous indentures which remain show with what minute care he planned every detail of his new foundation, providing large sums of ready money for the building, and for the monument to himself and his wife. The total cost was about £14,000. He endowed the chapel with estates obtained by the dissolution of other religious houses for the maintenance of the additional priests required, and for the charities established in connection with it. The king also bequeathed crucifixes and costly services of plate for the different altars, embroidered draperies, and other ornaments, so that the interior must have presented a very rich and splendid appearance. The windows were filled with painted glass, by the hand of the famous Bernard Flower, whose designs for these were copied soon after his decease in the splendid glass now to be seen in King's College Chapel, Cambridge. The upper windows were filled with large figures, the lower with the Tudor badges. Some fragments of these remain in the west window and in the aisles. The royal badges recur in every part of the chapel; prominent among them are the red rose of Lancaster and the white rose of York, both separately and conjoined; the portcullis of the Beauforts, which Henry VII inherited through his mother, and to which he added the motto *Altera securitas*, perhaps implying that as the portcullis gave additional security to the gate, so his descent through his mother added strength to his other titles; daisies, Margaret of Richmond's especial cognisance; the lions of England; the fleurs-de-lis; the Welsh dragon; the initials R. H. surmounted by a crown; a crown on a bush, perhaps alluding

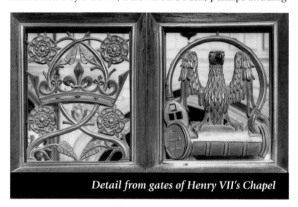

Detail from gates of Henry VII's Chapel

to the story of the discovery of Richard III's crown after the Battle of Bosworth; the greyhound for Richmond; and a falcon within an open fetter-lock, a badge of Edward IV, father of Henry VII's queen.

The chapel was consecrated in 1519, but at the Reformation it was stripped of some of its splendid fittings. We do not know for certain when the altars were destroyed, but as if miraculously, most of the superb statues of the saints survived. The painted glass was destroyed early in the Civil Wars. In January 1540, the Abbey was surrendered to Henry VIII by Abbot Boston and was dissolved, like all the other religious houses throughout the country. After 1660 the 'early morning prayers' were held in this chapel and not in the choir. The consecration of various bishops also took place here until 1708, and periodical meetings of Convocation. But unfortunately the exterior and interior of the chapel were greatly neglected, and, by 1803, the outside had become an 'almost shapeless mass of ruins'. Owing chiefly to the exertions of Dean Vincent a Parliamentary grant was obtained for its restoration in 1807, the necessary repairs were immediately set on foot, and gradually carried on until completed in 1822. Thomas Gayfere, the Abbey Mason, working under the Surveyors of the Fabric, James Wyatt and his son Benjamin, practically renewed all that remained of the outside sculptures, and rebuilt the exterior.

NORTH AISLE

The small enclosure to the left on entering was probably used as a sacristy or vestry by the additional priests for the services of Henry VII's Chapel.

On the south side of the aisle is a monument to **Charles (Montague), 1st Earl of Halifax, KG**, b. 1661, d. 1715, a great Parliamentary orator; he was a brilliant financier as well as statesman; the founder of the Bank of England. A munificent patron of literature and science, he was the friend of Addison, and of Sir Isaac Newton. Buried in General Monck's vault in this aisle.

Also buried in the vault is **Edward (Montagu), 1st Earl of Sandwich, KG**, b. 1625, d. 1672, one of the 'architects' of the Restoration of Charles II and, like General Monck, previously a Commonwealth military commander. He was the cousin and patron of Samuel Pepys and thereby indirectly responsible for Pepys's great services to the Royal Navy. In the second Dutch War he showed himself a naval commander of great courage; commanded a squadron at the great victory of

Tomb of Elizabeth I and Mary I

Lowestoft in 1665. In 1672 at Sole Bay as Vice-Admiral of England and Admiral of the Blue he hoisted his flag in the *Royal James*. When his ship was blown up (see p. 17) Sandwich was either killed or drowned while shifting his flag. His body, scuffed by porpoises but still wearing the Star and George of the Order of the Garter, was recovered off the Suffolk coast and many days later was buried solemnly in the Abbey.

George (Saville), Marquess of Halifax, b. 1633, d. 1695, 'the Trimmer' Lord Keeper of the Privy Seal in the reigns of three kings – Charles II, James II, and William III. 'A man of very great and ready wit, full of life, and very pleasant, much turned to satire, but with relation to the public he went backwards and forwards and changed sides so often that in conclusion no one trusted him.'[1]

The white marble tomb of **Queen Elizabeth I** was erected by James I. She was born at Greenwich 7 September 1533, and died at Richmond 24 March 1603; crowned 15 January 1559, amidst the enthusiastic rejoicings of the people. On 'the 14th day of January, the Queene, with great majestie, rode through London to Westminster, against which time the Lord Mayor and citizens of London had furnished the streets with stately pageants, sumptuous showes and devices; the next day she was crowned by Dr Oglethorpe, Bishop of Carlisle', as the see of Canterbury was vacant and the Archbishop of York refused to officiate. Oglethorpe was assisted by Abbot Feckenham and the service was read partly in Latin and partly in English. Queen Elizabeth was the foundress of this Collegiate Church (1560), and her long reign was one of the most brilliant in English history. Her death was an occasion of universal mourning: 'The 28 day of Aprill being her funeral day at which time the citie of Westminster was surcharged with multitudes of all sorts of people in their streets, houses, windows, leads, and gutters, that came to see the obsequie, and when they beheld her statue or picture lying upon the coffin set forth in Royall robes, having a crown upon the head thereof and a ball and sceptre in either hand, there was such a general sighing, groning, and weeping as the like hath not beene seene or knowne in the memory of man.'

The monument by *M. Colt* and *J. de Critz*, is plainer and less sumptuous than that of Mary Queen of Scots; it was finished long before hers, in 1606, and cost less, only £765. The recumbent figure of the queen is fine, and resembles her later portraits. In October 1975 a gilded collar and pendant, created by *Mrs H. C. Hughes* (*Sah Oved*) from copper gilt with marble for the gems, after the design for the Burgundy or Three Brothers pendant, was added to the effigy to replace items stolen before 1723. The missing regalia were recently completed with a gilded crown designed by *J. Arnold*. These items were all the gift of Mr Brian Court-Mappin. A grate which formerly enclosed the tomb was removed in 1822, but a new grille, designed by *J. P. Foster*, has been added recently.

For some years the reputed 'Essex Ring' – a gold ring, with a sardonyx cameo portrait bust of the queen – was fixed to the tomb. It is now to be seen in the Undercroft Museum. This ring is traditionally the same which Elizabeth gave the Earl of Essex, and which should have been sent her from him as an appeal for pardon when under sentence of death. The ring through a mischance never reached her and the earl

---

1   Burnet, *History of My Own Time.*

Vaulting of Henry VII's Chapel

was executed. It was presented to the Dean and Chapter in 1927.

Beneath the coffin of Elizabeth rests that of her half-sister **Queen Mary**, b. 1516, d. 1558. The stones from the broken altars were piled upon Mary's grave during the whole of her sister's reign. The hearse, upon which lay an effigy of the queen in her royal robes, was a very grand one, adorned with wax angels and escutcheons. John White, Bishop of Winchester, and Abbot Feckenham, preached funeral sermons upon her in the Abbey. The striking words of the Latin inscription include both sisters. 'Partners both in throne and grave, here rest we two sisters, Elizabeth and Mary, in the hope of one resurrection.'

At the west end of the monument a floor-stone unveiled in 1977 commemorates those divided at the Reformation who 'laid down their lives for Christ and conscience sake'.

At the eastern end of the aisle, called by Dean Stanley 'the Innocents' Corner', are two small monuments of children of James I: **Princess Sophia**, d. 1606, aged three days, is represented as lying in a cradle. Her sister **Princess Mary**, d. 1607, aged two years, reclines on her elbow on a small altar tomb. *Maximilian Colt*, the sculptor of both monuments, received £140 for the 'Lady Sophia's' tomb. A small sarcophagus against the east wall contains the bones found at the foot of a staircase in the Tower of London, and placed here by order of Charles II in 1674, who presumed them to be the bones of **Edward V**, b. 1470, created Prince

of Wales in 1471, and his brother **Richard, Duke of York**, b. 1472, the sons of Edward IV, supposed to have been murdered by order of their uncle, Richard III, in 1483.

Against the south wall formerly hung three 'Morris' tapestries depicting St Edward the Confessor, St John the Evangelist and Henry III, the gifts of Mr H. Yates Thompson and Mr and Mrs A. Murray Smith. The tapestries were removed during the restoration of the chapel in 1995 and are to be re-hung elsewhere.

The graves of Joseph Addison, d. 1719 (p. 98), and James Craggs, d. 1721, Addison's successor as Secretary of State (p. 14), are near the entrance.

THE NAVE
• •

The fine gates at the entrance to the chapel are made of bronze mounted on a framework of wood. They resemble the screen round the founder's tomb, and are possibly by the same hand, that of *Thomas Ducheman*[1]

The oak stalls date from different periods. Originally they occupied only the first three of the bays on each side (the lower stalls being omitted in the third bay to allow space for the originally intended position of Henry VII's tomb), a stone screen dividing the body of the chapel from the eastern bay of each aisle. The additional stalls and seats were added

---

1   Not necessarily a Dutchman, but possibly a German or Fleming.

Statue of St Wilgefortis from Henry VII's Chapel

A range of statues of saints standing on pedestals in richly carved niches, surrounds the interior of the chapel below the clerestory windows. There were originally a hundred and seven figures, ninety-five of which remain. The most wonderful part of the chapel is the incomparable fan-vaulting with its carved pendants. The interior of the chapel, the roof, and the whole of the stonework were cleaned in 1934 and again during 1994–5.

In 1725 when this chapel was first used for the installations of the Knights of the Bath, George I presided in person; from that time until 1812 the installations took place here with great ceremony. After 1812 no installations were held for a hundred years, and the banners of the knights, which hung above their stalls, fell into decay, and the remnants were removed, and where possible returned to the knights' families. On 22 July 1913 the installation ceremony of Knights Grand Cross of the greatly enlarged Order was revived by King George V, with his uncle, the Duke of Connaught, as Great Master. The banners of the forty-six new knights then installed were hung over their respective stalls, and their stall-plates affixed to the back of each. Since 1920 further services of installation have taken place at approximately four-yearly intervals, the most recent being held in 1994. In 1975 the Prince of Wales was installed as Great Master.

In 1955 Queen Elizabeth II and Queen Elizabeth the Queen Mother presented **a sword which belonged to King George VI**. It was given to him by his father King George V when he entered the Navy, and was the sword which King George VI always wore when in naval uniform and with which he conferred the accolade of knighthood. It has been placed in a case not far from the Sovereign's stall. Below the Great Master's stall is the **Sword of Honour of the Bath**, used at the installation of new Knights. Presented by Air Vice Marshal Sir Charles Longcroft, KCB, Scarlet Rod (1923–48) and Secretary (1948–54).

A brass plate on the floor commemorates the presentation of the marble pavement by **Dr Henry Killigrew**, d. 1700, Prebendary of Westminster (1660–1700).

According to the Abbey's baptismal register the **font** was 'newly set up' in 1663 in the north transept. It was displaced by the monument to the Three Captains around 1788, and by 1819 had been placed on a modern base within the south-west tower (now St George's Chapel). In 1871 Dean Stanley had the font moved to its present position at the west end of Henry VII's Chapel. The basin was renovated by *Sir G. Scott*, who also designed the cover.

Buried in vaults beneath the floor are:

William Augustus, Duke of Cumberland, b. 1721, d. 1765, third son of George II, for some time Commander-in-Chief of the British forces; notorious as 'the Butcher of Culloden'.

Caroline Elizabeth, b. 1713, d. 1757, and **Amelia Sophia Eleanora**, b. 1711, d. 1786, unmarried daughters of George II.

Frederick Louis, Prince of Wales, b. 1707 at Hanover, d. 1751 at Leicester House, eldest son of George II, and father of George III. His wife, **Augusta of Saxe-Gotha, Princess of Wales**, d. 1772, married to him at St James's Palace in 1736. She lived to see her son George III on the throne. Five of their other children are buried here: **Elizabeth Caroline**, d. 1759, their second daughter; **Louisa Anne**, d. 1768, their third

when the chapel was fitted up as the Chapel of the Order of the Bath in 1725, when it was re-founded by George I, and the Deans of Westminster made Deans of the Order. The extra canopies required for the new stalls were obtained by cutting some of the canopies on the south side in half. The banner of each knight hangs over the stall appointed for his use, to the back of which is attached a stall-plate of brass or copper emblazoned with his arms. Below the stalls are seats for the knights' esquires (there used to be three to each knight), with their arms engraved on stall-plates. A small wooden figure of Henry VI is on a ledge of the Great Master's stall. These stalls retain the misericords of the monks, who used the Lady Chapel, and afterwards the present chapel, for the services of Our Lady. The seats are hinged in order to give support to the brethren who had to stand during the long hours of their services. They are decorated with carvings, which have some resemblance to the engravings by *Albrecht Dürer* and other German artists.

Effigy of Mary, Queen of Scots

daughter; **Edward Augustus, Duke of York**, d. 1767, their second son, brought home to be buried from Monaco; **Henry Frederick, Duke of Cumberland**, d. 1790, their fourth son; and **Frederick William**, d. 1765, their fifth son.

George II, born at Hanover, 1683, d. 25 October 1760, at Kensington Palace; and crowned here with Queen Caroline in 1727. His funeral (11 November) which was very stately, is graphically described by Horace Walpole, who walked in the procession.[1]

Queen Caroline of Anspach, b. 1683, d. 1737, Consort of George II, married at Hanover in 1705. Her husband, as a last proof of attachment to her, directed that his wife's remains should not be separated from his own in death. 'Accordingly the two coffins were placed in a large black marble sarcophagus inscribed with their joint names, and with their sceptres crossed, and one side of each of the wooden coverings withdrawn.'[2] Handel's anthem, 'The ways of Zion do mourn', was composed for her funeral.

Beneath the altar at the head of the tomb of Henry VII lies **Edward VI**, b. 1537, d. 1553, son of Henry VIII and Jane Seymour. It was at his funeral that the burial service of the English Prayer Book was used for the first time over a sovereign. In 1966 Christ's Hospital placed a stone in the floor to mark the place of burial of their royal founder.

The original altar, either by *Benedetto da Rovezzano* or by *Torrigiano* was broken down at the beginning (1643) of the Civil War, and afterwards a wooden table (now in the Chapter Library) was made to serve as an altar or Communion table.

There was no permanent altar in the chapel until the third quarter of the nineteenth century. Under Dean Stanley a new

altar, designed by *Sir G. G. Scott*, was set up in 1870 and remained until 1935. The altar slab of black marble lay upon a cedarwood structure of eight columns. Part of the frieze of the original altar had been found by Dean Stanley during the search for the coffin of James I in the vaults below, and this piece was laid on the new altar table, at the back, with the altar cross standing on it. Shortly afterwards two of the original pillars were discovered in the Ashmolean Museum at Oxford and incorporated in Scott's design. Three unusual relics, from ancient altars, were inserted into the new altar by Stanley's instructions: a piece of sacred stone from the altar of an Abyssinian church, brought to England from Magdala and acquired by the Dean, a fragment of jasper from the Norman altar of Prior Conrad's choir at Canterbury Cathedral, destroyed by fire in 1174, and a piece of mosaic from the Greek church at Damascus brought back by Stanley in 1862.

The present **altar** in Renaissance style was given by members of the Order of the Bath, and closely follows the original sixteenth-century altar as depicted in engravings. The two original pillars together with two reproductions support the black marble table. Above it the frieze round the canopy has been lengthened and reproduced with the addition of the Badge and Star of the Order of the Bath. It is supported on four Corinthian columns. The work was designed by *Sir W. Tapper*, and executed in 1935 by *L. Turner*, and his school of craftsmen. The altar-piece, presented by Viscount Lee of Fareham, GCB, is a fifteenth-century Madonna and Child by *Bartolommeo Vivarini*.

Restoration work on the chapel and the construction of the new altar having been completed, the chapel was reopened on 3 July 1935 by Dean Norris at a ceremony at which several Knights Grand Cross were installed.

Beyond the altar is the tomb of the founder and his queen.

Henry VII, b. 1457, d. 1509, the son of Edmund Tudor, Earl of Richmond, and Margaret Beaufort, the descendant of

---

1 Toynbee (ed.) *Walpole's Letters,* vol IV, pp. 455–7.

2 Stanley, *Historical Memorials of Westminster Abbey* (Eighth edition), p. 167.

Henry VII's Chapel looking east

John of Gaunt and Catherine Swynford. Tradition says that Richard III's crown was placed on Henry's head on the victorious field of Bosworth (1485); he was crowned again in the Abbey, after the battle. The first person to be buried in Henry's chapel was his wife, **Elizabeth of York**, b. 1465, d. 1503, eldest daughter of Edward IV, and the last of the House of York to wear the English crown. She died in the Tower about a month after the ceremony of laying the foundation-stone of the chapel and was temporarily buried in one of the side chapels until the new building was sufficiently advanced for her grave to be made in it. The magnificent funeral given her by Henry was considered a great proof of his affection. Her body was brought through the city on a gorgeous hearse, on which lay her effigy in royal robes.[1] Eight ladies on white horses followed behind, and 'a grand procession of the religious, and the Mayor and Commonalty of London'. At Charing Cross the procession was met by the abbots of Westminster and Bermondsey and escorted to the Abbey.

The king in his will gave minute directions for the monument to himself and his wife, and for Masses to be said for their souls; he also directed that his obsequies should have respect 'somewhat to our dignitie Roial, eviteng alwaies dampnable pompe and outeragious superfluities'. His funeral was, however, performed with great, if not with 'outeragious', magnificence. He died at Richmond, and his body was carried in state to the Abbey, where it rested on a hearse all

---

1   The head of this effigy is preserved in the Undercroft Museum.

night, and was buried the following day. The agreements between the executors of Henry VII and the Florentine artist *Pietro Torrigiano* for the construction of the tomb still exist. It was to cost £1,500, and appears to have been finished by 1518. The recumbent portrait effigies of the king and queen, executed in gilt bronze, lie side by side, as directed by the will. The black marble tomb has a beautifully carved frieze, and is adorned with medallions in copper gilt, representing the Virgin and Henry's ten patron saints; among them are St Michael and St George, St Christopher carrying the infant Christ, St Edward the Confessor, and St Barbara with her tower. At either end the king's arms are supported by gilt-bronze cherubs. A small altar where precious relics, such as the leg of St George and a piece of the true Cross, were kept, used to stand at the foot of the tomb. The fine screen of bronze by *Thomas Ducheman* was partly erected before Henry's death. Some of the upper part of it has gone, and all but six of the thirty-two statues have disappeared from the niches, but on it may be seen the badges of Henry VII, the Welsh dragon, the greyhound for Richmond, and Tudor roses. Elegiac verses by Skelton, court poet to Henry VIII, used to hang on this screen.

James I, b. 1566, d. 1625, the son of Mary Queen of Scots and Henry, Lord Darnley. He succeeded to the Scottish throne as James VI and upon the death of Elizabeth I in 1603 united both countries under the English crown. He was crowned with the new style of 'King of Great Britain, France, and Ireland'. His exact burial-place in the Abbey was not quite certain until Dean Stanley in 1869 brought to light the coffin, resting in the vault below, beside those of Henry VII and his queen. James died at his country palace, Theobalds, on 27 March 1625, and his funeral took place on 5 May. Dean Williams preached the sermon, his eldest surviving son and successor, Charles I, attended in state as chief mourner, and a grand hearse with the late king's effigy upon it was placed in the Abbey before the ceremony.

Five small chapels form the apse of Henry VII's Chapel.

The chapel to the north is filled by the tomb of **George (Villiers), 1st Duke of Buckingham**, b. 1592, d. 1628, the favourite of James I and Charles I, fourth son of Sir George Villiers (q.v.). Clarendon says of his rapid rise to power, 'his ascent was so quick that it seemed rather a flight than a growth . . . And as if he had been born a favourite, he was supreme the first month he came to Court.' The effects of his rash and disastrous counsels soon made him as increasingly unpopular with the nation as he was dear to the king. On the eve of leading an expedition for the relief of La Rochelle, he was assassinated (23 August 1628) at Portsmouth by a discontented soldier named John Felton, who believed 'he should do God good service if he killed the duke'. Charles I buried his friend in the Chapel of Henry VII, hitherto reserved for those of royal descent, but the funeral was performed with little ceremony for fear of a popular uproar. The splendid monument, by *H. Le Sueur*, was erected by the **duchess**, formerly **Lady Katherine Manners**, d. 1643, daughter of the Earl of Rutland. She afterwards married the Marquess of Antrim. The small statues, by *N. Stone*, represent their children, some of whom were buried in their father's vault, including the youngest, **Lord Francis Villiers**, b. 1629, d. 1648, a posthumous child, 'a youth of rare beauty and comeliness of person', killed in a skirmish with the Parliamentary forces near Kingston upon Thames. **George**

Villiers, b. 1628, d. 1687, the only surviving son, succeeded his father, as **2nd Duke of Buckingham**, but had no issue; he was satirised by Dryden as 'Zimri' in *Absalom and Achitophel*.

In the north-eastern chapel is the monument of **John (Sheffield), 1st Duke of Buckingham**, b. 1648, d. 1721, only son of the 2nd Earl of Mulgrave, early distinguished for his political and military services under Charles II, and James II. He took the oath of allegiance to William and Mary, by whom he was created successively Marquess of Normanby and Duke of Buckingham. He ended his days in political disgrace as a consequence of having plotted for the return of the Stuarts during the reign of Queen Anne. Sheffield is also remembered as man of letters, the friend of Pope and of Dryden, to whom he erected a monument in Poets' Corner. His own productions earned him a place in Johnson's *Lives of the Poets*, where, however, he is spoken of as 'a writer that sometimes glimmers but rarely shines'. He built Buckingham House for himself on the site of the present Buckingham Palace. Pope wrote an epitaph for him which was never inscribed on the monument; the concluding lines of the Latin one by himself are striking – the following is a contemporary translation of them: 'I lived doubtful but not dissolute; I died unresolved, not unresigned. Ignorance and error are incident to human nature; I trust in an Almighty and all-good God. Oh thou Being of Beings, have compassion on me!'

The monument was erected by his widow, **Catherine, Duchess of Buckingham**,[1] d. 1743, who is also buried here. Catherine was the illegitimate daughter of James II by Catherine Sedley. She always insisted on being treated with royal state, and on the anniversary of the 'martyrdom of her grandfather, Charles I, received Lord Hervey in the great drawing-room of Buckingham House, seated in a chair of state, attended by her women in like weeds in memory of the royal martyr'.[2] Her ladies were made to promise that if she should become insensible at the last they would stand up in her presence until she was actually dead. The duke is represented in Roman armour, the duchess in the ordinary costume of her time. Principal figures by *P. Scheemakers*, allegorical by *L. Delvaux*. Designed by *D. Plumière*.

With the above are buried their four children, three of whom Time is represented as bearing away. The fourth, **Edmund, 2nd** and last **Duke of Buckingham**, d. 1735, in Rome, aged nineteen.[3]

In the same chapel lies **Anne of Denmark**, b. 1574, d. 1619, Queen of James I, and daughter of Frederick II, King of Denmark and Norway.

Anne, Duchess of York, b. 1472, d. 1481, daughter and heiress of the last Mowbray Duke of Norfolk; she had been

---

1 Her wax effigy is in the Undercroft Museum.
2 Walpole, *Reminiscences*.
3 His wax effigy is in the Undercroft Museum.

Tomb effigies of Henry VII and Elizabeth of York

RAF Chapel showing altar and Battle of Britain window

which was unveiled by King George VI and dedicated on 10 July 1947, is a stained and painted glass window designed and made by *Hugh Easton*. The lower lights contain the badges of the fighter squadrons that took part in the battle. In four panels are shown visions which symbolise the Redemption, while above these are the Seraphim with hands outstretched. At the foot of the window are words from Shakespeare's *Henry V*: 'We few, we happy few, we band of brothers'. Below the window, in the stonework, is a hole now covered with glass, which was made by a fragment of a German bomb during the Battle of Britain in September 1940. The names of six RAF war leaders are painted below the window. The altar, designed by *Sir A. E. Richardson*, is of English walnut. Below are sculptured figures of King Arthur and St George by *A. F. Hardiman*. The Cross, candlesticks, candelabra, and altar rails are of silver-gilt designed by *J. Seymour Lindsay*. In the chapel the Roll of Honour, illuminated by *Miss D. Alcock*, was presented by Captain B. S. Ingram. It contains the names of 1,495 pilots and air crew killed or mortally wounded in the battle. The names include men from the United Kingdom and the Colonies, Australians, Canadians, South Africans, Belgians, Czechoslovaks, Poles, and one American.

Here are buried **Hugh Montagu (Trenchard), 1st Viscount Trenchard**, b. 1873, d. 1956, Marshal and 'Father' of the RAF and **Air Chief Marshal Hugh Caswall Tremenheere (Dowding), 1st Baron Dowding, GCB**, b. 1882, d. 1970, who was Air Officer Commanding-in-Chief of Fighter Command at the time of the Battle of Britain. Both by his foresight in building up Fighter Command between the two world wars and by his strategy and firmness during the battle he was responsible more than any one man for the successful defence of Great Britain in 1940. Also his wife, **Muriel**, d. 1993.

married (1477) in childhood to Richard, Duke of York, son of Edward IV, the bridegroom's age being only five years. She was originally buried in the *old* Chapel of St Erasmus and, when that was pulled down to make way for Henry VII's Chapel, it was believed she was still buried here or in the *new* Chapel of St Erasmus. In 1964, however, her coffin was found on the site of a medieval nunnery near St Clare Street, Stepney, and on 31 May 1965 she was reburied in Henry VII's Chapel near Queen Anne of Denmark.

RAF CHAPEL

Battle of Britain Memorial Window. In 1947 the easternmost chapel was dedicated to the memory of the men of the Royal Air Force killed in the Battle of Britain (July–October 1940). The principal part of the memorial,

A stone in the pavement of the chapel records the burial here of **Oliver Cromwell**, of some of the regicides, and several of Cromwell's family. After the Restoration the bodies of Cromwell, Ireton, and Bradshaw were dug up and dragged to Tyburn, where they were hanged and decapitated, the heads being set on Westminster Hall. The others were reinterred on the north side of the Abbey. The remains of **Elizabeth Claypole**, d. 1658, Cromwell's favourite daughter, were left undisturbed north of Henry VII's tomb.

Among the bodies ejected was that of **Isaac Dorislaus**, of Leyden, d. 1649, a Judge of the Court of Admiralty, who was involved in Charles I's 'trial'. He went as Parliamentary Envoy to The Hague, and was murdered there by Royalists. His body was originally buried near Elizabeth I's monument.

The chief of those buried in 'Oliver's Vault' were:

Oliver Cromwell, b. 1599, d. 1658. Cromwell was

PRINCEPS ILLUSTRISSIMUS ET SERENISSIMUS
ANTONIUS PHILIPPUS, DUX DE MONTPENSIER,
REGIBUS ORIUNDUS,
DUCIS AURELIANENSIS FILIUS NATU SECUNDUS;
A TENERA JUV
IN ARMIS STR
IN VINCULIS INI

Utcunque Fortunæ viciss
Expertus.

Tomb of the Duc de Montpensier

installed Lord Protector in the Court of Chancery, Westminster Hall (1653). The body of the Protector lay in state at Somerset House, from thence it was escorted to the Abbey by an immense train of mourners, including the City Companies with their insignia draped in black, through streets lined with soldiers. 'The effigy or statue of the dead, made most lifelike, in royal robes, crown on head, in one hand the sceptre and in the other the globe, was laid out on a bier richly adorned, and borne hither in a coach made for the purpose, open on every side and adorned with many plumes and banners.' Little more than two years elapsed before his body was exhumed.

The bodies of the following were also removed after the Restoration and thrown into a pit on the north green.

General Henry Ireton, b. 1611, d. 1651, the Protector's son-in-law. He died in camp while with the forces in Ireland, and was brought here for burial.

John Bradshaw, b. 1602, d. 1659, and his wife **Mary**, (*née* Marbury). He was president of the tribunal which condemned Charles I and died in the Deanery which had been granted to him as a residence.

Elizabeth Cromwell, d. 1645, mother of the Protector. Jane Desborough, d. 1656, sister of the Protector and wife of the Parliamentary General. Anne Fleetwood, probably grandchild of the Protector.

Richard Deane, Admiral and General-at-Sea, b. 1610, d. 1653, killed by a cannon-ball in a naval engagement with the Dutch off the east coast. His body lay in state at Greenwich, and was given a public funeral here by order of Cromwell.

Colonel Humphrey Mackworth, d. 1654, a member of Cromwell's Council, and Governor of Shrewsbury during the Civil Wars.

Sir William Constable, Bt (1611); d. 1655, as a young man he received a knighthood in Ireland from Elizabeth's favourite, the Earl of Essex; at Edgehill he fought under the 3rd Earl of Essex and afterwards was made Governor of Gloucester. As a regicide his estates were especially exempted from the general pardon after the Restoration.

Robert Blake, Admiral and General-at-Sea (see p. 33).

Dennis Bond, d. 1658, one of Cromwell's Council and another regicide.

After the ejection of the above, the vault was used as a place of burial for **James (Butler), 1st Duke of Ormond**, b. 1610, d. 1688, and his family, as well as for various noblemen whose names are inscribed on the slab, including several of Charles II's illegitimate descendants: **Charles, Earl of Doncaster**, d. 1674, son of the Duke of Monmouth; **Charles (Fitzroy), Duke of Cleveland and Southampton**, d. 1730; **Charles (Fitz-Charles), Earl of Plymouth**, d. 1681. Besides these, **William (Bentinck), 1st Earl of Portland**, b. 1649, d. 1709, the friend of William III, whom he accompanied to England from Holland; also **Meinhard (Schomberg), 3rd Duke of Schomberg**, b. 1641, d. 1719, who rose to the rank of General in the English Army. The remains of **John (Churchill), 1st Duke of Marlborough**, were interred in this vault on 9 August 1722; then removed to the chapel at Blenheim twenty-four years afterwards.

In the south-east chapel are buried the following:

Arthur Penrhyn Stanley, b. 1815, d. 1881, Dean of Westminster (1864–81). The ideal for which he laboured unceasingly was to make the Abbey a national church. His *Historical Memorials of Westminster Abbey* (1868) laid the foundations for this *Guide*. Sculptor: *Sir J. E. Boehm*.

The coffin of Stanley's wife, **Lady Augusta**, b. 1822,

Tombs of the Countess of Lennox (foreground) and Mary Queen of Scots (beyond)

d. 1876, daughter of Thomas (Bruce), 7th Earl of Elgin, rests beneath her husband's in the vault below. She was lady-in-waiting first to the Duchess of Kent, and afterwards to her daughter, Queen Victoria, who was much attached to her and personally attended the funeral.

Antoine Philippe, Duc de Montpensier, d. 1807, when an exile in England; younger son of Philippe Égalité, 5th Duke of Orleans and brother to Louis-Philippe, afterwards King of France, who erected this monument, executed by *Sir R. Westmacott*. The Latin inscription was written by Dumouriez, the exiled General. The remains of **Queen Louise** of Savoy, d. 1810, wife of Louis XVIII, rested in this vault for a time after her death at Hartwell, but were afterwards removed to Sardinia.

On the south side is the tomb of **Ludovic (Stuart), Duke of Richmond and Lennox**, b. 1574, d. 1624, cousin to James I, and his widow **Frances**, d. 1639 (widow of Edward Seymour, Earl of Hertford), who erected this monument. The enormous bronze figures supporting the canopy are Hope, Truth, Charity, and Faith. Against the east wall, an urn, mounted on a pyramid, contains the heart of **Esmé (Stuart), Duke of Richmond and Lennox**, d. 1660, in Paris, aged eleven. In the vault below lies Esmé's father, **James (Stuart), 4th Duke of Lennox**, b. 1612, d. 1655, created **1st Duke of Richmond** by James I, and other members of the family. These include **Charles (Stuart), Duke of Richmond and Lennox**, b. 1639, d. 1672, the last of the House of Lennox, and his widow, **Frances Theresa**, b. 1647, d. 1702. When the titles and honours of this family became extinct they were conferred by Charles II upon one of his illegitimate children, **Charles** (son of the Duchess of Portsmouth), who became **Duke of Richmond and Lennox;** he died in 1723 and was buried in this vault.

SOUTH AISLE

Evelyn (Baring), 1st Earl of Cromer, GCB, OM, b. 1841, d. 1917, statesman, diplomat, and administrator; 'regenerator of Egypt'. A white marble tablet with medallion portrait. Unveiled 1920. Sculptor: *W. Goscombe John*.

Alfred (Milner), 1st Viscount Milner, KG, b. 1854, d. 1925; Under-secretary of Finance in Egypt (1889–92), Secretary of State for War (1918–19). A medallion portrait inscribed 'Servant of the State'. Milner rendered great services to South Africa as High Commissioner (1897), and Governor of the Transvaal (1901). Buried at Great Wigsell, Bodiam, Sussex. A memorial tablet was also placed in Canterbury Cathedral. Sculptor: *G. Ledward*.

Cecil Rhodes, b. 1853, d. 1902; Imperialist and founder of the Rhodes Scholarships. Unveiled 1953. Buried in Zimbabwe.

George Nathaniel (Curzon), 1st Marquess Curzon of Kedleston, KG, GCSI, GCIE, b. 1859, d. 1925; statesman and writer. Curzon was Under-secretary of State for India (1891); Viceroy of India (1899–1905); Secretary of State for Foreign Affairs (1919–24). Chancellor of Oxford University and Lord Warden of the Cinque Ports. He gave to the nation the castles of Bodiam in Sussex and of Tattershall in Lincolnshire. White marble tablet, with portrait bust by *Sir B. McKennal*, the Curzon crest and the arms of Oxford University erected by the Curzon Memorial Committee. Buried at Kedleston, Derbyshire.

The first tomb is that of **Margaret, Countess of Lennox**, b. 1515, d. 1578, wife of Matthew (Stewart), Earl of Lennox and daughter of Margaret Tudor, widow of James IV of Scotland, by her second husband, Archibald (Douglas), Earl of Angus. She was niece to Henry VIII, and grandmother to James I through her son Lord Darnley's marriage with Mary Queen of Scots. Lady Lennox was extremely beautiful, and was the cause of Lord Thomas Howard's imprisonment in the Tower by Henry VIII for becoming engaged to her without her uncle's consent. She was imprisoned for a time, but on the death of Lord Thomas she was released, and married Lord Lennox on 6 July 1544. She died in poverty at Hackney, and was buried at the expense of her cousin, Queen Elizabeth. An elaborate altar tomb was erected for her by James I, after he had succeeded to the English throne. Her painted and gilt alabaster effigy in robes of state lies upon it, and at the sides are the kneeling figures of her four daughters and four sons. Foremost of the latter is Henry, Lord Darnley, dressed in armour and a long cloak, with a crown over his head. Behind him kneels **Charles, Earl of Lennox** (d. 1576), (father of Arabella Stuart) buried in his mother's grave.

Mary Queen of Scots, b. 1542, d. 1587, daughter of James V of Scotland and Mary of Guise; born a week before her father died, just after his defeat at Solway Moss. Mary was betrothed to the Dauphin and educated at the French Court. Her husband, who succeeded as Francis II, died within a year of his accession to the throne, and Mary left France in 1560, never to return. She married Darnley in 1565, and had one child, James VI of Scotland and I of England. After Darnley's mysterious murder (1567) Mary married James (Hepburn), Earl of Bothwell (d. 1578), one of the men who was suspected of having contrived Darnley's death, but was shortly after obliged to divorce Bothwell. A fervent Roman Catholic and a claimant to the English Crown, she was a great danger to Elizabeth I. She was captured by the English in 1568, and, after nineteen years' imprisonment, executed at Fotheringhay Castle on 8 February 1587. The remains of the queen were first buried in Peterborough Cathedral with great solemnity by Elizabeth's orders, but afterwards by royal warrant from James I they were brought to Westminster in 1612, that the 'like honour might be done to the body of his dearest mother and the like monument extant to her that had been done to others and to his dear sister the late Queen Elizabeth'. The two queens rest opposite one another in the aisles of this chapel; their monuments were both erected by James I. The fine white marble effigy of Mary lies on a sarcophagus, under an elaborate canopy. She wears a close-fitting coif, a laced ruff, and a long mantle fastened by a brooch. At her feet sits the Scottish lion crowned. The tomb was not completed for several years; in 1607 a royal warrant ordered the payment of £825 10s. and 'all further sums as the marble shall amount to', to *Cornelius Cure*, Master Mason of the Works, and as late as 1611 a pattern for this tomb, to cost £2,000, is mentioned as ready to show the king. The grille, which originally protected it, has been replaced round the tomb. The sculptors were *William* and *Cornelius Cure*.

An inscription in the floor records the burial in Queen Mary's vault of the following:

Henry Frederick, Prince of Wales, b. 1594, d. 1612, the eldest son of James I. A prince of great promise, and the hope of the Protestants because of his violent anti-Catholic opinions.

Lady Arabella Stuart, b. 1575, d. 1615, the daughter of Charles, Earl of Lennox, and Elizabeth Cavendish. She was always looked upon as a possible claimant to the throne, and was the centre of many political intrigues. Her marriage, without permission, in 1610 with Sir William Seymour (afterwards Duke of Somerset), a representative of the Suffolk branch of the Royal Family, contributed to make her doubly dangerous in the eyes of James I, who imprisoned her in the Tower, where she lost her reason and died. Her body was brought to the Abbey at midnight by river, and laid upon the coffin of Mary Queen of Scots.

Four children of Charles I: **Prince Charles**, d. 1629, his first-born, an infant; the **Princess Anne**, d. 1640, aged three; **Henry, Duke of Gloucester**, b. 1639, d. 1660, the youngest son; he came over to England with his elder sister, **Mary, Princess Royal**, b. 1631, d. 1660, wife of William II, Prince of Orange and mother of William III, Prince of Orange and King of England; and both died of smallpox at the Palace of Whitehall.

Elizabeth, Queen of Bohemia, b. 1596, d. 1662, at Leicester House, Strand. The grandmother of George I, she was the eldest daughter of James I, and wife of Frederick V, Elector Palatine of the Rhine, the unhappy 'Winter King' of Bohemia. After his death Lord Craven placed his London house at her disposal and thus enabled her to have a peaceful end to her life. Her son **Prince Rupert, Count Palatine of the Rhine, Duke of Cumberland and Bavaria, KG**, b. 1619, d. 1682; most popularly known for his success as the commander of Charles I's horse and inventor of the all-out cavalry charge. In addition, Rupert was a talented artist who introduced the art of mezzotint engraving into this country; a founder Fellow of the Royal Society and a practising amateur

Effigy of Lady Margaret Beaufort

scientist. He was Admiral of the Fleet during the Anglo-Dutch Wars under Charles II and founded the Hudson's Bay Company (1670). First Lord of the Admiralty (1673–9).

Anne, Duchess of York, b. 1637, d. 1671, first wife of James II, whose accession she did not live to see. She was the daughter of Lord Clarendon, and the mother of the two queens, Mary II and Anne. In this vault also are buried many **children of James II**, and also of **Queen Anne**, none of whom survived infancy excepting **William, Duke of Gloucester**, who died in 1700, aged eleven.

Margaret (Stanley), Countess of Richmond and Derby, b. 1443, d. 1509, best known as the Lady Margaret Beaufort; she was the mother of Henry VII by her second husband,[1] Edmund Tudor, Earl of Richmond (d. 1456), the oldest son of Owen Tudor and Henry V's widow, Catherine de Valois. Margaret's third husband was Lord Henry Stafford, son of the Duke of Buckingham. She married fourthly Thomas, Lord Stanley, who deserted Richard III, and crowned his stepson Henry with Richard's coronet, on the battlefield of Bosworth; he was afterwards created Earl of Derby. Lady Margaret was the foundress of two colleges at Cambridge – Christ's and St John's – and of Chairs of Divinity at both Oxford and Cambridge. She was a great lady, to whom the king her son owed much; the patroness of Caxton, whose printing-press was in the Abbey almonry and of Wynkyn de Worde. Lady Margaret not only contributed to the endowment of her son's new chapel, but also established charities of her own in connection with it, one of which – a small weekly dole of alms and bread to poor widows – still exists. The epitaph upon her tomb was composed by Erasmus, for which St John's College paid him 20 shillings. As her friend and confessor Bishop Fisher said in her funeral sermon, 'Every one that knew her loved her, and everything that she said or did became her.' She died on 29 June 1509 at the Abbot's House, Cheyney Gates, now the Deanery. The tomb[2] resembles that of Henry VII; patterns were prepared for it by *Meynnart Wewyck*, a Fleming, but the work was carried out by *Pietro Torrigiano*, who was then at work on Henry VII's monument. The greater part of the cost (£4,000) was defrayed by Margaret's executors, Sir Thomas Lovell and Bishop Fisher, and Torrigiano undertook to finish the work by 1 February 1513. The portrait effigy of Margaret in her old age is Torrigiano's masterpiece: she wears a widow's dress with a hood and long mantle, her feet rest on the Beaufort beast – the yale; the delicate and most characteristic wrinkled hands are raised in prayer. The effigy and canopy are of gilt bronze, as are the coats of arms arranged within flowered wreaths, like those on the tomb of Henry VII; traces of coloured paint remain on the inside of the hands and on the wimple.[3] The tomb itself is of black marble. The iron grate or grille has been replaced, after having been lost for over ninety years. In 1823 the Surveyor of the Fabric, Wyatt, sold this and other grates on behalf of the Dean and Chapter for about £100. The pieces of two of these were put away in a country residence, those of Margaret and Mary Queen of Scots being mixed up together, until they were discovered and reassembled by a London dealer. The National Art

---

1 She was first married as a child to the Earl of Suffolk.
2 See R. F. Scott, 'On the contracts for the tomb of the Lady Margaret Beaufort . . . ', *Archaeologia*, vol. LXVI, 1915.
3 Information kindly supplied by Dr John Physick.

side, as joint sovereigns, carrying the sword between them. The queen's funeral on 5 March 1695, was attended by both Houses of Parliament, the Lords robed in scarlet and ermine, the Commons in long black mantles. Purcell wrote a special anthem and Archbishop Tenison preached the sermon.

William III, b. at The Hague, 1650, d. 1702, the grandson of Charles I, by his daughter Princess Mary's marriage with William of Orange. William founded Greenwich Hospital in memory of his wife. Both added much to Hampton Court Palace.

Queen Anne, b. 1665, d. 1714, the second daughter of James II by his first wife, Lady Anne Hyde. She was married at Whitehall in 1683 to **Prince George of Denmark**, d. 1708, youngest son of Frederick III, King of Denmark. Their many infants also rest in the vault below.

On the wall near by is a **bronze plaque** presented by Trinity Church in the city of New York to commemorate the 900th anniversary of Westminster Abbey and in grateful memory of King William III and of Queen Anne, who by grants of land established Trinity Church as the first Anglican church in New York.

George Monck ('General Monck'), **1st Duke of Albemarle**, b. 1608, d. 1670, who was principally responsible for the Restoration of Charles II. He first distinguished himself when a Captain in many actions against the Dutch Fleet, under their famous admirals de Tromp and de Ruyter. During the Commonwealth he was appointed General-in-Chief of the Forces on land and Admiral and General-at-Sea. He retained both these posts after the Restoration by the king's wish. But at the end of his career disaster overtook him. In June 1667 the Dutch broke the chain laid by his orders across the Medway, burnt eight great warships, and captured Monck's flagship, the *Royal Charles*. From this time Monck took little part in naval battles, an old wound received in the Civil Wars tormented him, he became increasingly infirm, and died on 3 January 1670, 'standing (it is said) upright in his chair like a Roman soldier, his chamber like a tent, open with all his soldiers about him'. His funeral was delayed for nearly four months, the king having offered and failed to pay the expenses. It finally took place on 30 April 1670, with great pomp, in the north aisle of Henry VII's Chapel. Charles himself attended as chief mourner. His son **Christopher, 2nd Duke of Albemarle**, b. 1653, d. 1688, was buried in the same grave. Monck's funeral armour is in the Undercroft Museum. The monument was not put up until the 1740s, the expenses defrayed by the bequest of Monck's son. Designed by *W. Kent* and executed by *P. Scheemakers*. The model for Monck's head, by *J. Bushnell*, perhaps based on a death-mask, is in the Chapter Library.

Above the altar in a frame is a tapestry, woven of wool, silk, and silver gilt, representing the Descent from the Cross. It is thought to be Flemish work and perhaps dates from the early part of the sixteenth century. Given in 1929 by the Duke of Westminster in memory of his mother the Countess Grosvenor. The black marble altar is by *D. Blow*, 1929. A Latin inscription commemorates **Percy Wyndham** (Countess Grosvenor's son by her second marriage) and **Horatio Herbert (Kitchener), 1st Earl Kitchener of Khartoum**, b. 1850, d. 1916. Altar cross presented by the Royal Stuart Society in 1987 to commemorate the death of Mary Queen of Scots in 1587. Designed by *G. Benney*.

One of the windows recording donors to the restoration appeal in Henry VII's Chapel

Collections Fund purchased Margaret's grate in 1915 and presented it to the Dean and Chapter, by whom it was re-erected in its original position. It was constructed by an English smith, *Cornelius Symondson*, and the cost was defrayed by St John's College, Cambridge, and paid in instalments; it was finished and gilded in 1529. Originally the whole, which was made of Bilbao iron, was elaborately painted and decorated with coats of arms, crests, fleurs-de-lis, and other ornaments. The stone supports were made by *Raynold Bray*, Citizen and Freemason of London, and cost £2 13s. 4d.

In 1902 Sir J. C. Robinson presented to the Dean and Chapter a bronze *rilievo* bust of **Sir Thomas Lovell** (d. 1524), Chancellor of the Exchequer, by *Torrigiano*. This used to hang on the wall close by and is now in the Undercroft Museum. Lovell, as executor to King Henry VII and to Lady Margaret, superintended the design and erection of their tombs.

Lady (Catherine) Walpole, d. 1737, daughter of John Shorter of Bybrook (in Kennington), Kent, first wife of Sir Robert Walpole. The statue, copied from a Roman figure of Modesty, was erected by Horace Walpole to his mother in 1754; he also wrote the inscription. Sculptor: *F. della Valle*.

In the royal vault below, although they have no monuments in the Abbey, are buried:

Charles II, b. 1630, d. 1685. The magnificence of his coronation on 23 April 1661 is described by Pepys and Clarendon. 'It is impossible', says Pepys, 'to relate the glory of this day, expressed in the clothes of them that rid [in the procession] and their horses and horsecloths.'

Queen Mary II, b. 1662, elder daughter of James II, died of smallpox at Hampton Court on 28 December 1694. She was crowned here with her husband, William of Orange, in 1689 and her Coronation Chair is now to be seen in the Undercroft Museum. The king and queen walked side by

The South Ambulatory & its Chapels

See plan, page 36

CHAPEL OF ST NICHOLAS

The chapel is separated from the ambulatory by a fine stone screen, erected probably in the reign of Henry VII; the frieze is decorated with shields and roses. A finger of Saint Nicholas and other relics were presented to the Abbey by Queen Eleanor of Castile. Those who attended Mass at this altar were granted indulgences of three years and sixty days. The chapel contains the private vault of the Percy family, members of which have still a right to be interred there. Several of the monuments were shifted in order to make room for the new Percy vault constructed in 1776.

The first tomb on the right as you enter the chapel is that of **Philippa, Duchess of York**, d. 1431, daughter of John, Lord Mohun, and successively wife of Walter, Lord Fitzwalter, of Sir John Golofre (q.v.), and of Edward, 2nd Duke of York (grandson of Edward III). After the death of the Duke of York at Agincourt, his widow was allowed to hold the lordship of the Isle of Wight, which had been granted to her husband. Her body was brought in great state from Carisbrooke Castle

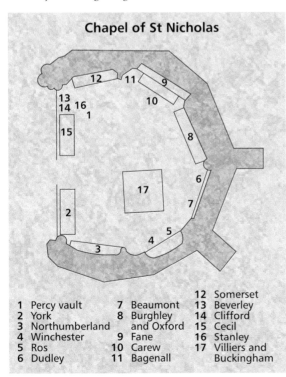

Chapel of St Nicholas

1	Percy vault	7	Beaumont
2	York	8	Burghley
3	Northumberland		and Oxford
4	Winchester	9	Fane
5	Ros	10	Carew
6	Dudley	11	Bagenall

12	Somerset
13	Beverley
14	Clifford
15	Cecil
16	Stanley
17	Villiers and
	Buckingham

to be buried here. Her tomb is the earliest in the chapel, and formerly stood in the centre. The recumbent figure is in a long cloak and robes and she has a wimple and plaited veil. An engraving is preserved of a fine triple canopy in wood, which has disappeared.

Elizabeth, Duchess of Northumberland, d. 1776, 'In her own right Baroness Percy, Lucy, Poynings, Fitz Payne, Bryan, & Latimer sole heiress of Algernon Duke of Somerset & of the ancient Earls of Northumberland'. She married Sir Hugh Smithson, who took the name of Percy and was created Duke of Northumberland in 1766. Her funeral was the occasion of an uproar. The crowd that collected to witness it broke down the canopy of John of Eltham's tomb. Several persons were injured, and the ensuing confusion was so great that the burial-service could not be resumed until after midnight. Designed by *R. Adam* and executed by *N. Read*.

Winifred, Marchioness of Winchester, d. 1586, daughter of Sir John Brydges, Lord Mayor of London. Figures of the children by her first husband (Sir Richard Sackville) kneel beneath: Thomas Sackville, Lord Buckhurst, the poet, and Anne, Lady Dacre, d. 1595, widow of Gregory, 10th Lord Dacre. Lady Dacre bequeathed her fortune to found a hospital for sick women and children in Tothill Fields, Westminster (the Emmanuel Hospital), schools, and the pensions for poor women still called the Dacre Bequest. Winifred married as her second husband, John Paulet, 2nd Marquess of Winchester.

Above is a portion of a monument with reclining figure which was removed to make way for the Percy monument, **Elizabeth Cecil**, d. 1591, daughter of the Earl of Rutland, *suo jure* **Baroness Ros** or Roos, mother of Lord Ros, and wife of William Cecil, afterwards Earl of Exeter, a grandson of the great Lord Burghley.

William Dudley (also called Sutton), d. 1483, Bishop of Durham (1476–83) and previously Dean of Windsor (1473–8). He was the third son of John, Lord Dudley, and uncle to Edmund Dudley, Henry VII's minister. A brass of the bishop in his vestments, together with the inscription, has disappeared from the tomb.

A pyramid of black and white marble supports a vase containing the heart of **Anne Sophia**, d. 1605, infant daughter of the **Comte de Beaumont**, ambassador from the French Court to James I.

Against the south wall is a large monument erected by Lord Burghley to his second wife, **Mildred Cecil**, d. 1589, and their daughter **Anne, Countess of Oxford**, d. 1588. Lady Burghley was one of the four learned daughters of Sir Anthony Cooke; she was also well known for her philanthropy. She died at Burghley House, in the Strand. The Latin inscriptions, by Lord Burghley himself, commemorate his grief. He is represented in the upper storey, kneeling in his robes of State. He was buried at Stamford, but a funeral service was held here in his honour. Below, on the sarcophagus, are the effigies of his wife and daughter. Lady Burghley's son, Robert Cecil, kneels at her feet, and her three granddaughters, Elizabeth, Bridget, and Susannah, at her head. The monument is twenty-four feet high and is composed of different coloured marbles.

Sir George and Lady (Elizabeth) Fane, d. 1618, a mural monument with kneeling figures beneath a canopy. It was erected by her husband 'who, as his effigy is placed near hers, so intends their ashes shall be united'.

Nicholas Carew, d. 1470, feudal Baron of Carew in Pembrokeshire, and his wife, **Margaret**, d. 1470, daughter of John, Lord Dinham. A grey marble altar tomb, from which the brass shields and inscription have disappeared.

Nicholas Bagenall, d. 1688, an infant two months old, 'by his Nurs, unfortunately overlayd', the son of Nicholas Bagenall, of the Isle of Anglesey.

Anne, Duchess of Somerset, d. 1587, widow of the Protector Somerset, sister-in-law to Queen Jane Seymour and aunt by marriage to Edward VI. She was a daughter of Sir Edward Stanhope of Rampton, Notts. Her eldest son, Lord Hertford, 'in this dolefull dutie carefull and diligent, doth consecrate this monument to his deere parent'. 'A mannish, or rather a devilish woman,' says Sir John Hayward, 'for any imperfectibilities intolerable, but for pride monstrous, exceeding subtle and violent.' An alabaster effigy of the duchess in her robes lies under a recessed arch with richly decorated soffit. Erected by her eldest son, Lord Hertford.

Isabella Susannah, Countess of Beverley, d. 1812. Sculptor: *J. Nollekens*.

Lady Jane Clifford, d. 1679, great-granddaughter of the Protector Somerset. Black marble monument with alabaster heads of cherubim at the corners, is probably by *J. Bushnell*.[1]

Elizabeth Cecil, d. 1597, daughter of Lord Cobham, and wife of Sir Robert Cecil, afterwards 1st Earl of Salisbury, son of Lord Burghley. She was Lady of the Bedchamber to Queen Elizabeth. An alabaster tomb with black marble slab, erected by her husband, who wrote the epitaphs in rhyme on either side, recording the mutual affection of husband and wife.

In the pavement near the above monument is the brass figure of **Sir Humphrey Stanley**, d. 1505, in plate armour.

In the centre of the chapel is the altar tomb of **Sir George Villiers**, d. 1605, and **Mary** (**Beaumont**), his second wife, d. 1632, the parents of George Villiers, Duke of Buckingham (q.v.). At her son's request Lady Villiers was made Countess of Buckingham in her own right by James I in 1618. Clarendon relates the story of Sir George Villiers's ghost appearing shortly before the assassination of his son at the bedside of an old servant, bidding him to go to the duke 'and tell him if he did not do somewhat to ingratiate himself to the people or at least to abate the extreme malice they had against him, he would be suffered to live but a short time'.[2] Lady Buckingham also had so strong a presentiment of her son's end that she was quite calm on hearing of his murder. The white marble tomb, with recumbent figures in the costume of the time, was set up by the Countess, a year before her death, at the cost of £560. Sculptor: *N. Stone*.

Outside in the ambulatory:

Gravestones commemorate **Sir Allen Apsley**, d. 1683, Falconer to Charles II, and his wife **Frances**, d. 1698; **Anne, Lady Apsley**, d. 1681 and her son **Allen**, d. 1691.

A tablet to **Sir Thomas Ingram**, d. 1672, 'for his eminent loyalty, suffering, and services' to Charles I and Charles II, made Chancellor of the Duchy of Lancaster. Buried below with his only child, Mary, aged twelve.

A bust by *F. Fanelli* of **Sir Robert Ayton**, b. 1570, d. 1638, poet and philosopher, a friend of Ben Jonson and Thomas Hobbes. He was secretary to Anne of Denmark and Henrietta Maria.

---

1 Information kindly supplied by Dr John Physick.
2 Clarendon, *History of the Rebellion*, vol. I, p. 74.

Monument to Anne, Duchess of Somerset

Beneath is a much-injured thirteenth-century **retable**, representing the ministry and majesty of Christ, which is believed to have formed part of the thirteenth-century High Altar. George Vertue mentioned it in his notes made between 1721 and 1725, but it was about 1827 before Edward Blore, the Surveyor, rediscovered it in use as a lid to one of the cases containing the wax effigies at that time in the Islip Chantry Chapel. The central figure, Christ in Glory, holds a small globe upon which are painted in miniature the sea, with men in a boat; the land, with sheep feeding; a stork and other birds in the sky; the sun and moon; on either side are figures of the Virgin and St John the Evangelist. The background is decorated with gilding and coloured glass. In star-shaped panels are represented the miracles of Christ and on one side stands St Peter with his keys.

Near by is the **Wyatt frontal**, made for the High Altar by Harriet Wyatt (d. 1906). The frontal, which depicts the Transfiguration of Our Lord, took eight years to embroider and was first used at the Abbey on Easter Day 1905.

Richard Harweden, d. 1441; Abbot of Westminster from 1420 until his resignation in 1440. He was one of the treasurers of the money given by Henry V for rebuilding the west part of the nave. His grave was at the foot of the steps to Henry VII's Chapel on the south side, and the large Purbeck marble slab there is known to have had a brass on it with a mitred effigy.

CHAPEL OF ST EDMUND

A fine wooden screen, with a doorway in the centre, separates the chapel from the ambulatory. This St Edmund is the King of East Anglia, martyred by the Danes in 870, and not St Edmund, Archbishop of Canterbury. **William de Valence, Lord of Pembroke and Wexford**, d. 1296, was a half-brother of Henry III, being son of Hugh de Lusignan, Comte de la Marche (d. 1249), by Isabella of Angoulême, King John's widow. Valence near Lusignan was probably his birthplace. William, in addition to his French lordships, acquired vast estates in England and Ireland by his marriage with Joan, daughter and in her issue heir of Warin de Munchensy, Lord of Swanscombe, whose first wife Joan was in her issue a co-heir of the Marshals, Earls of Pembroke; but William de Valence was never created earl nor invested with the earldom. The tomb is the only existing example in England of Limoges champlevé enamel-work. The effigy and the chest on which it lies are of oak, and both were once covered with enamelled copper plates. Most of these have been lost from the tomb-chest but the five small shields on round plates should be noted. The decoration on the figure is more complete, and the finely diapered cushion under William's head and the large shield at his side are especially remarkable. William's arms, as on the great shield, occur on the pillow, on small shields powdering the surcoat and on one of the roundels on the tomb-chest. The stone base bears the arms of England, Valence, and Valence dimidiating Clermont-Néelle, commemorating the first marriage of William's son Aymer (q.v.).

Edward (Talbot), 8th Earl of Shrewsbury, d. 1618, and **Jane**, d. 1626, his wife, daughter of Cuthbert, 7th Lord Ogle; she erected this fine Jacobean tomb, with the recumbent figures of herself and her husband; the effigy of their daughter is kneeling near her father. The monument, which was once protected by an iron grate, is by *William Wright*.

Sir Richard Pecksall, d. 1571, kneels between his two wives; Master of the Royal Buckhounds, a post he inherited from the Brocas family. The four small kneeling figures are his daughters by his first wife.

Sir Bernard Brocas, d. 1395. The man commemorated here is the father of the Sir Bernard Brocas who was executed in 1400 for conspiring to reinstate Richard II. The inscription now above the tomb is of the eighteenth century and is erroneous. The head rests on a helmet surmounted by his crest, a crowned Moor's head. The story of his cutting off the King of Morocco's head, mentioned by Addison, is a legend of later days. This Sir Bernard Brocas, like his son, held office at the Court of Richard II. He became hereditary Master of the Royal Buckhounds in right of his wife, the daughter and heiress of Sir John de Roche. The monument was repainted about the middle of the eighteenth century. The fine brass inscription is original.

John (Russell), Lord Russell, d. 1584, son of the 2nd Earl of Bedford. The inscriptions in Latin, Greek, and English were composed by his wife, the daughter of Sir Anthony Cook and sister of Lady Burghley. Lord Russell is represented reclining on his left elbow. At his feet is the figure of his infant son, Francis. His daughter, **Elizabeth Russell**, b. 1575, d. 1601, was born within the precincts and baptised in the Abbey; Queen Elizabeth and the Countess of Sussex were the godmothers, and Robert (Dudley), Earl of Leicester, was godfather. Elizabeth afterwards became maid of honour to the queen and died young of consumption. The monument, put up by her sister Anne, Lady Herbert, represents Elizabeth as seated upright on a basket-weave chair on a decorated pedestal.

Two mural tablets, the first of their kind in the Abbey: **Lady Jane Seymour**, d. 1560, aged nineteen, daughter of the Protector Somerset, and cousin to Edward VI; **Dame Catherine Knollys**, d. 1569, sister of Lord Hunsdon, and niece to Anne Boleyn. She died aged thirty-nine at Hampton Court, while in attendance on Queen Elizabeth I.

Francis Holles, d. 1622, aged eighteen, having already served through the Flemish campaign. The monument, a seated figure in Roman armour on a pedestal, put up by his father, the Earl of Clare, may be compared to that of his uncle Sir George Holles (q.v.). Sculptor: *N. Stone*.

On the east side of the chapel is the tomb of **Frances, Duchess of Suffolk**, b. 1517, d. 1559, daughter of Charles (Brandon), Duke of Suffolk, by the Lady Mary, daughter of Henry VII of England, and widow of Louis XII of France. Frances married Henry (Grey), 3rd Marquess of Dorset, created Duke of Suffolk, and was the mother of Lady Jane Grey, b. 1537, d. 1554. Suffolk himself was executed eleven days after his eldest daughter, and his widow lived in poverty throughout the reign of Mary I. She married about 1557 her groom of the chamber, Adrian Stokes (d. 1585); he put up the tomb with recumbent effigy of the duchess wearing her coronet.

Close by lies the daughter of Frances's only sister, Lady Cumberland, **Margaret, Countess of Derby**, d. 1596. She

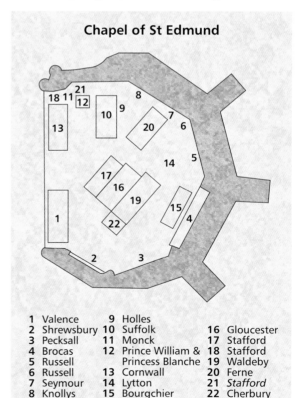

Chapel of St Edmund

1	Valence	9 Holles
2	Shrewsbury	10 Suffolk
3	Pecksall	11 Monck
4	Brocas	12 Prince William &
5	Russell	Princess Blanche
6	Russell	13 Cornwall
7	Seymour	14 Lytton
8	Knollys	15 Bourgchier

16	Gloucester
17	Stafford
18	Stafford
19	Waldeby
20	Ferne
21	*Stafford*
22	Cherbury

Effigy of William de Valence

was accused of witchcraft, and imprisoned by her cousin, Queen Elizabeth, in 1590, and when released forbidden to approach the Court or live with her husband.

A monument to **Nicholas Monck**, Bishop of Hereford, b. 1610, d. 1661, brother of General Monck, who at the Bishop's repeated instigations undertook the restoration of Charles II. The monument was erected by the Bishop's grandson in 1723. Sculptor: *W. Woodman*.

Beneath a diminutive altar tomb lie two children of Edward III, **William of Windsor**, d. 1348, and **Blanche of the Tower**, d. 1342, both surnamed from their birthplaces, that of Blanche being the Tower of London. The alabaster effigies, for which *John Orchard*, stonemason of London, received 20 shillings, in 1376, are only twenty inches in length; they are interesting examples of the civilian costume of the time. A brass inscription has disappeared from the ledge, and also the small figures with which the panels were adorned.

John of Eltham, Earl of Cornwall, d. 1336, second son of Edward II. In spite of his youth he was three times Regent of the kingdom during his brother Edward III's absence; he also took a prominent part in quelling the border raids of the Scots. He was born at the palace of Eltham in Kent, and died, aged nineteen, at Perth, from whence his body was brought in great state to be buried in the Abbey. The alabaster effigy is probably by the same sculptor as that of his father Edward II in Gloucester Cathedral. The feet rest on a lion; two angels, which support the head cushions, are ready to bear away the soul of the deceased. The small crowned figures round the sides of the tomb perhaps represent the kings and queens to whom he was related. Those on the south side are sadly

mutilated, but those on the north are in a better state. The canopy was unhappily broken down in 1776, and afterwards removed.

Edward (Bulwer-Lytton), 1st Baron Lytton, b. 1803, d. 1873, author of *The Caxtons, The Last Days of Pompeii*, and many other novels.

Sir Humphrey Bourgchier, d. 1471, killed fighting for Edward IV at the Battle of Barnet. He was the son of one John, Lord Berners, and his own son, John, Lord Berners (d. 1533) was Chancellor of the Exchequer to Henry VIII. The brass effigy in armour has disappeared from the low altar tomb, but the helm, with Saracen's head crest, shields, and heraldic badges remains.

In the centre of the chapel is a low altar tomb, on which is the finest brass in the Abbey, to **Eleanor, Duchess of Gloucester**, d. 1399. She was the wife of Edward III's youngest son, Thomas of Woodstock, Duke of Gloucester and daughter and co-heir of Humphrey de Bohun, Earl of Hereford, Northampton, and Essex, and Constable of England. After her husband's death, the duchess spent the remainder of her life, two years only, in the nunnery at Barking. She is represented in her widow's dress, under a triple canopy; above her head is the Bohun badge, a swan, afterwards adopted by Henry V.

Near hers is the tomb of her lineal descendant, **Mary, Countess of Stafford**, d. 1694; created Countess in her own right eight years after the attainder and execution of her husband, Viscount Stafford, for alleged treason, in 1680. In the corner is a tablet to **John Paul Howard**, b. 1700, d. 1762, grandson of the above and last **Earl of Stafford**. On the south of the Duchess of Gloucester's tomb lies **Robert de Waldeby**, Archbishop of York, d. 1397, the learned friend and companion of the Black Prince. A fine brass figure under a canopy, in mitre and robes, his right hand raised in benediction, his left holding a cross.

Next to the Waldeby brass a stone marks the grave of **Edward (Herbert), Lord Herbert of Cherbury**, b.c. 1633, d. 1678.

Under a blue slab with five shields of arms and a mitre in brass lies **Henry Ferne**, Bishop of Chester, b. 1602, d. 1662, who attended Charles I during his imprisonment.

Here also is buried a naval hero, **Sir Frescheville Holles**, b. 1641, d. 1672, knighted by Charles II after the victory over the Dutch off Lowestoft (1665); killed at Sole Bay (1672).

Outside in the ambulatory are:

Robert Tounson, b. 1575, d. 1621, Dean of Westminster (1617); Bishop of Salisbury (1620). While he was Dean, Sir Walter Raleigh was imprisoned in the gatehouse, which formerly stood at the entrance of what is now Tothill Street. Dean Tounson went to pray with Raleigh before his execution, and was amazed at the gaiety with which he faced death.

Sir Robert Anstruther, d. 1645, Privy Councillor, a favourite at the Courts of James I and Charles I, and a successful ambassador during both reigns.

Sir Henry Spelman, b. 1564?, d. 1641, antiquary, was buried by order of Charles I with much state close to the entrance of St Nicholas's Chapel. He wrote several learned works on legal and ecclesiastical history, and was an intimate friend of Archbishop Laud.

Richard de Berkyng, Abbot of Westminster (1222–46), one of the witnesses to the Magna Carta. He held several high offices in the State, and was a great favourite with Henry III, from whom he obtained important charters and grants for the Abbey. He was first buried in the old Lady Chapel, but on its demolition for the building of Henry VII's Chapel, his remains are said to have been removed here, but the actual place is unknown.

On the south wall of the ambulatory between the Chapels of St Edmund and of St Nicholas is a monument to **Richard Tufton, Esq.**, d. 1631, a younger son of Sir Thomas Tufton, Bt, of Hothfield, Kent. The family name is preserved in Tufton Street close to the Abbey.

CHAPEL OF ST BENEDICT

• •

This little chapel adjoins the south transept. It is dedicated to the founder of the Benedictine Order, to which the monks of Westminster belonged. The head of St Benedict, a much-valued relic, was presented to the Abbey by Edward III in 1335; he is said to have brought it from the Abbey of Fleury,[1] in France. There are heraldic tiles to be seen in the pavement. Against the south wall is a mural monument with the kneeling figure of **Gabriel Goodman**, b. 1529, d. 1601, Dean of Westminster. He addressed the House of Commons in defence of the rights of sanctuary at Westminster, and in consequence of his opposition to the Bill for their suppression, they were preserved, in cases of debt only, until the reign of James I. He was chaplain to Lord Burghley and a friend of William Camden, the antiquary, whose expenses he defrayed in some of his antiquarian journeys. Lady Burghley founded two scholarships for Old Westminsters at St John's College, Cambridge, which bear the name of Dean Goodman. Goodman founded the Grammer School, Ruthin, and left money to several Cambridge colleges.

George Sprat, b. 1682, d. 1683, second son of Dr Thomas Sprat (q.v.).

The place of the altar is occupied by the monument of **Frances, Countess of Hertford**, b. 1554, d. 1598, wife of Edward (Seymour), Earl of Hertford and sister of William, Lord Howard of Effingham, the Lord High Admiral who in 1588 defeated the Spanish Armada.

Cardinal Simon de Langham, d. 1376, Abbot of Westminster from 1349 to 1362 and Chancellor of England (1362–6). In 1366 he was made Archbishop of Canterbury, the only Westminster abbot to attain to that dignity. On receiving a cardinal's hat from Pope Urban V, Langham was

---

1   Widmore, *A History of . . . Westminster Abbey* (1751), p. 65.

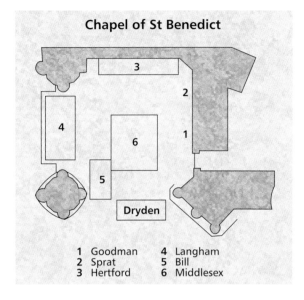

Chapel of St Benedict

1 Goodman   4 Langham
2 Sprat   5 Bill
3 Hertford   6 Middlesex

obliged to give up the archbishopric (1368) and go abroad to the papal court, and returned to England only twice after that. He was made Bishop of Palestrina in 1373, and died at Avignon three years later. He was buried by his own desire in the Abbey, to which he was a great benefactor. Besides many gifts in money, plate, and vestments during his lifetime, including £200 a year during his life towards the rebuilding of the nave, Langham bequeathed the residue of his vast fortune to the monastery, and his successor, Abbot Litlyngton, ably administered the funds. The monument, erected about 1395, is by *Henry Yevele* and *Stephen Lote*; the canopy was destroyed at the coronation of George I, but much remains of the brass inscription round the ledge. A statue of St Mary Magdalene (on whose Feast Day, 22 July, Langham died) was presented by one William 'de Reliquiis' and originally stood near the Cardinal's feet, and his cardinal's hat formerly hung above his tomb.

William Bill, d. 1561, the first Dean of Westminster after the establishment of the Abbey as a collegiate church by Elizabeth I in 1560. A brass figure of a man in a doctor's habit with Latin epitaph, rests on the low altar tomb. Another inscription in brass letters ran round the margin.

In the centre is the large altar tomb of **Lionel Cranfield, Earl of Middlesex**, b. 1575, d. 1645, and **Anne**, his second wife, who erected the monument. Cranfield rose from one

Tomb of Cardinal Simon de Langham

Dean Goodman's Monument

post to another through his great business capacity, and was finally made Lord High Treasurer under James I. He was impeached at the instigation of the Duke of Buckingham, whose extravagance he had opposed, and to whom he was indebted both for his rise and for his fall. He was pardoned in 1625.

William de Curtlyngton, Abbot of Westminster (1315–33), was buried before the altar. The brass figure and inscription which formerly marked the place have disappeared.

John Spottiswoode, Archbishop of St Andrews, b. 1565, d. 1639, historian, was buried in this chapel. In 1633 he crowned Charles I King of Scotland at Edinburgh. His younger brother **James Spottiswoode**, b. 1567, d. 1645, Bishop of Clogher (1621) is also buried in this chapel.

In 1878 an old doorway of the chapel, which had long been concealed by a tablet, was again opened to view, and is now known to have led to the Abbey anchorite's cell. Above the doorway a monument erected in 1968 commemorates the **monks of Westminster**. Executed by *A. Siegenthaler*.

SOUTH AMBULATORY
See plan, page 36

Underneath a segmental arch in the wall between the Chapels of St Edmund and St Benedict is a small altar tomb over the remains of **Katherine**, d. 1257, aged five years, and

of **four other children of Henry III**; with these were afterwards laid **four children of Edward I**. The loss of their daughter Katherine caused much grief to Henry III and his queen. He ordered a richly decorated monument for her, inlaid with precious marbles and mosaics, perhaps the remains of those brought over for St Edward's Shrine; however most of this decoration has disappeared except from the slab where something of the design can still be traced. There were also two images, lost long since; one of brass, which *Master Simon of Wells* came to London to set up, and one of silver (probably representing St Catherine), for which *William de Gloucester*, the king's goldsmith, received seventy marks. The back of the recess was painted with four kneeling figures; these may have been either the Princess Katherine and her brothers, or have been added later by Edward I when his children were laid to rest in the same grave. The space between the arches over the tomb was elaborately painted and gilt; an image of a saint occupied the centre.

In the pavement are the graves of:

Thomas Bilson, b. 1547, d. 1616, Bishop of Winchester (1597–1616). He 'put the completing hand' to the Authorized Version of the Bible by command of James I.

Sir John Golofre, d. 1396, the second husband of Philippa, Duchess of York. He was ambassador to the Court of France in the time of Richard II, by whose orders his remains were brought here from their burial-place at Wallingford. A few fragments of the original brass are preserved in the Muniment Room. The original large Purbeck marble slab, badly cracked, can be seen south of Richard II's tomb.

Philip Ludlow, d. 1650. A note on his will records that he died 'on the high seas on board ye ship Sephier . . . he being commander-in-chief of the Brazeele merchant ships homeward bound'.

Immediately within the gates of the ambulatory to the right is the recess containing the supposed tomb of **King Sebert**, d. *c*. 616, legendary founder of the Abbey. Although the story which connected this King of the East Saxons with Westminster has no historical foundation, the tomb has always been shown as his since the erection of the building, and was reputed to contain also the bones of Sebert's queen, Ethelgoda, and his sister Ricula. The segmental arch, with its mouldings, once painted and gilt, is early fourteenth century. The decoration at the back of the recess contains the *rose en soleil*, the badge of Edward IV. During the rebuilding of the church by Henry III the stone coffin was removed and deposited on the southern side of the Chapter House entrance until after the completion of the choir, when it was placed with great ceremony by the monks in its present position. Above it are remains of the painted figures of the Confessor and pilgrim, contemporary with those on the north side of the sedilia (about 1308); restoration has uncovered traces of a painting of the Annunciation in the other recess.

Ralph Selby, d. 1420, a learned Westminster monk, the favourite of two kings, Henry IV and Henry V, is buried beneath a stone, which formerly had on it a brass, between Sebert's tomb and that of Cardinal Langham.

In 1960 a bronze tablet, designed by *J. S. Comper*, was erected on the wall by Sebert's tomb to **Queen Anne Nevill**, b. 1456, d. 1485, wife of Richard III and daughter of Richard, Earl of Warwick, 'the Kingmaker'. She lies buried in front of the sedilia with nothing to mark her grave.

The North Transept

See plan below

The north entrance, or 'Solomon's Porch'. The name of 'Solomon's Porch' recalls a large porch erected against the central portal *c.* 1342, of which no trace remains. The whole was much decayed at the beginning of the eighteenth century, when Wren and Dickinson recased it in Oxfordshire stone, paring and altering the details until the ancient character of the entrance was quite lost. The eighteenth-century front was entirely remodelled under Pearson (1884),

who designed the upper part himself, and carried out Scott's plans for the triple portico, with slight modifications.

After the interment of William Pitt, Lord Chatham, the north transept became known as 'The Statesmen's Aisle', the burial-place of statesmen.

WEST AISLE

Hugh Boulter, Archbishop of Armagh, b. 1672, d. 1742, statesman and philanthropist; consecrated Bishop of Bristol (1719), translated to Armagh in 1724, when he became Primate of All Ireland. At the time of his death he was serving for the thirteenth time as a Lord Justice of Ireland. Sculptor: *Sir H. Cheere.*

Samuel Bradford, b. 1652, d. 1731, Dean of Westminster and Bishop of Rochester (1723). Succeeded Atterbury in these posts while the latter was in the Tower. He was the first

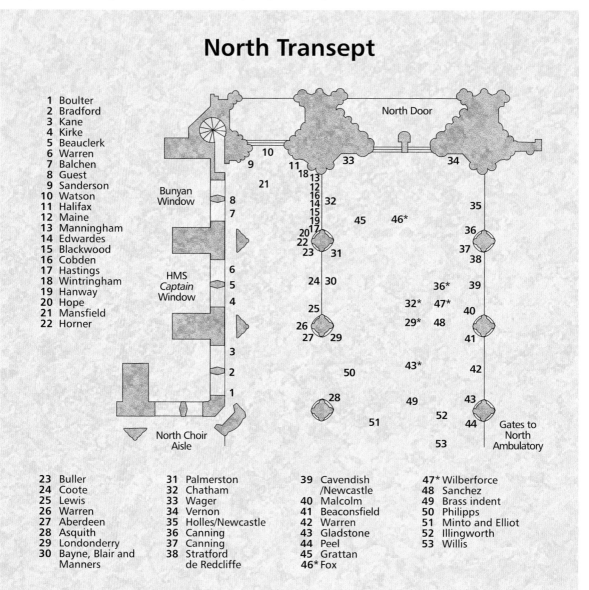

North Transept

1 Boulter
2 Bradford
3 Kane
4 Kirke
5 Beauclerk
6 Warren
7 Balchen
8 Guest
9 Sanderson
10 Watson
11 Halifax
12 Maine
13 Manningham
14 Edwardes
15 Blackwood
16 Cobden
17 Hastings
18 Wintringham
19 Hanway
20 Hope
21 Mansfield
22 Horner

North Door

Bunyan Window

HMS *Captain* Window

North Choir Aisle

Gates to North Ambulatory

23 Buller	31 Palmerston	39 Cavendish	47* Wilberforce
24 Coote	32 Chatham	/Newcastle	48 Sanchez
25 Lewis	33 Wager	40 Malcolm	49 Brass indent
26 Warren	34 Vernon	41 Beaconsfield	50 Philipps
27 Aberdeen	35 Holles/Newcastle	42 Warren	51 Minto and Elliot
28 Asquith	36 Canning	43 Gladstone	52 Illingworth
29 Londonderry	37 Canning	44 Peel	53 Willis
30 Bayne, Blair and	38 Stratford	45 Grattan	
Manners	de Redcliffe	46* Fox	

Dean of the revived Order of the Bath. Buried close by. Sculptor: *Sir H. Cheere.*

Brigadier-General Richard Kane, b. 1662, d. 1736, military commander and historian, and Governor of Minorca; distinguished himself when besieged at Londonderry (1689); wounded at the taking of Namur (1695); fought at Blenheim (1704); commanded regiment at Malplaquet (1709); Lieutenant-Governor of Minorca (1712), and later defended Gibraltar (1725); Governor of Minorca (1730–6); Brigadier-General (1734). Monument with bust by *J. M. Rysbrack.* Buried at Fort St Philip, Minorca.

Lieutenant-General Percy Kirk(e), b. 1684, d. 1741, succeeded his father as commander of the regiment which was derisively called 'Kirke's Lambs' because of their cruelty to Monmouth's adherents at Sedgmoor; the regimental badge was a Paschal Lamb. Kirke was a distinguished soldier, who fought under Marlborough and was wounded at Almanza (1708). In later life he was made Keeper of Whitehall Palace. Buried in this transept. Monument by *P. Scheemakers.*

Captain Lord Aubrey Beauclerk, RN, b. 1710, d. 1740, youngest son of Charles, 1st Duke of St Albans (illegitimate son of Charles II by Nell Gwynne) by Diana, daughter of Aubrey (de Vere), Earl of Oxford; killed commanding the *Prince Frederick* on Admiral Vernon's expedition to Cartagena; both his legs were shot off during the bombardment of Boca-Chica. The lines of verse are by Edward Young. Sculptor: *P. Scheemakers.*

Dr John Warren, Bishop of Bangor, b. 1730, d. 1800; previously (1779–83) Bishop of St David's. On the monument by *Sir R. Westmacott*, the Bishop's epitaph is incised on a rock 'on one side of which, in a mournful attitude . . . Religion [is] bearing a Cross, and on the other . . . an Angel [is] pointing to it as a source of consolation'. Erected by the Bishop's widow Elizabeth (q.v.), daughter of Henry Southwell, Esq., of Wisbech, Cambs. Buried near by.

Admiral Sir John Balchen, b. 1670, d. 1744, Commander-in-Chief of the fleets of England and Holland, lost with his ship, the *Victory*, in a violent storm in the Channel. The monument, executed by *P. Scheemakers*, also commemorates the Admiral's son **George Balchen**, d. 1745, aged twenty-eight; commander of the *Pembroke*.

Lieutenant-General Joshua Guest, b. 1660, d. 1747, 'who closed a Service of Sixty Years by faithfully defending Edinburgh Castle against the Rebells, 1745'. Sculptor: *Sir R. Taylor* (q.v.). Buried in the east cloister.

Sir William Sanderson, d. 1676, historian of Mary Queen of Scots, James I, and Charles I; Gentleman of the Bedchamber to Charles I. 'After great hardships sustained under the late Tyranny of Rebels' and 'after a full length of 90 years of this troublesome Life', he 'went to a better'. His wife, **Dame Bridget**, d. 1681, daughter of Sir Edward Tyrell, erected the monument, and is buried in his grave in front of Chatham's monument.

On the north wall above the door is the monument, designed by *J. Stuart* and executed by *P. Scheemakers*, to **Vice-Admiral Charles Watson**, b. 1714, d. 1757. It consists of three human figures and an inscription; the central figure is a standing one of the Admiral in a toga and holding a palm branch in his right hand. With his left he indicates an oriental woman representing 'the Genius of Calcutta'. On his right is a native of Gheriah seated in chains. Formerly Watson

stood beneath an arcade, the columns of which were transformed into palm trees so as to unite the design. On one tree there was a shield with the arms of France and behind it a sword and battle-axe. The son of John Watson, Prebendary of Westminster, he was educated at Westminster School and entered the Navy in 1728. As Commander-in-Chief, East Indies, in co-operation with Clive (q.v.) he reduced Gheriah (1756), liberated Calcutta, and captured Chandernagore (1757). He died and was buried at Calcutta. His monument was put up by the East India Company.

George (Montague-Dunk), 2nd Earl of Halifax, KG, b. 1716, d. 1771. First Lord of the Admiralty (1762); Lord-Lieutenant of Ireland (1761–3); twice Secretary of State (1762, 1771); styled the 'Father of the Colonies' for his success in extending American commerce. He also helped in the foundation of the colony of Nova Scotia; the capital was called Halifax after him. Monument by *J. Bacon* (1782).

Sir Henry James Sumner Maine, KCSI, b. 1822, d. 1888. Legal Member of Council in India for seven years. Master of Trinity Hall, Cambridge, and Professor of International Law. Author of *Ancient Law.* Sculptor: *Sir J. E. Boehm.*

The monument by *J. Bacon, Jun.*, erected 1813 by Lieutenant-General Thomas Hislop to **Major-General Coote Manningham**, d. 1809, Colonel of the 95th Foot, is near by.

Major-General Sir Herbert Benjamin Edwardes, KCB, KCSI, b. 1819, d. 1868, soldier and Indian official. He distinguished himself in the Punjab (1848), and again in the Indian Mutiny (1857); Commissioner of Peshawur (1853–9); KCB (1860); Commissioner of Umballa (1862); KCSI (1866). Monument, by *W. Theed, Jun.*, erected by the Secretary of State for India in Council.

Vice-Admiral the Hon. Sir Henry Blackwood, 1st Bt, KCB, GCH, b. 1770, d. 1832. He entered the Navy (1781); Captain of the frigate *Euryalus* at Trafalgar (1805); distinguished himself at the blockade of Toulon (1810); Baronet and Rear-Admiral (1814); KCB (1819); Commander-in-Chief, East Indies (1819–22); Vice-Admiral (1821); Commander-in-Chief, The Nore (1827–30). Tablet by *W Behnes*, put up by his widow.

Richard Cobden, b. 1804, d. 1865, statesman, hero of the repeal of the Corn Laws and the successful champion of free trade. Bust by *T. Woolner.* Buried at West Lavington, Sussex.

The Rt Hon. Warren Hastings, LLD, FRS, b. 1732, d. 1818; Governor-General of Bengal (1774–85), King's Scholar at Westminster School. He entered the service of the East India Company (1750). After a distinguished career in India, Hastings retired (1785); in 1788 he was impeached on charges of cruelty and corruption during his Indian administration. His trial lasted over seven years, and resulted in his triumphant acquittal, but the immense cost, £70,000, practically ruined him. Monument, by *J. Bacon, Jun.*, erected by his second wife, formerly Baroness Imhoff. Buried at Daylesford, Worcs.

Sir Clifton Wintringham, 1st Bt, FRS, b. 1710, d. 1794, physician; entered the Army medical service; Physician in Ordinary to George III and knighted (1762); Bt (1774); Physician-General to the Forces (1786); FRS (1792). Monument, by *T. Banks*, erected by his widow Anne.

Jonas Hanway, b. 1712, d. 1786, philanthropist. He is said to have been the first person in England to carry an umbrella; one of the founders of the Marine Society (1756), to which he gave the first training ship in the world, commemorated here by Britannia giving sailors' clothes to three boys; founder of the Magdalen Hospital. Monument by *J. F. and J. Moore*. Buried at Hanwell, Middx.

Brigadier-General Henry Hope, d. 1789; Lieutenant-Governor of Quebec. The monument, executed by *J. Bacon* in 1793, incorporates a female in North American dress lamenting over a sarcophagus, in company with a beaver and emblems of government, plenty, wisdom, integrity, and industry.

William (Murray), 1st Earl of Mansfield, b. 1705, d. 1793; Lord Chief Justice of England (1756–88); educated at Perth Grammar School and Westminster School; Solicitor-General (1742); Attorney-General (1754); Lord Chief Justice and Baron Mansfield (1756); Earl of Mansfield (1776); retired in 1788, and lived thereafter at Kenwood, Highgate, designed for him by Robert Adam (q.v.). This large monument, executed in 1801 by *J. Flaxman*, with seated figure of Mansfield from a portrait by *Reynolds* and flanked by figures of Wisdom and Justice, was paid for by A. Bailey of Lyon's Inn. It originally occupied the space between the columns in the bay south of that where the monument to The Three Captains stands. Buried in the transept.

Francis Horner, b. 1778, d. 1817; politician and economist. MP successively for St Ives (1806), Wendover (1808) and St Mawes (1813). Monument by *Sir F. Chantrey* (1823). Inscription by Sir Henry Englefield. Buried at Leghorn.

Charles Buller, b. 1806, d. 1848; politician. MP for West Looe (1830) and for Liskeard (1832); Chief Commissioner of the Poor Law (1847) and instigator of the Record Commission. Bust by *H. Weekes*. Inscription by Lord Houghton.

Lieutenant-General Sir Eyre Coote, KB, b. 1726, d. 1783; fought the Jacobites (1745); led a division at Plassey (1757); captured Pondicherry (1761); MP for Leicester (1768); Commander-in-Chief, Madras (1769), but resigned; KB (1771); Major-General (1775); Lieutenant-General (1777); Commander-in-Chief, India (1777); routed Hyder Ali at Porto Novo and elsewhere (1781); died at Madras. Fine monument by *T. Banks*, with seated Hindu captive, erected by the East India Company and finished in 1789. Buried at Rockbourne, Hants.

Sir George Cornewall Lewis, b. 1806, d. 1863, successively Chancellor of the Exchequer (1855–8); Home Secretary (1859–61); and Secretary for War (1861–3). Editor of the *Edinburgh Review* and author of political pamphlets. Bust by *H. Weekes*. Buried at Old Radnor church.

(Mrs) Elizabeth Warren, d. 1816, aged eighty-three, philanthropist and widow of Bishop John Warren (q.v.). The monument by *Sir R. Westmacott* is known as 'The Distressed Mother', because of the figure of a scantily clad woman nursing her baby. Buried near by.

George (Gordon), 4th Earl of Aberdeen, KG, b. 1784, d. 1860, statesman, Foreign Secretary (1828–30 and 1841–6); Prime Minister (1852–5) and classical scholar. Bust by *M. Noble*. Buried at Stanmore, Middx.

CENTRAL AISLE

Against the southernmost pillar is the memorial to: **Herbert Henry (Asquith), 1st Earl of Oxford and Asquith, KG, FRS**, b. 1852, d. 1928, statesman and Prime Minister; MP (Liberal) (1886–1918); QC (1890); PC (1892); and Home Secretary (1892–5); Chancellor of the Exchequer (1905–8); Prime Minister (1908–16) (resigned); MP (Independent Liberal) (1920–4); created Earl and KG (1925). Tablet, by *Puiker*, unveiled (1934) by Leader of the House of Commons (Baldwin). Buried at Sutton Courtenay, Berks.

Robert (Stewart), 2nd Marquess of Londonderry, KG, b. 1769, d. 1822, statesman: best known as **Viscount Castlereagh**; son of Robert (Stewart), 1st Marquess of Londonderry (1739–1821); MP (1794); Chief Secretary for Ireland (1799–1801); Secretary for War (1807–9); Foreign Secretary (1812–22); concluded first Peace of Paris (1814); KG and Senior British Plenipotentiary at First Congress of Vienna (1814); concluded triple peace alliance with France and Austria (1815); succeeded father as 2nd Marquess (1821). His mind having become unbalanced, he committed suicide on 12 August 1822. Standing figure on pedestal, executed by *J. E. Thomas* and erected (1850) by his brother (3rd Marquess) and friends. Buried in centre of transept near Chatham's grave. His widow **Amelia Ann** (*née* Hobart), **Dowager Marchioness of Londonderry**, b. 1772, d. 1829, is buried in the north-east angle of the cloisters.

Northwards is the large monument, known as 'The Three Captains', commemorating: **Captain William Bayne, RN**, b. *c*. 1732, d. 1782; **Captain William Blair, RN**, b. *c*. 1741, d. 1782; and **Captain Lord Robert Manners, RN**, b. 1758, d. 1782, all mortally wounded while commanding three of Rodney's ships at the second Battle of Dominica and of Les Saintes in the Caribbean on 9 and 12 April 1782. The monument, executed by *J. Nollekens* and paid for by the Treasury, was finished and open to public view late in 1793. The design which eventually adopted had been made as early as 1784; it consists of a naval trophy backing on to a pyramid and surmounted by a figure of Fame. Portrait busts of two of the Captains are fixed to the column, and a putto is in the act of adding the third; Britannia with her lion stands on one side and at the base is Neptune sprawling on a seahorse. The monument, which cost £4,000, was in place in 1788, but not yet finished. All three Captains buried at sea.

Next to the last-mentioned monument is one to **Henry John (Temple), 3rd Viscount Palmerston, KG, GCB**, b. 1784, d. 1865, statesman and twice Prime Minister (1855–8 and 1859–65). Standing figure in Garter robes on a pedestal; erected by Parliament. Sculptor: *R. Jackson*. His widow **Emily Mary, Viscountess Palmerston**, b. 1787, d. 1869; widow previously of the 5th Earl Cowper (d. 1837) and daughter of Peniston (Lamb), 1st Viscount Melbourne; was buried near him in this transept.

The next bay north is also occupied by one monument: **William (Pitt), 1st Earl of Chatham**, b. 1708, d. 1778; statesman and twice Prime Minister. He was temporarily buried at Hayes, Kent, but Parliament decided that he should be buried in the Abbey and his body was reburied in the middle of this transept. The commission for the monument was given largely, it seems, due to the influence of George III, to *J. Bacon*, who received more than £6,000 for it. It is some thirty feet or more high; at the top, in a recess scooped out of the pyramidical background, stands Lord Chatham delivering an oration. Bacon, we are told, composed the inscription which says that in Chatham's administration 'DIVINE PROVIDENCE exalted *Great Britain* to an Height of *Prosperity* and *Glory* unknown to any former Age.' This is the

Monument to Viscount Palmerston

BORN 1784 _ DIED 1865

theme of the allegorical figures, for Chatham is 'extending the sway of Britannia by means of Prudence and Fortitude over Earth and Ocean'. Beneath Chatham are Prudence (with serpent and looking-glass) and Fortitude (wrapped in a lion's skin and holding a column). On a lower stage Britannia, seated, thrusts down with a trident Neptune riding on a dolphin, the tail of which is skilfully disposed to serve as a substitute for a fig leaf; on the right Earth reclines with fruit, corn, and flowers in profusion. Monument executed 1779–83.

Against the north wall to the left of the door: **Admiral Sir Charles Wager**, PC, b. 1666, d. 1743, who served chiefly in the Mediterranean; Captain (1692); Rear-Admiral of the Blue (1707); and in command in the West Indies (1707–9). The monument has a bas-relief of his most famous exploit, known as 'Wager's Action', on 28 May 1708 when in the *Resolution* he defeated and destroyed the Spanish treasure fleet at Cartagena. In this action he was unaided except for a single fireship, for the *Kingston* and the *Portland* failed to support him, conduct for which their respective captains were court-martialled; Rear-Admiral of the Red and knighted (1709); blockaded Cadiz (1728); Admiral of the White (1731); First Commissioner of the Admiralty (1733–42),

Treasurer of the Navy. Buried in the middle of this transept. His widow **Dame Martha** (*née* Earning), d. 1748, aged eighty-two, is also buried there. Francis Gashry erected (1747) the monument, by *P. Scheemakers*, to his 'patron' the Admiral; he had married the widow of Wager's nephew and heir.

Near by is buried **Thomas Blagge**, b. 1613, d. 1660; Colonel of a foot regiment in the Royalist Army and a Groom of the Bedchamber to both Charles I and Charles II. His black marble monument was removed to make way for that of **Admiral Edward Vernon**, b. 1684, d. 1757, which matches Wager's monument and stands to the right of the north door. His boat-cloak made of grogram gave rise to his nickname 'Old Grog', and this in turn was applied to the drink 'grog' – rum and water mixed, which he instituted in the Royal Navy instead of neat rum. The Admiral was second son of James Vernon, Secretary of State to William III; entered the Navy in 1700 and served first under Sir Clowdisley Shovell (q.v.); Captain (1706) under Sir George Rooke (1705–12); MP for Penryn (1722); captured Porto Bello (1739), but was unsuccessful at Cartagena, Santiago, and Panama; MP for Ipswich; Admiral of the White (1745), in command in the North Sea. However, he was of a choleric temper and he exposed in print and in Parliament abuses in the Navy, which led to his being cashiered in 1746. Monument by *J. M. Rysbrack* erected (1763) by his nephew Francis, Lord Orwell.

Near the north door formerly stood an oak and pearwood **model**, *c.* 1620, of Sir Christopher Wren's proposed central tower and spire for Westminster Abbey. It was removed to the triforium during 1997.

John (Holles), 1st Duke of Newcastle and 4th Earl of Clare, KG, b. 1662, d. 1711, statesman; under Queen Anne he was Lord Privy Seal and Chief Justice in Eyre of the royal forests north of Trent. His wife was Margaret, daughter of Henry (Cavendish), 2nd Duke of Newcastle. The large architectural monument designed by *J. Gibbs* and executed by *F. Bird* comprises a reclining figure of the duke in armour holding a baton in one hand, and looking upwards at two angels who are seated on the pediment, while with his other hand he holds his coronet. The columns are flanked by statues of Wisdom and Sincerity. The monument, erected in 1723, was commissioned by Newcastle's son-in-law Edward (Harley), Earl of Oxford. Buried in St John the Evangelist's Chapel near his kinsmen of the Vere and Holles families.

In the Duke of Newcastle's vault is buried **Edward (Harley), 2nd Earl of Oxford**, b. 1689, d. 1741; only son of the statesman Robert (Harley), 1st Earl of Oxford (d. 1724) who started the great Harleian Library by purchasing the manuscript collections of Stow, D'Ewes, and others to which the 2nd Earl added. Also his widow **Henrietta, Countess of Oxford**, d. 1755, aged sixty-two, daughter of John (Holles), Duke of Newcastle (q.v.). She sold the manuscript collections to the British Museum, where now they form the famous Harleian Manuscripts.

Next to the Holles/Newcastle monument is one to the **Rt Hon. George Canning**, b. 1770, d. 1827, statesman; Prime Minister (1827), Chancellor of the Exchequer (1827) and Foreign Secretary (1822-27). The statue is a replica of that by *Sir F. Chantrey*, now at Athens but formerly at Trentham, Staffs. Buried near by. Close by is a statue on a pedestal to the son of the last-named: **Charles John (Canning), 1st Earl Canning, KG, GCB**, b. 1812, d. 1862; first Viceroy of India

(1856–62) and statesman. Monument executed by *J. H. Foley*. Buried with his father.

Stratford (Canning), 1st Viscount Stratford de Redcliffe, KG, GCB, b. 1786, d. 1880, diplomat; styled 'the Great Elchi' or ambassador *par excellence*; 'for 50 years the honoured representative of his sovereign in Turkey and other foreign countries'. Statue by *Sir J. E. Boehm*. Lines of verse by Tennyson are incised on the monument. Buried at Frant, Sussex.

Next is the large monument erected in his lifetime by **William (Cavendish), 1st Duke of Newcastle, KG**, b. 1592, d. 1676; to himself and his second wife **Margaret**, b. *c*. 1624, d. 1674, daughter of Sir Thomas Lucas of Colchester. For his devotion to Charles I, Newcastle was known as 'the Loyal Duke', he spent vast sums (about £1,000,000) on the Royalist cause, raising a regiment himself. He went into exile abroad after Marston Moor. A great patron of learning and the friend of Ben Jonson and Dryden, Newcastle himself wrote plays, poems, and works on horsemanship. The duchess also was a writer: of verses, essays, plays, a life of her husband, and an autobiography. The monument by *Grinling Gibbons* is somewhat old-fashioned, having recumbent figures of the duke (in armour and holding a baton) and duchess. The latter holds an open book, a pen-case, and an inkhorn, and books are represented again on the south side of the tomb, while martial emblems are on the north. Both buried near by.

South of the Cavendish/Newcastle monument is a standing figure by *Sir F. Chantrey* of **Major-General Sir John Malcolm, GCB**, b. 1769, d. 1833; soldier, statesman, and one of the founders of the Indian Empire. He began his Indian career as an ensign, aged fourteen, and concluded it as Governor of Bombay (1827–30). On his return to England he became MP for Launceston and vigorously opposed the Reform Bill.

Near by is a memorial statue on a pedestal to **Benjamin (Disraeli), 1st Earl of Beaconsfield, KG**, b. 1804, d. 1881, statesman and writer. Twice Prime Minister (1868 and 1874–6). He was highly regarded by Queen Victoria who assumed the title of Empress of India during his premiership. Sculptor: *Sir J. E. Boehm*. Buried at Hughenden, Bucks.

South of Disraeli is a drastically mutilated monument, executed by *L. F. Roubiliac*, to **Vice-Admiral Sir Peter Warren, KB**, b. 1703, d. 1752. He entered the Navy in 1717; Captain (1727); Commodore (1744); served on the American Station and in the West Indies; naval commander at the taking of Louisburg (1745); as Rear-Admiral he distinguished himself under Anson at the first Battle of Finisterre (1747); invested KB and promoted to Vice-Admiral of the Red (1747); MP for Westminster (1747–52). On the monument Hercules is represented as placing a fine portrait bust of the Admiral on the pedestal; on the right Navigation with a withered olive branch is seated on a cornucopia and regards the bust 'with a mixed look of veneration and melancholy'. Warren's bust wears the Star of the Order of the Bath; the pedestal or base of the monument is decorated with naval emblems, and formerly behind the monument there was a large Union Flag 'expanded pyramidically'. This last was removed in order to reveal the medieval screen of the Chapel of St John the Evangelist.

The Rt Hon. William Ewart Gladstone, b. 1809, d. 1898; statesman and four times Prime Minister (1868, 1880, 1886, 1892). Leader of the Liberal Party. He retired from public life (1894), and was buried in this transept at the public charge, by order of Parliament. The first State funeral here since that of Pitt, similar honours having been offered and declined in the case of Lord Beaconsfield. **Mrs Catherine Gladstone** (*née* Glynne), d. 1900, was buried in her husband's grave. Standing figure on pedestal by *Sir T. Brock*.

Sir Robert Peel, Bt, b. 1788, d. 1850; Prime Minister (1834 and 1841–6); the repeal of the Corn Laws (1846) was the marked feature of Peel's last administration, though he is perhaps best known for his reorganisation of the London Police force. His death was caused by a fall from his horse on Constitution Hill, and he was buried by his own wish at Drayton Bassett, Staffs. Standing figure in classical dress executed by *J. Gibson*.

Henry Grattan, b. 1746, d. 1820, statesman, the defender of the rights of Ireland. He endeavoured, though unsuccessfully, to gain full emancipation for Roman Catholics. He first wished to be buried in his native country, but ultimately consented to have his grave in the Abbey; a plain stone marks the spot at the head of the grave of **Charles James Fox** (see p. 23).

Near the Canning gravestone is that of **William Wilberforce** (q.v.) and close by, to the east of Londonderry's gravestone, is a now-defaced one to a noble Spaniard: **Didachus Sanchez**, d. 1557. Not far away there is another ancient stone with **the indents of a lost brass to an unknown man and woman** wearing a butterfly head-dress (*c*. 1490).

In this transept are also buried: **General Richard Philipps**, b. 1661, d. 1750; Governor of Nova Scotia (1720–49).

Gilbert (Elliot), 1st Earl of Minto, b. 1751, d. 1814; Governor-General of India (1806–13), and his brother **Hugh Elliot**, b. 1752, d. 1830, a distinguished diplomat, Governor of the Leeward Islands and of Madras successively, lie in one vault.

Mary Illingworth, d. 1758, daughter of **Elizabeth Illingworth**, d. 1760, who is buried with her. Elizabeth's great-grandson, Standish Haly, provided their stone.

Dr Thomas Willis, b. 1621, d. 1675, physician and author of works on the brain and nervous system; the first to distinguish the form of diabetes known as diabetes mellitus; an early Fellow of the Royal Society; FRCP 1664. The stone, dedicated in 1961 to replace a former one which was sent to Canada, also covers his first wife, **Mary**, d. 1670, daughter of Dr Samuel Fell, Dean of Christ Church, Oxford, and their daughter **Catherine**, b. 1663, d. 1667.

Buried in an unmarked grave is **Charles (Abbott), 1st Baron Colchester**, b. 1757, d. 1829; Speaker of the House of Commons (1802–16).

Also buried in an unmarked grave, near the gates leading to the north ambulatory, is **Sir Edward Broughton**, d. 1665, Keeper of the gatehouse prison. He was of Marchwiel, Co. Denbigh, and during the Commonwealth had been imprisoned in the gatehouse. The Keeper of the prison then was Aquila Wykes II (d. 1659), and Broughton in 1660 married the widow Wykes, Mary, daughter of William Knightley of Kingston upon Thames. Broughton was mortally wounded at the Battle of Lowestoft on 3 June 1665 and was brought back to the gatehouse to die; he was buried on 26 June. His widow **Dame Mary Broughton**, d. 1695, was also buried in the Abbey.

The South Transept

See plan, page 92

POETS' CORNER

Although nowadays the whole of this transept is generally called 'Poets' Corner', for many years it has contained tombs and memorials of men of letters other than poets, such as scholars, antiquaries, and divines. It was because of the burial of Chaucer in the east aisle and of Spenser not far away, that from the end of the sixteenth century it became increasingly common for poets and dramatists to be buried or commemorated there. In time these graves and monuments overflowed into the whole transept.

On the north side, backing on the tomb of Queen Anne of Cleves, is the fine monument executed by *F. Bird* of **Dr Richard Busby**, b. 1606, d. 1695, Prebendary of Westminster and Head Master of Westminster School. He was the most celebrated schoolmaster of his time and held the post for fifty-five years. 'He used to declare that the rod was his sieve, and that whoever could not pass through that was no boy for him.' The bulk of his academic library remains at the school, and among his other benefactions was the black and white pavement of the choir (1677), beneath which he was buried.

East of Busby is the memorial of **Dr William Vincent**, b. 1739, d. 1815, Dean of Westminster (1802–15); educated at Westminster School, and subsequently an Usher, then Under Master there; Head Master (1788–1802); Canon of Westminster (1801–2), then Dean. His name is preserved in Vincent Square which he gave to the school. Buried in St Benedict's Chapel near by. Also commemorated by a tablet, formerly in the Chapel of St John the Evangelist, is his wife (**Mrs**) **Hannah Vincent** (*née* Wyatt), b. 1735, d. 1807. Buried in the north transept. The same tablet commemorates their second son **George Giles Vincent**, d. 1859, for fifty years Chapter Clerk of the Abbey. Buried in the north cloister.

Separated from Busby by the Vincent memorials is another monument *by F. Bird* to a favourite pupil of Busby: **Dr Robert South**, b. 1634, d. 1716; Prebendary of Westminster and Archdeacon. He was a famous preacher, and the violence of an attack on Cromwell in one of his sermons so amused Charles II that he fell into a violent fit of laughter, and vowed Dr South should have a bishopric if he was put 'in mind of him at the next death'. The next death was, however, the king's own. Buried at his own request close to Busby.

Against the pillar at the corner of St Benedict's Chapel is a bust by *H. H. Armstead* of **Archibald Campbell Tait**, b. 1811, d. 1882; Archbishop of Canterbury (1869–82). Buried at Addington, Kent.

Near by a slab on the floor, recently reincised, covers the grave of **William Spottiswoode, PRS**, b. 1825, d. 1883; printer to Queen Victoria.

Not far south of Spottiswoode is buried **Dr Peter Birch**, b. *c.* 1652, d. 1710; Prebendary of Westminster (1689–1710); Sub-dean and Archdeacon; Chaplain to the Duke of Ormond

and to the House of Commons. His first wife Mary was the daughter of the poet Edmund Waller. His second wife **Martha**, b. *c.* 1653, d. 1703, widow of Francis Millington, and daughter of Samuel Vyner, Esq., is commemorated by a baroque cartouche near by.

In the middle of the bay at the west end of St Benedict's Chapel is the bust of **John Dryden**, b. 1631, d. 1700, Poet Laureate and dramatist. He was educated at Westminster School under Dr Busby. In early life an admirer of Cromwell, after the Restoration Dryden became a Royalist, and held several offices under the Crown. Soon after the accession of James II he became Roman Catholic. His finest works, the tragedy *All for Love* (1678) and the political satire *Absalom and Achitophel* (1681), were published before he changed his religion, but his poem *The Hind and the Panther* (1687) was written after his conversion. In consequence he was deprived of his laureateship, died in poverty in Gerard Street, Soho, but was buried on 13 May 1700, with much ceremony, near Chaucer's empty grave. This monument (which has since been altered) was erected in 1720 by Dryden's friend John Sheffield, Duke of Buckingham, whose widow replaced the first bust in 1731 with the present fine one by *P. Scheemakers*.

Starting from Dryden's monument we find the following gravestones in the floor. A stone with the indent of a lost brass of a man in armour, a marginal inscription, and symbols of the Evangelists at the corners, covers the grave of **Robert Haule(y)**, d. 1378. He and a fellow squire John Shakel took a hostage for the payment of the ransom of the Count of Denia, a great Aragonese nobleman whom Hauley had captured at the Battle of Najera in 1367. In 1377 Hauley and Shakel were thrown into the Tower of London for refusing an order to hand over the hostage, who was, in fact, the Count's elder son Alphonso. The Count had been adjudged by the Black Prince to be the prisoner of Hauley, and his ransom was fixed at a vast sum of money, in which London merchants had become financially interested. Also, since the Count was of the Blood Royal of Aragon, his son's captivity in England was a political and diplomatic embarrassment. In 1378 Hauley and Shakel, using violence, escaped from the Tower and took sanctuary at Westminster. A royal letter to Abbot Litlyngton having failed to secure their surrender, the Constable of the Tower (Sir Alan de Buxhall, KG) broke into the Abbey sanctuary with fifty soldiers on 11 August and succeeded in capturing Shakel. This breaking of sanctuary was in itself sacrilege, but far worse was done when Hauley, having shown fight, was killed together with a sacrist named Richard in the choir during High Mass. Archbishop Sudbury excommunicated the malefactors and their confederates, excepting only the boy-King Richard II, his mother (the Princess of Wales), and his uncle John of Gaunt. In fact Gaunt was widely suspected of having been implicated because of his claim to be King of Castile and his consequent interest in Spanish politics. Hauley was buried in this transept before the altar of St Benedict, and four months after its desecration by bloodshed the Abbey was reconsecrated. Buxhall, the Constable, had his excommunication lifted on payment of a substantial fine. When **John Shakel**, d. 1396, came to make his will, he desired to be buried next to his comrade Hauley and gave to the building of the Abbey £100 – if he should recover the ransom money.

Near Dryden lie **Sir John Beaumont**, b. *c.* 1583, d. 1627,

South Transept

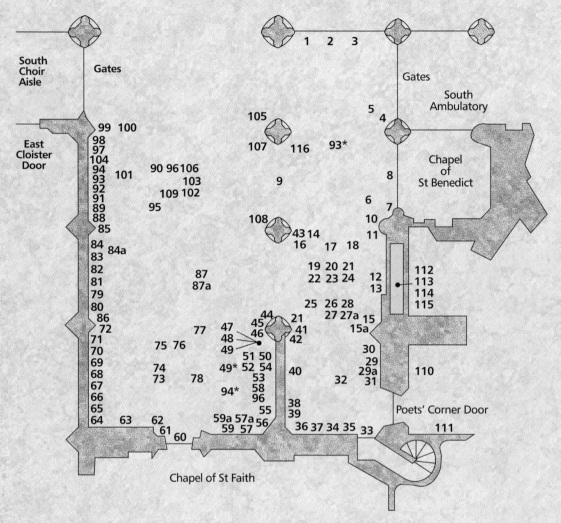

South Choir Aisle

Gates

East Cloister Door

Gates

South Ambulatory

Chapel of St Benedict

Chapel of St Faith

Poets' Corner Door

a minor poet, and his better-known brother, **Francis Beaumont**, b. 1584, d. 1616, the dramatist. The latter wrote chiefly in conjunction with John Fletcher; the two friends lived in Southwark not far from the Globe Theatre. Their best-known joint production is *The Knight of the Burning Pestle*. The lines on the Abbey tombs are usually ascribed to Francis Beaumont:

> Mortality, behold and fear
> What a change of flesh is here!
> Think how many Royal bones
> Sleep within these heaps of stones.

Not far from Dryden's monument is one to **Henry Wadsworth Longfellow**, b. 1807, d. 1882, the American poet; perhaps best known for his *Hiawatha*. Bust, by *Sir T. Brock*, erected in 1884 by his English admirers. Buried at Cambridge, Mass.

Abraham Cowley, b. 1618, d. 1667, a poet whose great contemporary reputation quickly waned, to which the epitaph (by his friend and biographer Dean Sprat) calling him the 'Pindar, Horace, and Virgil of England', bears witness. For several years Cowley worked in Paris as confidential secretary to Queen Henrietta Maria. He returned to England after the Restoration expecting recognition of his services, and died in retirement a few years later. Monument by *J. Bushnell*. To Cowley's gravestone near by Dean Stanley added the names of eight other writers buried in Poets' Corner (all separately noted in this *Guide*). Stone re-cut by *T. Metcalfe*, 1993.

Near his friend Cowley, on whose death he wrote a fine elegy, lies **Sir John Denham**, b. 1615, d. 1669. His poem *Cooper's Hill*, an early example of English descriptive poetry, was praised by Dryden, Pope, and Dr Johnson.

We now come to the tomb to which Poets' Corner owes its origin: **Geoffrey Chaucer**, b. *c*. 1343, d. 1400, poet and civil servant. As the author of *The Canterbury Tales* he is, next to Shakespeare, perhaps the most famous English poet. He began his career in the service of Lionel, third son of Edward III, and subsequently held various offices in the king's household. He was sent abroad on several diplomatic missions, including twelve months in Italy, which exercised a marked influence on his writings. His patron and constant friend was John of Gaunt, whose first wife's death was the occasion of Chaucer's poem *The Book of the Duchess*. Gaunt's third wife is said to have been the sister of the poet's wife. For a short time Chaucer held the office of Clerk of the King's Works at Westminster. During the last years of his life he took a long lease of (and seems to have lived in) a house near the old Lady Chapel which was later pulled down to make room for Henry VII's Chapel. It was probably owing to these circumstances that he was buried in the Abbey, at the entrance of St Benedict's Chapel. For 150 years his only memorial was a leaden plate 'whereon', Caxton tells us, 'was wreton his epitaphye, maad by a Poet-laureate' (Surigonius of Milan), which hung on the adjacent pillar. In 1556 Nicholas Brigham, a minor poet, erected the present tomb. Behind it was a portrait of Chaucer, and there were in the eighteenth century traces of another figure, possibly that of Brigham, who is said to have been buried near Chaucer.

Above Chaucer's tomb is a tablet (1776) to **John Roberts**, b. *c*. 1712, d. 1772, politician. Sculptor: *R. Hayward*.

Chaucer's tomb

John Philips, b. 1676, d. 1708, poet. Author of a poem called *Cyder*. His epitaph is memorable for its early mention of Milton. Dean Sprat had the epitaph erased on account of this allusion, but it was restored by Dean Atterbury four years later. Buried in Hereford Cathedral.

A stone in the floor commemorates **Wystan Hugh Auden**, b. 1907, d. 1973, poet. Designed by *J. P. Foster* and executed by *Messrs Whitehead*. Unveiled on 2 October 1974. Buried at Kirchstetten, Lower Austria.

Near by a stone covers the ashes of **John Masefield, OM**, b. 1878, d. 1967, Poet Laureate (1930), novelist and dramatist. Masefield is known best for his poems concerning the sea.

Robert Browning, b. 1812, d. 1889, poet. He married the poetess Elizabeth Barrett, in 1846, and lived in Italy until her death in 1861. Browning died at Venice, whence his body was brought to the Abbey. His last work, *Asolando*, was published on the day (16 December) of his death. The gravestone is composed of Italian marbles and porphyry.

Stones in the floor commemorate: **George Eliot** (**Mary Ann Cross**, *née* Evans), b. 1819, d. 1880, novelist. Among her best-known works are *The Mill on the Floss* and *Middlemarch*. Stone unveiled 21 June 1980, cut by *J. Skelton*. Buried at Highgate.

Gerard Manley Hopkins, SJ, b. 1844, d. 1889, 'Priest and Poet'. His best-known poem is probably *The Wreck of the Deutschland*. Designed by *D. Peace* and executed by *Messrs Whitehead*. Unveiled on 8 December 1975. Buried at Glasnevin, Dublin.

Alfred (**Tennyson**), **1st Baron Tennyson**, b. 1809, d. 1892, succeeded Wordsworth in 1850 as Poet Laureate. *In Memoriam* (of his friend Arthur Hallam) was published the same year. His poem 'Crossing the Bar', set to music by Sir Frederick Bridge, was first sung at his own funeral in the Abbey. Bust by *T. Woolner*, set up in 1895.

Part of Poets' Corner showing monuments to Shakespeare, Wordsworth and others

A floor slab of green Penrhyn stone commemorates **Dylan Marlais Thomas**, b. 1914, d. 1953, poet. He became well known to a wide public through his verse-play *Under Milk Wood*; his *Collected Poems* appeared in 1952. He died in America and was brought back for burial in Laugharne, Dyfed. The memorial stone, cut by *J. Jones*, was unveiled on St David's Day 1982. The inscription includes two lines from 'Fern Hill'.

An adjacent stone commemorates **Henry James, OM**, b. 1843, d. 1916, novelist and writer of short stories. Born in New York he was naturalised British in 1915. His novels include *The Portrait of a Lady* and *The Ambassadors*. His short story, *The Turn of the Screw*, was used as the basis of an opera by Benjamin Britten (q.v.). He died in London, but is buried in Cambridge, Mass. The memorial, by *W. Carter*, was unveiled on 17 June 1976.

Close by a floor-slab by *R. Stone*, in memory of **Thomas Stearns Eliot, OM**, b. 1888, d. 1965, poet, dramatist, and critic, was unveiled on 4 January 1967. Born in St Louis, Missouri and educated at Harvard University, he settled in London and took up British nationality. His principal works are *The Waste Land*, *Four Quartets*, and the verse drama *Murder in the Cathedral*. He was awarded the Nobel Prize for Literature in 1948. Buried at East Coker, Som.

The memorial stone to **George Gordon (Byron), 6th Baron Byron**, b. 1788, d. 1824, was given by the Poetry Society and dedicated on 8 May 1969. *Childe Harold* and *Don Juan* are probably his best-known poems. After his marriage failed in 1816 the poet lived abroad. In 1823 Byron joined the Greek insurgents, but he died of fever at Missolonghi in 1824. For many years the open profligacy of his life proved an obstacle to his commemoration in the Abbey, but his poetic genius and mastery of the art of letter-writing at length prevailed. Buried at Hucknall Torkard, Notts.

Lewis Carroll (Charles Lutwidge Dodgson), b. 1832, d. 1898. Educated at Rugby School and Christ Church, Oxford, where he later became a lecturer in mathematics. Best known for his children's book *Alice's Adventures in Wonderland*, first told to Alice Liddell and her sisters on a boating trip at Oxford. Stone by *E. Rees*, unveiled 17 December 1982. Buried at Guildford, Surrey.

The stone designed by *D. Parsley* in memory of **David Herbert Lawrence**, b. 1885, d. 1930, novelist and poet, was unveiled on 16 November 1985 by the president of the D. H. Lawrence Society. The son of a Nottinghamshire coal-miner, Lawrence's works are infused with a rich quality of feeling and sensitivity. Perhaps the two most influential are *Sons and Lovers* and *The Rainbow*. Buried at Vence, France, where the phoenix which he regarded as his emblem is also in mosaic on the grave.

The memorial stone to **Poets of the First World War**, with its quotation from Wilfred Owen's *Collected Poems*, was unveiled by another poet, Ted Hughes, on 11 November 1985. It commemorates: **Richard Aldington**, b. 1892, d. 1962; **Laurence Binyon**, b. 1869, d. 1945; **Edmund Blunden**, b. 1896, d. 1974; **Rupert Brooke**, b. 1887, d. 1915; **Wilfrid Gibson**, b. 1878, d. 1962; **Robert Graves**, b. 1895, d. 1985; **Julian Grenfell**, b. 1888, d. 1915; **Ivor Gurney**, b. 1890, d. 1937; **David Jones**, b. 1895, d. 1974; **Robert Nichols**, b. 1893, d. 1944; **Wilfred Owen**, b. 1893, d. 1918; **Herbert Read**, b. 1893, d. 1968; **Isaac Rosenberg**, b. 1890, d. 1918; **Siegfried Sassoon**, b. 1886, d. 1967; **Charles Sorley**, b. 1895, d. 1915, and **Edward Thomas**, b. 1878, d. 1917. Designed by *H. Meadows*.

Adjacent are memorials to two nineteenth-century writers. **Edward Lear**, b. 1812, d. 1888, poet. A skilled ornithological artist, Lear is, however, best known for his so-called nonsense verse including *The Owl and the Pussy-Cat*. Unveiled in June 1988, executed by *M. Bury*.

Anthony Trollope, b. 1815, d. 1882, novelist. Trollope spent much of his career working for the Post Office and was responsible for the introduction of the pillar-box for letters. He wrote over fifty books, including the 'Barchester' novels set in the fictional cathedral city of that name. Stone designed by *S. More*; unveiled by the Prime Minister, John Major, in March 1993. Buried at Kensal Green.

On the window-sill is a bust by *B. Joy* of **Matthew Arnold**, b. 1822, d. 1888, poet and essayist. It was presented by his relatives and friends, unveiled by Lord Coleridge on 31 October 1891, and originally stood in St George's Chapel. A commemorative tablet, *designed by D. Buttress* and unveiled in February 1989, includes a quotation from Arnold's memorial poem to Dean Stanley.

Beside it a mural tablet of limestone and slate commemorates **John Clare**, b. 1793, d. 1864, one of the finest of English nature poets, unparalleled in his sensitive evocation of country life. Buried at Helpston, Northants. Designed by *D. Buttress*, lettered and executed by *J. Skelton*, unveiled June 1989.

Next is a monument to **Barton Booth**, b. 1681, d. 1733, actor; he succeeded Betterton in public estimation. Sculptor: *W. Tyler*. Buried at Cowley, Middx. Barton Street, Westminster, recalls his connection with this area.

Michael Drayton, b. 1563, d. 1631, poet. Bust by *E. Marshall*. The epitaph (attributed both to Quarles and Ben Jonson) testifies to the poet's contemporary fame, but his chief work, *Polyolbion*, is now little read.

A stone set into the floor commemorates the early Northumbrian poet **Caedmon**, *fl.* 670, 'who first among the English made verses'.

Ben Jonson, b. 1574, d. 1637, dramatist and poet. Educated at Westminster School, under Camden, he was the friend of Shakespeare and Bacon. Later he was tutor to Sir Walter Raleigh's son, and in 1619 became Poet Laureate. Jonson was always improvident and, in spite of gifts from the King, died in great poverty in a house between the Abbey and St Margaret's church. Of his many tragedies and comedies, *Volpone, Every Man in his Humour*, and *Bartholomew Fair* are the most celebrated. He was also well known as a writer of masques. He was buried in the nave (see p. 25), under a stone bearing the same inscription as his monument, which was erected before 1728 by the Earl of Oxford. Monument designed by *J. Gibbs* and executed by *J. M. Rysbrack*.

Samuel Butler, b. 1612, d. 1680, satirist, buried at St Paul's, Covent Garden, because there was no money to pay the Abbey fees for a grave here. The author of *Hudibras* did not reap much profit from its popularity, and, after passing from the service of one great person to another, died in dire poverty. The monument was erected in 1721 by John Barber, Lord Mayor of London.

Edmund Spenser, b. 1553, d. 1599, poet, author of *Faerie Queene*, which he dedicated to Queen Elizabeth. He spent his latter years on an estate granted him in Ireland, but this was finally devastated by the natives, his house set on fire, and he and his wife obliged to flee with their four young children. He died, it is said, in King Street, Westminster.

A memorable gathering of his contemporaries assembled at the funeral, and all, probably including Shakespeare, threw their elegies, with the pens which wrote them, into the grave. Anne Clifford, Countess of Dorset, erected his monument in 1620; but this falling into decay, was replaced in 1778 by an exact copy, for which the poet Mason set on foot a subscription.

John Milton, b. 1608, d. 1674, poet, buried in St Giles's, Cripplegate, born in London. He was educated at St Paul's School and at Christ's College, Cambridge. The earlier part of his life was spent in study, but in 1639 the gathering of the political storm and his own strong Puritan bias called him home from a journey in Italy. For ten years he was Latin Secretary to the Council of the Commonwealth, during which time he published many controversial writings on political, social, and religious subjects. After the Restoration Milton was forced to conceal himself for a short time. He lived later on in London and, totally blind, devoted himself to the great works of his life, *Paradise Lost* (1667), *Paradise Regained*, and *Samson Agonistes* (1671). Until 1737, when this monument was erected by Auditor Benson, the Abbey contained no memorial of Milton, the strength of Royalist feeling against him having delayed public recognition of his genius. Addison in his *Spectator* criticism led the way for the inevitable reaction. Speaking of it, Dr Gregory remarked to Dr Johnson: 'I have seen erected in the church a bust of that man whose name I once knew considered as a pollution of its walls.' Sculptor: *J. M. Rysbrack*.

Thomas Gray, b. 1716, d. 1771, poet, buried at Stoke Poges, the scene of his 'Elegy written in a Country Churchyard'. The lyric muse holds a medallion with his portrait, and points to the bust of Milton. The epitaph is by **William Mason**, b. 1724, d. 1797, poet, the friend and biographer of Gray, buried at Aston, Yorks. Dr Hurd, Bishop of Worcester, wrote his inscription. The monuments to Gray and Mason are both by *J. Bacon*.

Thomas Shadwell, b. 1642?, d. 1692, poet. He was the rival of Dryden, and succeeded him as Poet Laureate. Dryden satirised him in *MacFlecknoe*. He died of opium-eating at Chelsea, where he is buried. Sculptor: *F. Bird*.

Matthew Prior, b. 1664, d. 1721, diplomat and poet. He held several offices under William III, and was for a time Plenipotentiary at the Court of Louis XIV. The very fine bust of Prior incorporated in the monument is by *C. A. Coysevox* and was a present from Louis. He was buried, as he desired, at the feet of Spenser. Dr Freind, Head Master of Westminster School, wrote the epitaph. Monument designed by *J. Gibbs* and executed by *J. M. Rysbrack*.

Charles de Saint Denis, Seigneur de Saint-Evremond, b. 1613, d. 1703, soldier, poet and essayist.

Granville Sharp, b. 1735, d. 1813, philanthropist, one of the earliest and most devoted opponents of the slave-trade. The monument was erected by the African Institution in gratitude for his efforts. Sculptor: *Sir F. Chantrey*.

Christopher Anstey, b. 1724, d. 1805. Buried at Bath. Widely known in his day as the author of the *New Bath Guide*. Sculptor: *C. Horwell*.

On the column near Tennyson is the bust of **Adam Lindsay Gordon**, b. 1833, d. 1870, poet and amateur steeplechaser; born in England but emigrated to Australia in 1853. His bush ballads are the best of his verses, among them 'The Sick Stockrider' and 'How we beat the Favourite'. The bust was unveiled by the Duke of York on 11 May 1934. Sculptor: *Lady Kennet*.

Thomas Campbell, b. 1777, d. 1844, poet, author of 'The Pleasures of Hope', 'Hohenlinden', 'Ye Mariners of England', and 'The Battle of the Baltic'. The lines engraved are from his own 'Last Man'. He died at Boulogne, whence his remains were brought here for interment. Sculptor: *W. Calder Marshall*.

Samuel Taylor Coleridge, b. 1772, d. 1834, poet, philosopher and critic. 'The Ancient Mariner', 'Christabel', and 'Kubla Khan' are his best-known poems. The bust was given by Dr Mercer, an American, and unveiled on 7 May 1885, by Mr Lowell, the United States Minister. Sculptor: *H. Thornycroft*. Buried at Highgate.

William Wordsworth, b. 1770, d. 1850, succeeded Southey as Poet Laureate (1843). All his poetry was inspired by an absorbing love of nature and written amidst the lakes and mountains where he spent most of his life. His *Lyrical Ballads* (1798) was a landmark in the development of a new style of English poetry, while *The Prelude*, first published 1805, contains much autobiographical material. Buried at Grasmere, Cumbria.

Robert Southey, b. 1774, d. 1843; Poet Laureate, and prose writer; educated at Westminster School; one of 'the Lake Poets'. His poetry was much admired by his contemporaries such as Scott and Byron, but today his shorter poems are best remembered, e.g. 'The Battle of Blenheim' and 'The Inchcape Rock'. Among other prose works Southey wrote biographies of Nelson (1813), Wesley (1820), and the poet Cowper (1833–7). Sculptor: *H. Weeke*s. Epitaph by Wordsworth. Buried at Crossthwaite, Cumbria.

Dr Samuel Johnson, b. 1709, d. 1784, lexicographer and critic, is, thanks to Boswell, one of the most living and familiar figures in the eighteenth century. He was born at Lichfield and educated at the grammar school there and at Pembroke College, Oxford. After an unsuccessful attempt at schoolmastering, in 1737 he went up to London accompanied by his pupil Garrick, in search of a career. The master's success, however, was much slower than that of the pupil, and continual struggles with poverty and ill-health lay before him. The great *Dictionary of the English Language*, the *Lives of the Poets*, and *The Rambler* are his chief works. The inscription was re-cut at the cost of his old college, Pembroke, Oxford. In 1939 a bust of Dr Johnson by *J. Nollekens* was placed on the wall above his grave.

A small tablet, unveiled in 1967, commemorates **Jane Austen**, b. 1775, d. 1817, novelist; the daughter of a country clergyman, she belonged to that society the life and manners of which she portrayed in her novels with acute perception, humour, and gentle irony. The volume of her major published work, though small, is the result of continued rewriting and polishing: *Sense and Sensibility* (1811), *Pride and Prejudice* (1813), *Mansfield Park* (1814), *Emma* (1816), *Northanger Abbey* (1818), and *Persuasion* (1818). Buried in Winchester Cathedral.

Near by are two small oval tablets, by *F. Dobson*, incised simply with the names 'Keats' and 'Shelley'; they were erected by the Keats-Shelley Memorial Association and unveiled in 1954. **John Keats**, b. 1795, d. 1821, poet and letter-writer; the youngest and shortest-lived of the Romantic poets. Among his best-known poems are his odes, 'To a Nightingale' and 'On a Grecian Urn' and the ballad 'La Belle Dame sans Merci'. His letters, published some years after his death, provide a valuable commentary on his poems and on contemporary events. In 1820 he left England for Italy and died of tuberculosis in 1821 in Rome, where he is buried in the Protestant Cemetery.

Percy Bysshe Shelley, b. 1792, d. 1822. He wrote his first important poem *Queen Mab* while he was leading a wandering life separated from his first wife Harriet. The latter drowned herself (1816) in the Serpentine, and Shelley married secondly Mary Godwin. In 1816 he published *Alastor* and began a friendship with Byron. His great drama *Prometheus Unbound* was published in 1819. To his last years belong his great odes and lyrics: 'To a Skylark', 'To the West Wind', and 'The Cloud'. Shelley was drowned while sailing near Spezzia in 1822 and was buried in the Protestant Cemetery at Rome. His avowed atheism for long prevented his commemoration in the Abbey.

William Shakespeare, b. 1564, d. 1616. Shortly after his death there was much talk of removing his remains from Stratford-upon-Avon to the Abbey; the idea was soon abandoned but it gave rise to Ben Jonson's famous lines:

> My Shakespeare, rise! I will not lodge thee by
> Chaucer or Spenser, or bid Beaumont lie
> A little further on to make thee room.

The monument, designed by *W. Kent* and executed by *P. Scheemakers*, was erected in 1740. On the scroll is written a variant of some of Prospero's most famous lines from *The Tempest*; the heads at the corners of the pedestal represent Elizabeth I, Henry V, and Richard III.

The continuing affection felt for the poet **Robert Burns**, b. 1759, d. 1796, for whom 'Burns Night' is still celebrated world-wide on 25 January, is shown also by this memorial, erected eighty-nine years after his death and paid for in shilling subscriptions contributed by people of every rank. The bust, sculptor *Sir J. Steell*, was unveiled by Lord Rosebery on 7 March 1885. Buried in Dumfries.

James Thomson, b. 1700, d. 1748, poet; author of *The Seasons*, which are represented in bas-relief on the pedestal. His most remembered composition now is probably 'Rule, Britannia'. The monument designed by *R. Adam* and executed by *M. H. Spang* was erected in 1762. Buried in Richmond parish church, Surrey.

The Brontës. A tablet to the three Brontë sisters (**Charlotte**, b. 1816, d. 1855, novelist, author of *Jane Eyre* and other novels; **Emily Jane**, b. 1818, d. 1848, author of *Wuthering Heights*; **Anne**, b. 1820, d. 1849, author of *The Tenant of Wildfell Hall*) was presented by the Brontë Society and unveiled in July 1947.

A floor stone commemorates two abbots of Westminster buried close by: **William Benson**, d. 1549, the first Dean of the Church (1540–49) who as William Boston had also been the last abbot (1533–40); **Abbot Nicholas de Litlyngton**, d. 1386, who succeeded Langham as abbot here (1362–86). Partly out of his predecessor's bequest and partly from his own money he rebuilt the west and south cloister, part of the abbot's lodgings including the Jerusalem Chamber and College Hall, the conventual buildings on the east side of Dean's Yard and the boundary wall of the monastery, part of which can be seen in Great College Street. He also enlarged the monastic frater or refectory. From 1376 he continued the rebuilding of the nave with the aid of Langham's money.

Sir Henry Irving, b. 1838, d. 1905, actor and actor-manager, who revolutionised the dramatic art of the nineteenth century by his revivals of Shakespeare and other plays at the old Lyceum Theatre (1878–99).

An adjacent stone of green slate covers the ashes of **Laurence Olivier, O. M., Baron Olivier of Brighton**, b. 1907, d. 1989. The greatest actor of his generation, celebrated in particular for his Shakespearean roles, and for his film of *Henry V*. Stone cut by *I. Rees*, unveiled by Sir John Gielgud in September 1991.

In 1936 **two wall paintings** representing St Christopher and the incredulity of St Thomas were discovered on the wall to the east of the door leading into St Faith's Chapel and immediately behind and hidden by the monuments to Gay and Rowe. These paintings, which date from 1280 to 1300 are among the most important to have survived in England. In consequence of their discovery the monuments, both by *J. M. Rysbrack*, to **John Gay**, b. 1685, d. 1732, poet and dramatist, author of *The Beggar's Opera* and to **Nicholas Rowe**, b. 1674, d. 1718, Poet Laureate, have been moved to the triforium.

Oliver Goldsmith, b. 1728, d. 1774, author of *The Vicar of Wakefield*, *She Stoops to Conquer*, and *The Deserted Village*. His life was a perpetual struggle with poverty, for he was incapable of managing money affairs, and died burdened with debt. Sir Joshua Reynolds chose the site for his monument, which is by *J. Nollekens*, and Dr Johnson wrote the epitaph. Buried in the Temple churchyard.

A bronze medallion portrait head commemorates **John Ruskin**, b. 1819, d. 1900, author of *The Stones of Venice*, *Modern Painters*, and other works; one of the greatest artistic and social influences of his generation. Sculptor: *O. Ford*.

Beside Goldsmith's monument a memorial to the author of the Waverley Novels, **Sir Walter Scott**, b. 1771, d. 1832, was placed in 1897. It is a replica by *J. Hutchinson*, of the *Chantrey* bust at Abbotsford.

John (Campbell), 2nd Duke of Argyll and 1st Duke of Greenwich, b. 1680, d. 1743, buried in Henry VII's Chapel. This orator and soldier, who figures in the pages of Scott's *Heart of Midlothian*, was one of the main instruments of the Union of England and Scotland. His allegorical monument, perhaps the finest eighteenth-century monument in the Abbey, blocks the place where once a staircase led up to the monks' dormitory. Minerva and Eloquence stand below the recumbent figure; History inscribing his titles, stops short at Gr – to show that the dukedom of Greenwich expired with him. Sculptor: *L. F. Roubiliac*.

A tablet by *R. Adam* commemorates **Mrs Mary Hope**, d. 1767 and near by is a tablet and medallion by *J. Nollekens* to the **Rt Hon. James S. Mackenzie**, d. 1800, Lord Privy Seal of Scotland.

General Sir Archibald Campbell, b. 1739, d. 1791. As Governor of Madras, at the end of his career, Sir Archibald Campbell arranged the important Arcot Treaty (1787). The monument also commemorates his nephew, **Lieutenant-General Sir James Campbell, Bt**, d. 1819. Sculptor: *J. Wilton*.

A monument to the **Atkyns** family, three of whom were Barons of the Exchequer in the seventeenth century. Their descendant, **Sir Robert Atkyns**, b. 1647, d. 1711, also commemorated on the monument, was the author of the classic history of Gloucestershire.

George Frederick Handel, b. 1685, d. 1759, the great composer. The statue is said to be an exact likeness; the face

South transept wall painting: The Incredulity of St Thomas

was modelled from a death-mask. A tablet above recalls the first Handel Festival held in the Abbey in 1784. Sculptor: *L. F. Roubiliac*.

Below the composer was placed in 1894 a portrait head of **Jenny Lind-Goldschmidt**, b. 1820, d. 1887, the well-known singer ('the Swedish Nightingale'). Sculptor: *C. B. Birch*.

Sir Thomas Robinson, b. 1700, d. 1777, architect, called 'long Sir Thomas', who ruined himself by his love of building. He was Governor of Barbados for a time.

William Makepeace Thackeray, b. at Calcutta 1811, d. 1863, novelist and essayist, editor of the *Cornhill* (1860–2) and a contributor to *Punch* (1842–52). *Vanity Fair* (1848) established his reputation. Buried at Kensal Green. Sculptor: *Baron C. Marochetti*.

Joseph Addison, b. 1672, d. 1719. The great English essayist, 'the noblest purifier of English literature', had no monument in the Abbey until this statue was erected in 1809. Addison's paper in *The Spectator* on the Abbey should be read by all who visit this church. Sculptor: *Sir R. Westmacott*. Buried in the north aisle of Henry VII's Chapel.

Richard Cumberland, b. 1732, d. 1811, dramatist, and friend of Dr Johnson. Satirised in Sheridan's *The Critic* as Sir Fretful Plagiary.

Charles Dickens, b. 1812, d. 1870, novelist, whose books have had perhaps the largest circulation of any English works of fiction. *The Pickwick Papers* and *David Copperfield* are the best known. Dickens edited two journals, *Household Words* and *All the Year Round*, and took part in advocating the abolition of the slave-trade, and in other philanthropic works.

Rudyard Kipling, b. in Bombay 1865, d. 1936, writer and poet. Kipling's voluminous output of short stories mainly concern the British Empire, and India in particular. His books included *The Jungle Books*, *Kim*, and *Just-So Stories*. Of his collections of poems *Barrack-Room Ballads* are probably the best known. He was awarded the Nobel Prize for Literature in 1907.

Thomas Hardy, OM, b. 1840, d. 1928, novelist and poet. His novels include *The Return of the Native*, *Tess of the D'Urbervilles* and *Jude the Obscure*. They are set in rustic 'Wessex' (mainly Dorset, Wiltshire, and Somerset), the background of his youth, and are powerful stories of the struggle between man and the forces of nature and the ironies of human life and love. The value of his poetry, written later in life, is increasingly recognised. Ashes buried in the south transept; heart at Stinsford, Dorset.

The **Reverend Henry Francis Cary**, b. 1772, d. 1844, the translator of Dante.

Richard Brinsley Sheridan, b. 1751, d. 1816, the eloquent parliamentary orator and dramatist, author of *The Rivals* and *The School for Scandal*. Notwithstanding his great reputation he died in extreme poverty, and the help which came too late served only to furnish him with a magnificent funeral.

Dr Stephen Hales, b. 1677, d. 1761, physiologist and botanist; the inventor of ventilators. Augusta, Princess of Wales, mother of George III, erected this memorial. The figures of Religion and Botany support the medallion portrait. Buried at Teddington. Sculptor: *J. Wilton*.

Dr Isaac Barrow, b. 1630, d. 1677, mathematician, and classical scholar. He was Master of Trinity College, Cambridge, and tutor to Sir Isaac Newton, in whose favour he resigned his Mathematical Professorship.

Dr Thomas Triplet, b. *c.* 1601, d. 1670, Canon and Sub-dean of Westminster, scholar, and philanthropist. His tablet fills the place previously occupied by a monument, destroyed at the Restoration, to **Thomas May**, d. 1650, the parliamentary historian. A tablet erected in 1880 commemorates May and three other preachers of the Commonwealth period: **William Twisse**, d. 1646, **William Strong**, d. 1654, and **Stephen Marshall**, d. 1655. The remains of all four were disinterred in 1661.

John Keble, b. 1792, d. 1866, author of *The Christian Year*. Keble College, Oxford, was founded in his memory. Keble, Newman, and Pusey formed the triumvirate of the Oxford Movement in 1832. Sculptor: *T. Woolner*.

Thomas Babington (Macaulay), 1st Baron Macaulay, b. 1800, d. 1859, the historian and poet was buried at the foot of Addison's statue. Bust by *G. Burnard*.

Thomas Parr, d. 1635, said to be aged 152 years, and to have lived in the reigns of ten sovereigns. One of his portraits, by Van Dyck, is at Dresden, another is in the National Portrait Gallery, London.

Mary Eleanor Bowes, Countess Dowager of Strathmore, b. 1749, d. 1800. She married as her first husband John, 9th Earl of Strathmore (d. 1776) and is thus the great-great-great-grandmother of HM Queen Elizabeth the Queen Mother. The countess is said to have been buried dressed in 'a superb bridal dress'.

Sir Robert Taylor, b. 1714, d. 1788, architect of the Classical Revival, who designed the Mansion House and part of the Bank of England.

Sir Richard Coxe, d. 1623, 'taster' to Queen Elizabeth I, and Steward of the Household to James I.

James Wyatt, RA, b. 1746, d. 1813, Surveyor of the Abbey Fabric (1776). Under his direction major repair work was carried out in Henry VII's Chapel.

John Ernest Grabe, b. 1666, d. 1711, the Prussian orientalist, whose veneration for the English Church led him to settle in this country. Buried at St Pancras. Sculptor: *F. Bird*.

Isaac Casaubon, b. at Geneva, 1560, d. 1614, classical scholar and editor of *Persius* and *Polybius*. The monument was erected at the cost of Thomas Morton, Bishop of Durham (1632–59). Notice the initials I.W. and date, 1658, traditionally said to have been scratched on the tablet by Izaak Walton, author of *The Compleat Angler*.

David Garrick, b. 1716, d. 1779, actor. He was Dr Johnson's only scholar when he set up a school near Lichfield, whence they came up to London together to seek their fortune. Garrick retired at the height of his fame and died three years later at his house in the Adelphi. His funeral cortège stretched from there to the Abbey. **Mrs Eva-Maria Garrick**, d. 1822, was buried in her husband's grave. Garrick's monument was erected in 1797 by his old friend, Albany Wallis, whose grave is in the east cloister, near the tablet which Garrick put up to commemorate Wallis's only son, a Westminster scholar. Sculptor: *H. Webber*.

Sir Robert Stapylton, d. 1669, dramatic poet and translator. A French Benedictine monk, he turned Protestant, became a servant of Prince Charles (later Charles II) and was knighted in 1642. His plays included *The Slighted Maid*, a comedy which Pepys saw in 1663.

Mrs Hannah Pritchard, b. 1711, d. 1768, the celebrated actress. William Whitehead, then Poet Laureate, wrote the

GEORGE FREDERICK HANDEL Efq.^r
born February XXIII. MDCLXXXIV.
died April XIV. MDCCLIX. *L.F.Roubiliac inv.^t et sc.^t*

Handel's monument in Poets' Corner

epitaph. Sculptor: *R. Hayward*. Monument now in the triforium.

John Henderson, b. 1747, d. 1785, called the 'Bath Roscius', an actor who was considered second only to Garrick.

Dame Mary Steele, d. 1718, the second wife of Sir Richard Steele, the 'dearest Prue' of his correspondence.

Thomas Chiffinch, b. 1600, d. 1666, and **John Osbaldeston**, d. 1667, Pages of the Bedchamber to Charles II. Chiffinch was also Keeper of the King's Private Closet and Comptroller of the Excise. He is said to have been brought to Charles I's Court by Bishop Duppa.

Richard Hakluyt, b. 1553, d. 1616, 'the father of modern geographers', educated at Westminster School, and later a Prebendary (1602–16), the compiler of the *Principal Navigations, Voyages, and Discoveries of the English Nation*. He was one of the promoters of the South Virginia colony. Buried probably in this part of the Abbey.

Sir Robert Moray, b. 1603, d. 1673, chemist and mathematician, the first President of the Royal Society, and one of its original founders. He fought for the king in the Civil Wars, and was knighted by Charles I at Oxford; he was in high favour at the Restoration Court, and Charles II paid the expenses of his funeral.

Joshua Ward, b. 1686, d. 1761, celebrated quack doctor, was the inventor of 'Friar's Balsam' and the first to manufacture sulphuric acid in England. In Westminster he founded a hospital for the poor and was philanthropic in intention, although some of his remedies proved lethal. Many allusions to him occur in contemporary literature and Pope satirised him in his *Imitations of Horace*. George II, Hogarth, and Fielding were among his patients. Buried near Camden.

Edward Tudor, son of Owen Tudor by Queen Catherine (widow of Henry V) and uncle of Henry VII. He is probably to be identified with Edward Bridgewater who was a monk of Westminster from 1468/9 to 1471/2.[1]

William Camden, b. 1551, d. 1623, the famous antiquary, author of *Britannia* and *Annals of the Reign of Queen Elizabeth*. Camden's father belonged to the Guild of Master Painters and William received a good education at Christ's Hospital and Oxford. As Second Master at Westminster School he pursued his antiquarian researches. Head Master of the school (1593–99). In 1597 he was given the post of Clarenceux King of Arms so that he might have greater leisure for his work. To him we owe the first Abbey guide-book, a Latin list of the chief monuments, published in 1600. He was buried in the south transept on 19 November 1623; his friend William Heather (q.v.) was his sole executor.

The two historians of Greece, **Connop Thirlwall**, Bishop of St David's, b. 1797, d. 1875 (bust by *E. Davis*), and **George Grote**, b. 1794, d. 1871, are buried in the same grave. A bust of Grote, by *C. Bacon*, is close by.

Between Grote's monument and his gravestone a stone covers the ashes of **Dr Adam Fox**, b. 1883, d. 1977, Canon of Westminster (1942–63); Archdeacon and Sub-dean; Warden of Radley College (1918–24); Dean of Divinity, Magdalen College, Oxford (1929–42); Professor of Poetry at Oxford (1938–43); Master of the Skinners' Company (1947–8).

Gilbert Murray, OM, b. 1866, d. 1957; classical scholar, renowned for his translations of Greek plays. His ashes were buried here in 1957.

James Macpherson, b. 1736, d. 1796, 'translator' of the alleged poems of Ossian.

Robert Adam, FRS, b. 1728, d. 1792, the celebrated architect; designer, with his brothers, of the Adelphi.

William Heather, b. 1563, d. 1627, musical composer, was a chorister and lay vicar in the Abbey choir, and a Gentleman of the Chapel Royal. In 1626 Heather founded the music professorship at Oxford called after his name, and himself appointed the first lecturer. In May 1926, a musical festival was held at Oxford, in commemoration of the tercentenary of the foundation of the Heather Chair, and on 18 June 1926 a special service was held here, at which the Chancellor of the University of Oxford, Viscount Cave, unveiled an inscribed stone close to Camden's monument, to mark Heather's grave.

Two tablets to Prebendaries of the Abbey are affixed to pillars, the graves being close by: **Dr Anthony Horneck**, d. 1696, aged fifty-six. Born and educated at Wittemberg, subsequently at Oxford; Chaplain in Ordinary to King William and Queen Mary (1689), Prebendary of Westminster (1693) and of Wells (1694). His wife **Jane** (*née* **Bolton**), b. 1649, d. 1703 and son **Captain William Horneck** (see

---

1 See E. H. Pearce, *The Monks of Westminster* (1916), p. 161.

Chapel of St Faith, painting of the saint

p. 23) are buried in the same grave.

Dr Samuel Barton, d. 1715, aged sixty-seven; sometime Chaplain to the House of Commons; Prebendary of Westminster (1696). Buried with him are his daughter by his first wife, Sarah, **Jane Wowen**, b. 1699, d. 1758, and her husband **John Wowen**, d. 1760, a sugar-refiner.

Sir William Chambers, b. 1723, d. 1796, the architect of Somerset House.

Sir William D'Avenant, b. 1606, d. 1668, the 'Sweet Swan of Isis', succeeded Ben Jonson as Poet Laureate and, himself a Cavalier, was buried in the grave from which his Roundhead rival Thomas May had been cast out at the Restoration. D'Avenant was manager of the Duke's Theatre, which was amalgamated after his death with the King's Company at Drury Lane. **Thomas Killigrew**, b. 1612, d. 1683, dramatist, manager of the King's Theatre, is buried close by.

A bronze bust of **William Blake**, b. 1757, d. 1827, poet and painter, was placed on a pillar in 1957 on the bicentenary of his birth. Buried at Bunhill Fields. Sculptor: *Sir J. Epstein*.

On the other side of the column is a memorial to **Sir John Betjeman, CBE**, b. 1906, d. 1984, poet, writer and broadcaster. Betjeman's poems enjoyed great popularity and together with his other writings, such as *Ghastly Good Taste* and *The Collins Guide to English Parish Churches*, reflect his passion for architecture and his devotion to the Church of England. He presented numerous television documentaries (notably *Metroland*) and used his popularity as a broadcaster to champion the cause of neglected buildings, especially

those threatened with demolition by developers. He had a life-long love of the Abbey, serving on its Architectural Advisory Panel and making it the setting of one of his best-known church poems. Buried at Trebetherick, Cornwall.

His memorial consists of an eighteenth-century cartouche supported by two newly sculpted books – the Book of Common Prayer and the Authorized Version of the Bible. The bell above the inscription recalls Sir John's verse autobiography *Summoned by Bells*. Designed by D. Buttress, inscription designed by *D. Peace*, executed by the workshop of *D. Reid* with decoration by *Messrs Howell & Bellion*. Unveiled November 1996.

CHAPEL OF ST FAITH

The Chapel of St Faith at the south end of this transept is reserved for prayer and meditation, and is also used occasionally for confirmations, marriages, and funerals. It formed the eastern portion of the monks' revestry, and has an altar dedicated to St Faith.

Some early wall-paintings still exist here. A figure of the saint herself, wearing a crown, holding a book and a gridiron, the emblem of her martyrdom, is above the altar; below is the Crucifixion. On the left is a small half figure of a praying Benedictine monk; from his lips issues a scroll with the words:

> Me quem culpa gravis premit, erige, Virgo suavis.
> Fac mihi placatum Cristum, delasque reatum.
> (From the burden of my sore transgressions,
> sweet Virgin, deliver me; make my peace with
> Christ and blot out my iniquity.)

On the north wall is a figure of Christ flanked by figures of St Peter and St Edward the Confessor. The figures are in teak, lightly gilded, and were carved by *M. Clark*. They were the gift of Mrs Sidney Hope of Virginia Water, Surrey, in memory of Mrs Martha D. Cavendish of Hove. They were originally placed over the inner west door of the nave in 1967 and were moved here in 1980.

On the south wall is a tablet to **Jocelyn Henry Temple Perkins**, b. 1870, d. 1962; Minor Canon and Sacrist (1899–1958). His ashes are in a casket behind the tablet. Part of the floor was repaired in his memory. The ashes of **Christopher Hildyard**, b. 1901, d. 1987, Minor Canon and Sacrist (1928–73) are also interred here.

Just within the south transept was an altar, the gift of the prior, Richard de Merston (1362–76). It was dedicated to St Blaise, an Armenian bishop, martyred with iron combs about 316, and hence the patron saint of woolcombers.

The **clock** above the entrance to St Faith's Chapel was installed by *Thomas Bray* of Westminster in 1808.

Outside the Poets' Corner door a tablet was placed in 1954 to commemorate the fact that near by **William Caxton** set up the first printing-press in England in 1476.[1]

In 1972 there was placed on the wall outside the Chapter House a tablet commemorating **John Charles Walsham (Reith), 1st Baron Reith**, b. 1889, d. 1971, first Director-General of the British Broadcasting Corporation.

---

1 H. M. Nixon, 'Caxton, his Contemporaries and Successors in the Book Trade from Westminster documents', in *The Library*, 5th ser., XXXI (1976), pp. 305–26.

The Cloisters

A great fire in 1298 probably destroyed or ruined most of the Norman cloisters. The present cloisters were not begun until the thirteenth century, when Henry III's church was being built and were finished in the late fourteenth century.

Of the **eastern cloister** the four bays nearest the church, including the Chapter House entrance (finished in 1253), were begun by Abbot Crokesley (1246–58) and the east cloister was continued by **Abbot Simon de Bircheston**, who died of the plague in 1349 and is buried in this walk. The east cloister door and the first four bays of the **north walk** coincide in date with the building of the choir aisle, in Abbot Ware's time. Notice the heads of Henry III and Queen Eleanor of Provence on either side of this door, and also the roses in the mouldings. The last two bays and the west cloister door are of mid-fourteenth-century date and were begun (1350) during the abbacy of Simon de Langham. They were finished (1366) four years after Langham became Bishop of Ely, by the next abbot, Nicholas de Litlyngton, who, when prior, had superintended the work for many years before; Litlyngton's initials and arms are carved upon some of the bosses.

Simon de Langham gave generously to the building of the cloisters. The **south walk** was rebuilt 1351–65 and the **west walk** was rebuilt a few years later. The cloisters have undergone restorations at various times. Blore practically rebuilt much of the south walk (1835) and Sir Gilbert Scott, in the later nineteenth century, refaced the stonework, and renewed much of the window tracery in the north walk. There has been recent restoration in the east and south walks.

In these cloisters the monks spent a great part of their time; at first only the upper half was glazed and the lower part was open to the wind and weather, but later on the whole was filled in with coloured glass. Carpets of hay and straw in winter, and rushes in summer covered the stone floor and benches. The walls were decorated with paintings, and lamps were suspended here and there by chains from the roof.

On Thursday in Holy Week the abbot held his Maundy in the east cloister; thirteen aged men were seated on the broad stone bench against the west wall; some of the rings to which the mats for their feet were hooked are visible just below the bench. The abbot himself washed their feet, which were carefully cleansed first, wiped them with a towel, and then kissed them; after which he gave each man threepence, seven red herrings, some ale, and three loaves apiece. The monks meanwhile washed the feet of children in the south walk, where their Maundy seat was.

At the west end of the south cloister the early fourteenth-century doorway used to lead into the monks' refectory; on one side are four recesses, which were originally closed with wooden doors and had hooks inside for hanging up the monks' towels. Round the corner in the west cloister is a recess much modernised, where was formerly the trough at which the monks washed their hands before entering the refectory. On some of the bosses in this south cloister are Litlyngton's initials and arms, and it was he who rebuilt the great dining-hall more than half a century after the fire of 1298. Part of the Norman dividing wall remains along the lower part of this walk, but the upper part of the wall arcading dates from Litlyngton's time.

The two vaulted bays leading to the entrance into Dean's Yard used to be the monks' parlour, where they received guests and were even allowed to entertain ladies of rank. The outer gateway itself belongs to Litlyngton's time; heads of Richard II and the abbot are on either side of the outer arch. In the niches over the gate used to be figures of the Confessor and the Pilgrim.

We now enter the **west walk**, where the novices were taught by a brother, called the 'Master of the Novices', who had his seat close to the west cloister door, above which was a picture of the Crucifixion, painted by order of Prior Merston (1376). Upon the sides of these cloisters were paintings, with verses alluding to the history of the foundation. A favourite game of the period – 'nine holes' – was evidently played by the novices in intervals of leisure, as traces of it are found both in this and in the first bay of the north cloister close by, where the holes are clearly visible on the stone bench near the prior's seat. The **north walk** was the place where the monks read and studied. A special room called the 'scriptorium' was set apart elsewhere in the monastery for the copying and illuminating of manuscripts. Bookcases were pegged against the wall, or stood on the floor and wooden partitions divided the 'carrells' in which the monks sat and studied. These little studies with wooden benches and tables were placed in the best-lighted bays, and it has been pointed out that this walk was chosen because of the warm south sun. The green or garth in the centre seems to have been used as a garden; the cemetery where the lesser brethren were buried was situated to the north-east, beyond where the Chapter House now stands. After the dissolution the Westminster boys held their fights on this green, and even played racquets and football in the cloisters. The walks also were haunted by beggars and all sorts of disorderly persons, 'idle boys playing cards and dice for money, cursing and swearing the while', until in the eighteenth century the Dean and Chapter appointed a constable to keep order.

WEST WALK

In the west walk are commemorated six Clerks of the Works: **Thomas Wright**, d. 1906, aged eighty-three, who was Clerk of the Works here, 1871–1906. Buried at Nunhead. Close by lies his son and successor, **Thomas James Wright**, b. 1851, d. 1928, who spent fifty-five years in the service of the Abbey. Also buried here are **William Bishop, MVO**, d. 1962, Clerk of the Works (1928–55), and **Ann**, his wife, d. 1971. **Harry Carter, MVO**, d. 1966, Clerk of the Works (1955–66); and **Nan Carter**, d. 1970, his wife. **Sidney Robert Andrews**, b. 1918, d. 1981, Clerk of the Works (1967–81); and his son, **Anthony Andrews**, b. 1955, d. 1979. At the north end of the walk lies **Benjamin Fidoe**, d. 1780, aged seventy-nine, Clerk of the Works (1748–80). His long association with the Abbey began with his appointment as a verger in 1735.

A tablet commemorates the **Civil Services of the Crown in India (1858–1947)**. Unveiled by HM The Queen on 6 March 1958. Designed by *S. E. Dykes Bower*.

On 21 May 1948 the then Mr Winston Churchill unveiled a monument in memory of (1) the officers and men of **The Submarine Service of the Royal Navy**, (2) **The Commandos**, and (3) all ranks of **The Airborne Forces and Special Air Service**, who fell in the Second World War. The memorial, designed by *G. Ledward*, comprises three bronze figures representing the three types of fighting men.

Thomas Sanders Dupuis, b. 1733, d. 1796, Organist and Composer to the Chapel Royal, is commemorated and buried in this walk. He was of a Huguenot family and had been a chorister at the Chapel Royal under Bernard Gates. Monument by *R. Wilford*.

Close by are tablets to two members of the Abbey choir buried in this walk: **John Freeman**, b. 1666, d. 1737, together with his wife, **Avis Freeman**, d. 1732; and **James Chelsum**, d. 1743, with his son **Thomas**, aged four, d. 1744. Both choirmen were also Gentlemen of the Chapel Royal and members of St Paul's Cathedral choir.

A white marble monument commemorates **William Dobson**, b. 1750, d. 1813. According to the journals of the day he was 'a man of singular mechanical ingenuity, and an excellent classical scholar', and it is said that 'in consequence of an asthmatic complaint he had not lain down in bed for the last sixteen years of his life'. Buried in this cloister.

Also commemorated here is **William Richard Lethaby**, b. 1850, d. 1931, architect; Surveyor of the Fabric (1906–28). In his two classic books, *Westminster Abbey and the Kings' Craftsmen* (1906) and *Westminster Abbey Re-Examined* (1925), Lethaby first traced in detail the history of the building of the Abbey and the names of the craftsmen who built it. Under his personal superintendence, the restoration of the exterior of the Chapel of Henry VII was begun. Buried at Hartley Wintney, Hants.

On 14 October 1976 a memorial was unveiled to **William Jocelyn Ian (Fraser), Baron Fraser of Lonsdale, CH, CBE**, b. 1897, d. 1974, Chairman of the Council of St Dunstan's (1921–74); blinded on the Somme (1916); MP (1924–9, 1931–6, 1940–58); knighted (1934); National President of the British Legion (1947–58); Life Peer (1958). The tablet, designed and executed by *D. B. McFall*, was erected by St Dunstan's and Lord Fraser's family. It includes a metal plate on which are Braille characters repeating the substance of the inscription.

Beneath the Fraser memorial are commemorated members of the **Special Operations Executive** who sustained resistance behind enemy lines during the Second World War. Stonework and lettering by *D. Dewey*, bronze work by *G. Cowell*. Unveiled by Queen Elizabeth the Queen Mother in February 1996.

A tablet to **William Malcolm (Hailey), Baron Hailey of Shahpur and Newport Pagnell, OM, GCSI, GCMG, GCIE**, b. 1872, d. 1969; Governor of the Punjab (1924–8); Governor of the United Provinces (1928–30, 1931–4). The memorial, designed by *S. E. Dykes Bower* and including a profile bust, was unveiled in May 1971.

A monument beneath, designed by *F. Belsky* commemorates members of the **Czechoslovak Army and Air Force** who died in the Second World War. Unveiled October 1993.

A mural monument unveiled by Queen Elizabeth the Queen Mother in July 1993 commemorates the **Old Contemptibles**, who prevented the German advance on the channel ports in 1914. Designed by *D. Buttress*, executed by *Rattee & Kett*.

Near by a stone commemorates **Emily Tennyson Bradley**, b. 1862, d. 1946, daughter of Dean Bradley and wife of **Alexander Murray Smith**; by her books and devotion to the Abbey, she did much to make its history more widely known; Mrs Murray Smith and her sister Lady Birchenough were the original compilers of this *Guide*.

Elizabeth Broughton, d. 1784, and her husband, **John Broughton**, b. 1703, d. 1789, Yeoman of the Guard and the most famous pugilist of his day. It was John Broughton's arms that Rysbrack used as models for his statue of Hercules. Buried in the same grave are their relations, **Roger Monk**, d. 1831, Yeoman of the Guard and tallow-chandler, and his wife **Catherine**, d. 1832.

Close by is the grave of **Sir Walter Tapper, RA**, b. 1861, d. 1935; President of the Royal Institute of British Architects (1927–8), and Surveyor of the Abbey Fabric (1928–35). The important work of the cleaning and repair of the roof and interior of the Chapel of Henry VII, completed in 1935, was carried out under his direction. He designed the alterations by means of which the Chapter Library and Muniment Room were connected.

John Thomas Micklethwaite, b. 1843, d. 1906, Surveyor of the Fabric, who devoted himself to the preservation of the church and buildings in the precincts.

The original wall tablet to **Frances Louisa Parnell**, d. 1812, aged six, was replaced in 1981 by a new one designed by *J. P. Foster*.

A mural monument with portrait medallion but now without inscription to **Sir Richard Jebb, FRS, FSA**, b. 1719, d. 1787, physician at the Westminster Hospital; physician to the Royal Family and a favourite of George III. He died at his house in Great George Street close by, from a fever caught when attending one of the princesses. Buried in this walk.

A portrait medallion is also above the tablet to another physician buried here: **William Buchan**, b. 1729, d. 1805; best known as the author of *Domestic Medicine*, the first work of its kind in England; 80,000 copies were sold in the author's lifetime.

A mural monument commemorates **John Laurence**, d. 1685, in his sixty-sixth year; he was sometime Chancellor of the Exchequer and fought for Charles I in the Civil Wars. Buried near by. His daughter Anne (d. 1690) married first Sir Lumley Robinson, Bt (q.v.).

Buried near by are **Thomas Gayfere**, d. 1812 in his ninety-second year, stonemason to the Abbey, together with his wife, **Frances**, d. 1770 and their daughter, **Frances Elizabeth Gayfere**, b. 1753, d. 1807.

A mural monument by *T. Banks* commemorates **William Woollett**, b. 1735, d. 1785, the most celebrated English engraver of his time, with an international reputation. His best-known work was an engraving of West's *Death of General Wolfe* (1776), which so pleased George III that he gave Woollett the title of 'Historical Engraver to His Majesty'. Buried in Old St Pancras churchyard.

Some Abbey organists are buried/commemorated near by:

James Turle, b. 1802, d. 1882, Organist and Master of the Choristers for fifty years. Buried at Norwood.

Sir Frederick Bridge, CVO, b. 1844, d. 1924, succeeded Turle as Organist, a post he held for nearly forty years. During this period he arranged and superintended the music at the coronation of King Edward VII and Queen Alexandra (1902), and of King George V and Queen Mary (1911), and composed many anthems and chants besides secular works. Tablet by *E. Gill*. Buried at Glass, Aberdeenshire.

Benjamin Cooke, b. 1734, d. 1793, Organist (1762–93), and Master of the Choristers. He took part in the Handel Commemoration of 1784. His son **Robert**, d. 1814, Organist here 1802–14, lies near his father.

Sir Sydney Hugo Nicholson, MVO, b. 1875, d. 1947, Organist of Westminster Abbey (1919–28). Founder and Director of the Royal School of Church Music.

Osborne Harold Peasgood, CVO, b. 1902, d. 1962, Sub-organist (1924–41 and 1946–62); Acting Organist (1941–6). Also his wife **Dora**, d. 1968.

Douglas Guest, b. 1916, d. 1996, Organist and Master of the Choristers (1963–1981).

The stone to **Thomas Greatorex**, b. 1758, d. 1831, Organist of the Abbey (1819–31), has been recut.

Sir William Neil McKie, MVO, b. 1901, d. 1984, Organist and Master of the Choristers (1941–63); he revitalised the choir after the Second World War and was director of music at the coronation of Queen Elizabeth II in 1953. His wife, **Phyllis**, d. 1983, is also buried here.

Above and to the left of Cooke's memorial is a tablet to one of his former choristers, **James Bartleman**, b. 1769, d. 1821, later lay vicar at Westminster Abbey and Gentleman of the Chapel Royal. Buried near Cooke.

A portrait bust tops the tablet to **Arthur O'Keeffe**, d. 1756, on which he is described as 'lineally descended from the Kings of Ireland'; his wife **Isabella**, d. 1762, is buried with him.

Tablets also commemorate **Jeremiah Lewis**, d. 1761 and **Enoch Hawkins**, d. 1847, a lay vicar of the Abbey, who is buried in the same grave as **Thomas Vaughan**, d. 1843. His small memorial in the next bay records that he was a member of the choir for over forty years.

Below is a tablet commemorating the **Reverend Edward Smedley**, b. 1750, d. 1825, an Usher at Westminster School (1774–1820) and his wife **Hannah**; also their son **Francis Smedley**, b. 1791, d. 1859, High Bailiff of Westminster for twenty-two years.

A small black marble tablet commemorates **John Banester** (or Bannister), b. *c*. 1625, d. 1679, musician. He is said to have been the first Englishman to distinguish himself on the violin and was dismissed from the service of Charles II after making an impertinent remark about the appointment of French musicians to the royal band. Buried in this cloister.

A memorial to **Charles Godolphin**, b. 1651, d. 1720, brother to Sidney, 1st Earl of Godolphin; MP and Commissioner of Customs, records the 'benefactions' of himself and his wife **Elizabeth** (d. 1726), daughter of Francis Godolphin of Coulston, Wilts., to the education of 'young gentlewomen of small fortunes' in Wiltshire. The Godolphin School, near Salisbury, was started sixty years after the death of Mrs Godolphin, and continues to flourish.

A mural monument commemorates **George Vertue**, b. 1684, d. 1756, engraver and art-historian. Vertue, who was a Roman Catholic, is buried in the north cloister, near **William Vertue**, a monk of Westminster (1509/10–1535?) whom he claimed as a member of his family. He was official engraver to the Society of Antiquaries, and executed most of the plates in *Vetusta Monumenta*, and for the Oxford

Almanacks, besides engraving many valuable portraits. For forty years Vertue collected materials for a history of the fine arts in England; these were purchased from his widow by Horace Walpole who compiled his *Anecdotes of Painting* from them. His widow **Margaret**, d. 1776, aged seventy-six years is buried in the same grave.

Edward Wortley Montagu, b. 1750, d. 1777, a son of the traveller, Edward Wortley Montagu, and a grandson of Lady Mary Wortley Montagu, was shipwrecked on his voyage home from the East Indies. The tablet, of artificial stone by *Mrs E. Coade*, was put up (1787) by Sir John English Dolben, to mark a friendship begun at Westminster School, 'continued at Oxford, not lessened by the barrier of half the world, a friendship unbroken by death, to be renewed in heaven, if God so will'.

Samuel Foote, b. 1720, d. 1777, actor, was buried in the west cloister in an unmarked grave. He was well known as a mimic and made Dr Johnson laugh against his will. Foote was also a writer of burlesque comedies and was notorious for his cruel wit.

NORTH WALK

A tablet commemorates all those of '**the British race who served Malaya, 1786–1957**'. Unveiled by Queen Elizabeth the Queen Mother on 1 November 1962.

A stone in the floor marks the grave of **Basil Wilberforce**, b. 1841, d. 1916, Canon (1894) and Archdeacon (1900) of Westminster and rector of St John's Church, Westminster; also his wife, **Charlotte**, b. 1841, d. 1909.

A tablet commemorates the work of those '**of our Race who laboured to serve the People of the Sudan, 1898–1955**'. Unveiled 1960.

A stone in the floor commemorates **Vernon Faithfull Storr**, b. 1869, d. 1940, Sub-dean of Westminster and rector of St Margaret's. Buried at Matfield, Kent.

Robert Henry Charles, DD, b. 1855, d. 1931, Canon (1913) and Archdeacon (1919) of Westminster; a great scholar and author of commentaries on the Apocalypse and on the Book of Daniel; his wife **Mary Lilian**, b. 1857, d. 1935, is also buried here.

Percy Dearmer, DD, b. 1867, d. 1936, Professor of Ecclesiastical Art, King's College, London (1919); Canon of Westminster (1931–6). Author of many books and pamphlets on ecclesiastical art and church history, and editor of the hymn-book *Songs of Praise* (1931).

William Boyd Carpenter, b. 1841, d. 1918; Bishop of Ripon (1884–1911): Canon of Westminster (1911) and Sub-dean; his second wife, **Ann**, b. 1854, d. 1915.

Kenneth Augustus (Muir-Mackenzie), 1st Baron Muir-Mackenzie, GCB, b. 1845, d. 1930; High Bailiff of Westminster (1912–30).

In 1960 the gravestone of **General John Burgoyne**, b. 1722, d. 1792, Commander-in-Chief of the British forces in the American War of Independence, was identified and his name and dates were cut upon it. He was forced to surrender to Horatio Gates, the American General, early in the war, and returned to England in disgrace. Although restored to royal favour, he never fought again, but spent the remainder of his life in a house near the Abbey, surrounded by his books.

A somewhat mutilated tablet, removed from the south walk, commemorates **Ephraim Chambers**, b. 1686, d. 1740.

He was the author of the second *English Encyclopaedia*. Buried in this walk.

The **Reverend Richard Gouland**, d. 1659, the first Keeper of the Chapter Library (1626) after Dean Williams had reinstituted it in the old dormitory. His epitaph states that he was 'well skill'd in the languages, and otherwise very well furnished with the best and choicest learning'.

Charles St Clare Bedford, b. 1810, d. 1900; Chapter Clerk for thirty years and Westminster coroner for forty-three years.

Sir Edward Knapp-Fisher, CVO, b. 1864, d. 1940; Chapter Clerk, Receiver-General, and Custodian of the Abbey (1917–37).

A brass tablet to the **Most Reverend William Markham**, b. 1719, d. 1807; Head Master of Westminster School (1753–64); Dean of Christ Church, Oxford (1767–77); Bishop of Chester (1771–7); Archbishop of York (1777–1807), who is buried beneath with other members of the Markham family; including his brother **Enoch Markham**, d. 1801, who went to Canada as a volunteer and fought under Wolfe. He afterwards raised the 112th Foot (the Royal Musketeers) and fought throughout the American War of Independence. He was buried with the colours of his old regiment wrapped round his body.

Against the north wall is a tablet to the memory of seven of the **Queen's Westminster Volunteers** (13th Middlesex), who died in the Boer War of 1900. Unveiled on 22 June 1901.

Bernard Gates, b. 1685?, d. 1773, musician, lies with his wife and family in this walk. He was Master of the Children of the Chapel Royal for over forty years, and formerly a chorister of the Abbey. He married **Elizabeth**, d. 1737, the adopted daughter and heiress of **Elizabeth Atkinson**, d. 1726, body laundress to Queen Anne, whose monument is close by.

The ashes of **Tom Hebron, CBE, MVO**, b. 1894, d. 1980, Registrar (1948–64), Receiver General of the Abbey (1958–9), and his wife **Eva**, b. 1895, d. 1979, lie beneath a stone in this bay. Also those of his son-in-law **Sir Reginald Pullen, KCVO**, b. 1922, d. 1996, Receiver General (1959–1987); Deputy High Bailiff of Westminster from 1987.

On a mural monument is a curious epitaph to **William Laurence**, d. 1621, aged twenty-nine, who was private secretary or steward to one of the prebendaries.

> With Diligence and Trust most exemplary
> Did William Laurence serve a Prebendary;
> And for his Paines now past, before not lost,
> Gain'd this Remembrance at his Master's cost.
> O reade these Lines againe: you seldome find
> A Servant faithfull and a Master kind.
> Short Hand he wrote: his Flowre in prime did fade
> And hasty Death Short Hand of him hath made,
> Well couth he Nu'bers, and well mesur'd Land;
> Thus doth he now that Ground where on you stand,
> Wherein he lyes so Geometricall;
> Art maketh some, but thus will Nature all.

A black marble ledger-stone covers the supposed remains of **William Lyndewode**, Bishop of St David's, d. 1446. He was keeper of the Privy Seal and was consecrated a bishop in 1442. The coffin was discovered on 16 January, 1852 in the crypt of St Stephen's Chapel in the Palace of Westminster; the burial in this cloister took place on 6 March 1852.

Two authors are buried in this walk: **Dr William King**, b. 1663, d. 1712, under an unmarked stone, and **Sir John Hawkins**, b. 1719, d. 1789, who has only his initials, date of death, and age upon his grave. King had been a King's Scholar at Westminster School and was a miscellaneous writer of some merit, counting Swift and Pope among his friends, and Lord Burlington as a benefactor. Hawkin's principal work was *The General History of Music*. An ardent fisherman himself, he published an edition of Izaak Walton's *The Compleat Angler*, which went through five editions. Hawkins was an early friend and biographer of Dr Johnson. The wits of the day composed an epitaph upon Hawkins in allusion to his drawling voice:

> Here lies Sir John Hawkins
> Without his shoes and stawkins.

Near by is buried **Spranger Barry**, b. 1719, d. 1777, actor, Garrick's successful rival, especially in the parts of King Lear and Hamlet. He lost his health, his looks, and his fortune, and ten years before his death was glad to accept small parts at Drury Lane and a salary from Garrick. Twenty-five years later his grave was opened to receive the coffin of **Ann Crawford**, b. 1734, d. 1801, actress, his pupil and second wife, at one time the queen of comedy at Drury Lane. As a tragedian she also rivalled Mrs Cibber, Peg Woffington and Sarah Siddons.

Susannah Maria Cibber, b. 1714, d. 1766, actress, wife of Theophilus Cibber, lies close by. 'Barry and I remain, but tragedy is dead on one side', exclaimed Garrick when he heard of her death.

Also buried here is **Dr Christopher Gibbons**, b. 1615, d. 1676; son of Orlando Gibbons (q.v.); as Organist of the Abbey (1660–6) he re-formed the choir at the Restoration. He was one of the Children of the Chapel Royal; sometime organist of Winchester Cathedral, and a Royalist soldier in the Civil Wars; Organist of the Chapel Royal (1660–76).

EAST WALK

A tablet against the wall to **Bonnell Thornton**, b. 1724, d. 1768, author, and editor of *The Connoisseur* to which the poet Cowper, who was one of Thornton's school-fellows at Westminster, contributed; Dr Johnson was also a friend of Thornton. The Latin inscription was written by another friend, Dr Joseph Warton.

In contrast are the simple and poignant words on a tablet close by to '**Jane Lister**, deare child', d. 1688. She was the daughter of Dr Martin Lister, FRS, an eminent zoologist and physician of York. Her brother **Michael Lister** (d. 1676 and buried at York) is also commemorated on this tablet.

Albany Charles Wallis, who was drowned in the Thames in 1776, aged thirteen, 'being his father's only hope'. David Garrick (q.v.), a close friend of the boy's father, erected this memorial. The father, **Albany Wallis**, d. 1800, who was an eminent solicitor, is also buried here.

Sir John Kemp, Bt, b. 1754, d. 1771, who 'after passing through Westminster School with improvement and applause' is commemorated here by 'two young friends, who loved him'.

Aphara or Aphra Behn, b. 1640, d. 1689, dramatist and novelist. Charles II employed her as a spy at Antwerp in

1666. Although she sent information of the Dutch raid up the Medway, Behn's reputation was so bad that nobody believed her warning, and the raid was actually carried out by De Ruyter and De Witt.

A tablet to 'two affectionate brothers, valiant soldiers, and sincere Christians', both of whom were officers in the English Army, although of French birth. **Scipio Duroure** was Colonel of the 12th Foot, and was killed at Fontenoy (1745). His elder brother, **Alexander Duroure** rose to the rank of Lieutenant-General, and died in 1765. Alexander is buried here.

A mural tablet commemorates the burial of **George Whicher**, d. 1682, Yeoman of the Guard. He built and endowed almshouses for six poor men in St Margaret's parish.

Close by lies the famous actress, **Mrs Anne Bracegirdle**, d. 1748, aged eighty-five. She was brought up in Betterton's family, and began her career on the stage as a child of six. So popular was she that it is said of her that 'scarce an audience saw her that were less than half of them lovers, without a suspected favourite amongst them.'

Near by beneath an unmarked stone is **Thomas Betterton**, b. 1635?, d. 1710, actor, son of an under-cook in Charles I's kitchen; born, bred, and buried close to the Abbey. He was considered the best tragedian of his day, and for fifty years no actor surpassed him in the public favour. His wife **Bess Saunderson**, d. 1712, is buried in the same grave.

Charles Wellington Furse, b. 1821, d. 1900, Canon and Archdeacon of Westminster; formerly Principal of Cuddesdon College, Oxford.

John Troutbeck, b. 1832, d. 1899; Minor Canon (1869) and Precentor (1895); Chaplain in Ordinary to Queen Victoria; and his wife **Elizabeth**, b. 1832, d. 1923, sister of Canon Duckworth. Troutbeck personally superintended the arrangements for many special services, notably Queen Victoria's Diamond Jubilee (1897). Editor of the *Westminster Abbey Hymn Book*.

Farther south, a green diamond-shaped tile inlaid with a floral emblem marks the place where a freeze-dried floral arrangement was buried by the National Association of Flower Arrangement Societies on 26 July 1977 to mark the Silver Jubilee of HM The Queen.

Near the door at the foot of the spiral staircase which until 1932 was the main approach to the Muniment Room is buried **Herbert Francis Westlake**, b. 1879, d. 1925, Minor Canon (1909), Custodian, and Keeper of the Muniments. Westlake's researches into the records resulted in the publication of his scholarly and indispensable *Westminster Abbey, A History of the Church and Monastery*, in two volumes, as well as of several smaller works, notably a history of St Margaret's church, and a guide-book to the Abbey monuments.

Near by is a large mural monument with the name of **Edward Godfrey**, who died in 1640, aged twelve, just after his election as a King's Scholar at Westminster School. This memorial was repaired fifty-six years later by one of his nineteen brothers, Benjamin Godfrey, who placed a tablet beneath it with a Latin inscription recording the murder of **Sir Edmond Berry Godfrey**, b. 1621, d. 1678, the best known of this family. He was educated at Westminster School, became Justice of the Peace for Westminster, and was esteemed 'the best Justice in England' at that time. Godfrey

was a zealous Protestant, but lived on such excellent terms with the Catholics that Titus Oates pretended to betray the Popish Plot to him. Three weeks later the Judge's body was found in a ditch on Primrose Hill transfixed by his own sword, but with marks of strangulation. A reward of £500 was offered for the discovery of the murderers, and three of the Queen's Catholic servants were arrested and hanged, having protested their innocence. The probable assassin was an adventurer who went under the name of Colonel John Scott: he fled the country afterwards.

The satirist and essayist, **Thomas Brown**, b. 1663, d. 1704; it was said that he had less 'the spirit of a gentleman than the rest of the wits', but he was more of a scholar; an example of his humour is the famous epigram on Dr Fell, Dean of Christ Church ('I do not love thee Dr Fell', etc.).

A stone covers the grave of the **Reverend Clayton Mordaunt Cracherode, FRS, FSA**, b. 1730, d. 1799, bibliophile; an Old Westminster, Cracherode was from 1775 a great collector of books; a benefactor to Westminster School, Christ Church, Oxford, and the British Museum.

Near the library is buried the **Reverend Ambrose Fisher**, d. 1617, the blind scholar, author of the *Defence of the Liturgy*; he seems to have been a tutor in the family of Dr Grant, one of the prebendaries.

On the further side of the library door lies a former Librarian, **Howard Millar Nixon**, b. 1909, d. 1983. He was the younger son of the Reverend Leigh Hunter Nixon, Precentor (1912–33). Opposite are buried the ashes of **Burke St John (Trend), Baron Trend of Greenwich**; Secretary of the Cabinet (1963–73); Rector of Lincoln College, Oxford (1973–83); High Bailiff of Westminster from 1983.

Lieutenant-General Henry Withers, d. 1729, lies below his monument in the same grave as his friend **Colonel Henry Disney**, d. 1731, who erected the memorial; the inscription was written by Pope, and condemned by Johnson as 'full of commonplaces with something of the common cant of a superficial satirist'.

Under a defaced gravestone lies **Pelham Humfrey**, b. 1647, d. 1674, musician. He was one of the first Children of the Chapel Royal after the Restoration, and succeeded Dr Cooke as Master. In 1664 he and his fellow choristers, Blow and Turner, composed the anthem, 'I will give thanks unto the Lord', and later on he and Purcell held the joint patent of Lutenist to the King.

At the end of the east walk and facing down the south walk is the famous monument to **Daniel Pulteney**, b. *c*. 1683, d. 1731, politician. He, his wife, **Margaret-Deering Pulteney**, d. 1763, and daughter **Frances**, d. 1782, who succeeded to the Bath estates on the death of General Harry Pulteney, are buried near by. Monument designed by *G. Leoni* and executed by *J. M. Rysbrack*, erected 1732.

SOUTH WALK

Eight abbots were buried in the Norman predecessor of this walk: Vitalis of Bernay (abbot 1076–85); Gilbert Crispin (abbot 1085–1117); Herbert (abbot 1121–36?); Gervase de Blois (abbot 1138–57?); Laurence of Durham (abbot 1158?–73); Walter of Winchester (abbot 1175–90); William Postard (abbot 1191–1200); and William de Humez (abbot 1214–22).

Effigies of three of them are now beneath the bench. The easternmost is **Abbot Laurence**, d. 1173; he was a favourite of Henry II and succeeded in obtaining (7 February 1161) the canonization of King Edward. He was granted by Pope Alexander III the right to wear the mitre, ring, and gloves, but he died before they arrived.

The middle effigy is that of **Abbot Gilbert Crispin**, d. 1117; Gilbert was a Norman noble who had been a monk at Bec under St Anselm and then at Canterbury with Lanfranc. Abbot Gilbert's is the oldest monumental effigy in the Abbey and possibly in the country.

The westernmost figure (wearing a mitre) is **Abbot William de Humez**, d. 1222. Although Abbot Laurence had been afforded the mitre by 1173, and his successor (Walter of Winchester) granted the additional privilege of the dalmatic, tunicle, and sandals, Abbot Walter was inhibited from wearing the mitre, because the quarrel for precedence between the Archbishops of Canterbury and York took place at the Abbey during his abbacy. Abbot Postard was the first to wear the mitre, but he did not have a monumental effigy. Humez was abbot when the foundation of the new Lady Chapel was laid by Henry III.[1]

The very large slab of stone known as '**Long Meg**' was by the seventeenth century presenting a puzzle to Abbey guides. What was then a comparatively recent tale of a semi-legendary giantess 'Long Meg of Westminster', who lived in the time of Henry VIII, was linked with this stone and it was said that Meg was buried beneath it. At some time the Latin couplet recorded as having been on the grave of **Abbot Gervase de Blois**, d. 1160, appears to have been incised on Long Meg. Gervase, a natural son of King Stephen, was deposed about 1157; his grave was at the feet of Abbot Humez. Widmore suggested that the large stone covered the graves of monks who died of the Black Death in the mid-fourteenth century. Last century an inscription to that effect was cut. When the stone was lifted to be recut recently the coffin of the one person who is certainly buried beneath was revealed:

Henrietta Laura (**Pulteney**), *suo jure* **Countess of Bath**, b. 1766, d. 1808. She was the daughter and heir of Sir William Johnstone (afterwards Pulteney), 5th Bt, by Frances, daughter and eventually sole heir of Daniel Pulteney.

A monument with a portrait bust commemorates **Edward Tufnell**, b. 1678, d. 1719, Master Mason to the Abbey (1692–1719), under Sir Christopher Wren. Buried in this walk.

In the next bay a memorial signed *M:l Rysbrack fecit* 1758, to the **Hon. and Reverend John Hay**, d. 1751, aged thirty-two, the third son of George Hay, 7th Earl of Kinnoull.

Below, the depiction of a comet in Bombay slate, with a tiny inset representation of the spacecraft *Giotto*, memorialises **Edmond Halley**, b. 1656, d. 1742, Astronomer Royal, and also marks the reappearance in 1986 of the comet named after him. Halley's multiple achievements are named in the tail of the comet. Designed and cut by *R. Kindersley*.

A memorial, with urn and two putti, designed by *P. Scheemakers*, to **Magdalen Walsh**, b. 1684, d. 1747. She and her sister, Margaret Daly were the co-heiresses of the estate of Edmund Sheffield, Duke of Buckingham.

---

1 For the correct identification of these effigies, see J. Armitage Robinson, *Flete's History of Westminster Abbey*, pp. 22–4.

Below is the '**Defenders' Memorial**' of slate, with gold lettering, commemorating all those 'who in the face of violence have given their lives in the service of the crown'. This was unveiled by the Duke of Edinburgh in March 1982. Designed and cut by *S. Verity*.

A stone covers the grave of **Philip Clark**, d. 1707, 'Plumber to this Collegiate Church'.

A tablet commemorates **Colonel Francis Ligonier**, d. 1746, whose 'distemper could not confine him to his bed when his duty called him into the field': he insisted on fighting the Jacobites at Falkirk, and in consequence died after the battle. Monument put up by his brother General Sir John Ligonier, KB (afterwards 1st Earl Ligonier, q.v.). Executed by *L.F. Roubiliac*.

Close by is a memorial unveiled on St Francis's Day, 4 October 1979, to three circumnavigators of the world who all set out from Plymouth: **Sir Francis Drake**, b. 1540 (?), d. 1596, in the *Golden Hind* (1577–80); **Captain James Cook**, b. 1728, d. 1779, in the *Endeavour* (1768–71); **Sir Francis Chichester**, b. 1901, d. 1972, in *Gypsy Moth IV* (1966–7). Design in coloured Devon marbles by *E. Fraser*, executed by *Messrs Whitehead*, frame cut by *A. Ayres*.

Four **Wesley** children were buried here (1725–31); their father Samuel was a brother of the celebrated John and Charles Wesley, and a master at Westminster School.

A black marble stone covers the grave of **Max Alexander Cunningham Warren, DD**, b. 1904, d. 1977. After service as a missionary, he later became General Secretary of the Church Missionary Society, then Canon of Westminster (1963–73) and Sub-dean (1964). Also his wife **Mary**, d. 1987.

A grey marble tablet commemorates '**all those who served the Crown in the Colonial Territories**'. Unveiled by HM The Queen on 23 March 1966.

Three musicians are buried close by: **Johann Peter Salomon**, b. 1745, d. 1815, violinist and composer, a native of Bonn, where in later years he won the affection of the young Beethoven. His name is often connected with Haydn, whom he engaged to play at his concerts in London. Salomon took an active part in founding the Philharmonic Society and led the orchestra at their first concert (1813). **William Shield**, b. 1748, d. 1829. He was principal viola player at the Italian Opera for eighteen years, composer at Covent Garden and later became Master of the King's Musick. He was also an original member of the Philharmonic Society. Salomon and Shield are buried in the same grave. Also **Muzio Clementi**, b. 1752, d. 1832, called 'the father of the piano-forte'.

A stone covers the grave of **Dr William Whitfield Dakins**, b. 1767, d. 1850, Minor Canon and Precentor of the Abbey; chaplain to the Brigade of Guards; Principal Chaplain to the Forces (1830–44); founder of the Royal Military Chapel, Wellington Barracks. Also his wife **Susannah** (*née* Shorter), d. 1834, aged sixty-nine years, and their infant son William, d. 1800, aged five.

Near by lies **Samuel Flood Jones**, b. 1826, d. 1895, Minor Canon for thirty-six years (from 1859) and Precentor for twenty-five years; rector of St Botolph's, Aldersgate. His gravestone is that of General James Johnston (q.v.) removed from the nave and reused.

Extensive renovations of the walls of this walk are signed by *R. Powis*, mason.

Little Cloister: entrance and fountain

Outside the Song School door is a slate plaque with white and gold lettering in memory of **Harry Barnes**, b. 1909, d. 1985, 'who for more than forty years faithfully served this Collegiate Church as Chorister and Lay Vicar'. His ashes are buried near by, together with those of his wife, **Ann**, d. 1993.

THE LITTLE CLOISTER

Southwards the east cloister is continued past 'Kill-Canon-Corner' through the **Dark Cloister** to the Little Cloister.

On the walls are several memorials. One tablet, formerly over the entrance to the Chapter House, i.e. near the library, is to **Elizabeth Moore**, d. 1720, aged thirty-five, and was erected by 'her truly afflicted Husband Thomas Moore Gent Librarian of this Church'. Buried in the east cloister near the library door. Moore was Librarian from 1688 until his death in 1733.

In the west wall a small stained glass window unveiled in May 1988 commemorates **Robinson Duckworth** (*q.v.*). The design, by *F. Skeat*, is based on Duckworth's bookplate.

Turning left through the undercroft a dark vaulted passage leads directly to the **Little Cloister**. On the left are the school gymnasium and former armoury; the latter has a classroom above it. Formerly access to this area was obtained from the west through the Norman undercroft, but when Dean Robinson created the Museum a new entrance had to be made. These rooms, formerly part of a canon's house, were given to the school in 1861, when the present gymnasium was built. The site of the armoury appears to have been a twelfth-century **Chapel of St Dunstan**. A decorated niche, possibly for a statue of St Dunstan, and a piscina marking the position of the altar remain. The chapel appears to have been largely rebuilt in the fifteenth century. The gymnasium, which is on part of the **monks' cemetery**, is bounded on the west by the Norman wall of the Pyx Chapel (q.v.), the barred and blocked windows of which can be seen. The Tudor windows higher up formerly belonged to the canonical residence.

The present **Little Cloister** and the surrounding houses, flats, and other buildings, of various dates, stand on the site of the monastic infirmary. This seems to have consisted, in early times, of one large room, with smaller buildings round it for the sick, infirm, and aged monks. After the great fire of 1298, which damaged many of the monastic buildings, more temporary accommodation had to be found, but the new works do not appear to have been added until later in the fourteenth century. Portions of these and of the earlier work are incorporated in the modern buildings. The inner arcade of the cloisters appears to date from the end of the seventeenth century. All but two of the houses (No. 4 and No. 5) were destroyed or seriously damaged in an air-raid during the Second World War, and the present dwellings were built or modified after the war. The **Infirmarer's Hall** is in the south-east corner of the cloister.

In the east walk there remains the fine fourteenth-century doorway which led into the ancient **Chapel of St Catherine**. The original chapel was built in the twelfth century and consisted of a nave and two aisles. The north arcade partly survives in the form of the lower parts of columns alternately round and octagonal. On the south side all the columns stand to the height of the capitals; the three eastern arches

have been filled in, but each round arch still contains some of its original twelfth-century voussoirs. To the south of this blocked arcade the outer wall of the aisle has been demolished and the ground is taken up by the courtyard of No. 4 and No. 5 Little Cloister. At the west end, however, the outer wall of the south aisle stands and contains an original twelfth-century window-opening. The roof of the chapel was removed in 1578 and a house was built over part of it. The successor to this house was destroyed by bombs in 1941, and in the subsequent rebuilding as much of the original chapel as could be was left exposed.

The chapel was used for many important assemblies, both secular and clerical, including the consecration of various prelates. Here took place the quarrel (1176) for precedence between the Archbishops of Canterbury and York, which resulted in the one receiving the title of Primate of '*all* England', the other 'of England'. Fuller thus described the dispute: 'A Synod was called at Westminster, the Pope's Legat being threat; on whose right hand sat, as in his proper place, Richard of Canterburie, which in springs Roger of York and finding Canterburie so seated fairly sits him down in Canterburie's lap (a baby too big to be dandled thereon), yea Canterburie his servants dandled this lap-childe with a witness, who plucked him thence and buffeted him to purpose.'

It was also in this chapel that Henry III, surrounded by prelates, solemnly swore on the Gospels to maintain Magna Carta.

Overlooking the site of St Catherine's Chapel, in a niche on the north side, is a **statue of St Catherine** given in memory of **Henry John Alexander (Seely), 2nd Baron Mottistone**, b. 1899, d. 1963. Lord Mottistone was the architect of the rebuilding of the Deanery and the houses in Little Cloister following the war damage. The statue was presented by Dr Alan Don, Dean (1946–59), and Mr Paul Paget, Lord Mottistone's former partner. The inscription includes the date of unveiling (1966) and the initials of the donors.

In the east walk a tablet on the wall near the door of the chapel commemorates a former resident **John Charles Thynne**, b. 1838, d. 1918, Receiver General of the Abbey (1865–1902). He was a younger son of Lord John Thynne (q.v.).

Near by a stone marks the grave of **Dr John Wilson**, b. 1595, d. 1674, a distinguished lutenist, chamber musician to Charles I.

A tablet on the wall of the north walk is noticeable for the inscription to **Thomas Smith**, d. 1664, who 'through ye spotted vaile of the Small-Pox, rendred a pure, & unspotted soul to God'.

Henry Lawes, b. 1595, d. 1662, musician, lies somewhere in the cloisters. He was a member of the King's band in the reigns of both Charles I and Charles II, and 'betook himself to the teaching of ladies to sing' during the Commonwealth. Lawes was a friend of Milton whom he is believed to have recommended to the Earl of Bridgwater for writing the words of *Comus*; he himself composed the music for the masque. Lawes wrote the music to many well-known lyrics by Herrick, Lovelace, and other poets.

A simple tablet on the wall of the west walk was erected by the Dean and Chapter in memory of **Henry Quittenton Roper**, b. 1871, d. 1887, chorister (1879–84).

The Chapter House & its Surroundings

· ·

In the east cloister is the thirteenth-century entrance to the **Chapter House**. The carvings on the arch are sadly decayed – no traces remain of the brilliant colours, vermilion and gold on a blue background, which once made this doorway a 'gate beautiful'. The stone statues of the Virgin and Child over the arch crumbled away, and part only of one of the two angels is left. The vaulted passage within is very low, because the night path from the monks' dormitory to the south transept was above it.

Here are buried **Edwin**, the friend and adviser of Edward the Confessor, the first abbot of his church (1049–71), and **Hugolin**, the Confessor's chaplain and treasurer. When the cloisters were rebuilt their bones were removed to this dark passage, and placed with those of the monk Sulcard, d. 1076?, under a marble tomb on the south side, of which no trace remains. **Sulcard** wrote a history of the monastery, which he dedicated to Abbot Vitalis; two copies of this manuscript are extant in the Cottonian MSS in the British Museum.

Two early doorways on either side of the vestibule lead into the Chapel of St Faith on the left, and the monastic treasury (the Chamber of the Pyx) on the right. The latter entrance originally enclosed three doors, only one of which remains. The central door used to be covered with a human skin, tiny fragments of which can be detected at the back of the top hinge. This was probably the tanned skin of a thief, who had been caught robbing the treasury. Here are deposited the **RAMC Rolls of Honour** for the First and Second World Wars.

On the right of the Chapter House entrance is a window, with a portrait head beneath it, to **James Russell Lowell**, d. 1891, the American poet and prose writer, Minister of the United States in London (1880–5). 'Placed here by his English friends.'

Below this is a white marble tablet to **Walter Hines Page**, b. 1855, d. 1918, Ambassador of the USA to the Court of St James's (1913–18), the 'friend of Great Britain in her sorest need' during the First World War.

The 'incomparable' **Chapter House**, as Matthew of Westminster justly calls it, was begun in 1250 and finished before 1259; it belongs to the same time as the church of Henry III. The style is the traditional English form. The English mason who was employed by the king's chief mason, Master Henry, was probably *Master Aubrey*. The shape is octagonal with a central pillar; in size it is one of the largest in England, sixty feet in diameter.

There was room for eighty monks on the stone benches round the Chapter House walls, and on the east side were seats for the abbot and four of the chief brethren. Every morning the whole convent passed in solemn procession from the church to the Chapter House after early Mass, about nine o'clock. Here all took their places, the abbot beneath a great crucifix on the east side, and prayers were read from a valuable lectern, presented by Henry III, which stood near the central pillar. All were then given their appointed tasks for the day, and the novices and some of the lesser monks retired. After this the affairs of the monastery were discussed in solemn conclave. The mutual improvement of the community was sought, not only by catechising and reading, but also by penitential discipline; against the central pillar the elder monks were chastised for serious offences; the younger brethren and the novices were reprimanded and punished in the cloisters.

Considerable traces remain of the mural paintings. The earliest on the eastern wall, where the abbot sat, represented the Doom, i.e. the Last Judgment, and dates from about 1390. The western wall was decorated with scenes from the Apocalypse, which were executed by the order of John of Northampton, who was a monk here from 1372 to 1404. When the wooden flooring was removed early in the nineteenth century the original tiled pavement was found to be in an almost perfect state, the colours in many places as brilliant as when first laid down in the 1250s. Among the varied subjects, which will be found south of the central pillar, are represented: the Confessor giving his ring to a beggar (i.e. to the disguised St John the Evangelist); a king on a throne (Henry III), playing with his hound; a queen (his wife, Eleanor of Provence) with a hawk on her hand; an abbot (Crokesley) with hand upraised in blessing. On some of the outer tiles are curious Eastern patterns, a fine rose window, and also the royal arms.

The Chapter House was used as a parliament house for the Commons in the second half of the fourteenth century, and for other ecclesiastical assemblies besides those of the monastery. In 1540, on the dissolution of the monastery, the Chapter House passed under the jurisdiction of the Crown, and since that time the Dean and Chapter have had no rights over it. Until 1863 the Chapter House was an important repository for the Public Records. Its subsequent restoration was the work of *Sir G. G. Scott*.

Below the Chapter House, approached by a doorway and stone staircase in Poets' Corner, is a small crypt with a recess for an altar in the eastern bay and a thirteenth-century piscina and aumbry. This may have been intended for the Chapter House revestry, but it has been found that the walls, originally twelve feet thick, were increased to seventeen feet, and there seems no doubt that either Henry III or Edward I appropriated this strong-room for his private treasury: it is in fact described as the 'Treasury of the King's Wardrobe', about 1303. In that year, during Edward I's absence in Scotland, this treasury was broken into, the regalia and other Crown jewels, as well as a large sum of money, were stolen, and strong suspicion fell on the monks. The abbot and forty-eight brethren were sent to the Tower, but released after a long trial, two only of the lesser monastic officials having been proved guilty. Most of the valuables were found hidden round about the precincts, but the king afterwards removed his money-chests from the abbot's care. The regalia seems, however, to have been left in the precincts, but were probably removed to the monastic treasury in the Chamber of the Pyx, where they remained until the Commonwealth.

In this crypt are kept, under the care of the Sacrist, the vestments, copes, silk banners, and the ornaments of the altars.

Chapter Library, East Cloister

THE CHAPTER LIBRARY
& MUNIMENT ROOM

Adjoining the Chapter House entrance is a doorway opening on to a stone stair (formerly the day stairs to the monks' dormitory), leading up to the library. This room originally formed part of the great dormitory where all the brethren slept; later on, it may have been partitioned into cubicles, as

at Durham. At the north end a stone gallery crossing St Faith's Chapel led by a staircase into the south transept; by this way the monks used to descend into the church for the night offices. The staircase no longer exists and the entry to it from the gallery is now blocked by the monument of the Duke of Argyll (see p. 97). The room itself is lofty, and has a fine roof, supported by massive beams. It probably dates from the end of the fifteenth century. At the south end is a contemporary portrait of Dean Williams (appointed Dean in 1620) who entirely remodelled this room and fitted it up as a library, furnishing it with valuable books and manuscripts at his own cost. Almost all these manuscripts were unfortunately destroyed by a fire in 1694. In the reign of Edward VI an order was published by Council for 'purging the library of all missals, legends, and other superstitious volumes'. Fortunately, however, a few are still extant. Among these are the famous *Liber Regalis*, which contains the recension used at the coronation of Richard II, and followed in its main features at every subsequent coronation, and the grand Missal commissioned by Abbot Nicholas de Litlyngton in 1383.

The Muniment Room is on the west side of the south transept, overlooking the choir and Poets' Corner; within it is the vast collection of documents concerning the business life first of the medieval Abbey and later of the Collegiate Church. Here is a bronze tablet erected by the Dean and Chapter to **Dr Edward John Long Scott**, b. 1841, d. 1918, sometime Keeper of Manuscripts and Egerton Librarian at the British Museum and subsequently Keeper of the Abbey muniments (1893–1918), whose labours in the arrangement and cataloguing of the Abbey documents are thus commemorated.

THE PYX CHAMBER

Next to the library entrance a heavy oak doorway with six locks leads into the so-called 'Chapel of the Pyx'.

Within is a vaulted chamber, built between 1065 and 1090, which formed part of the early monastic buildings. An altar, the only stone altar left *in situ* at Westminster, with a thirteenth-century piscina on the column near by, shows that this must have been used as a chapel at some time before the fourteenth century, when it was no doubt the monastic treasury. The altar was dedicated to St Dunstan in 1988. The tiled floor dates from the thirteenth century. After the dissolution the chamber passed into the possession of the Crown, and was never restored to the Abbey authorities.

In this chamber, was kept the 'pyx', or box containing the standard pieces of gold and silver. The trial of the pyx – the testing of the current gold and silver coinage – which now takes place at Goldsmiths' Hall, was not held here, but elsewhere in Westminster, usually in the Star Chamber.

THE UNDERCROFT & UNDERCROFT MUSEUM

A wall divides the two and a half vaulted bays which form the Pyx Chamber from the five and a half bays of the so-called 'undercroft', a name which applies to both of these substructures of the monks' dormitory. The undercroft is approached from the east cloister. It is about a hundred and ten feet long by forty-five feet wide. On two of the pillars the original twelfth-century carving remains, the others have been modified by slightly later decorations.

In monastic times it was probably the common-room of the monks. In 1908 it was turned into a museum in memory of the late Mr John T. Micklethwaite who was for many years the Abbey's Surveyor of the Fabric.

A separate guide to the contents of the museum is available.

Dean's Yard & the Precincts

The area which is now Dean's Yard was partly covered by monastic buildings and the northern portion called 'The Elms' was part of the abbot's garden. The approach from the broad sanctuary is now beneath a gateway built by Sir Gilbert Scott. The column (designed by Scott) erected in memory of the Old Westminsters, who fell in the Crimean War and in the Indian Mutiny, is opposite this entrance. It is surmounted by a figure of St George slaying the dragon and also has statues of Queen Victoria, Queen Elizabeth I, Henry III, and St Edward the Confessor. It stands on part of the site of the old gatehouse prison pulled down in 1776, where Sir Walter Raleigh spent the night before his execution (29 October 1618). John Hampden, Sir John Eliot, Richard Lovelace, the Cavalier poet, who wrote the lines: 'Stone walls do not a prison make,/Nor iron bars a cage',[1] and Lilly, the astrologer, were some of the notable persons imprisoned here. The sanctuary tower stood to the north. It contained two chapels, where those who had taken sanctuary were expected to attend service. Close beside it was the belfry tower, 'whose ringings, men said, soured all the drink in the town'. The right of sanctuary had been a privilege belonging to the monastery from the earliest times, but the sanctuary area gradually became a scandal to the neighbourhood, where all the thieves, murderers, and vagabonds took refuge from the law. The sanctuary rights were, therefore, much restricted under Queen Elizabeth, and finally abolished by James I.

On the east side of Dean's Yard the chapter office and the school houses incorporate much of the fourteenth-century monastic guest house and cellarer's quarters. Other monastic buildings filled up much of the square now known as Dean's Yard, and it was not until 1756 that these together with the monks' granary, then practically a ruin, were pulled down, and the materials used to construct the terrace. But a row of ancient buildings still blocked up the 'green', and it was not until 1815 that these were cleared away, the space in the centre sown with grass, and railings added. The pump, which formerly supplied the school with water, was left in its place opposite the Head Master's House until 1872, although it had been dry over twenty years before. The original use of the green as a playground for the boys of Westminster School was somewhat modified as the numbers increased, and it is now only occasionally used for this purpose.

During the Second World War the precincts of the Abbey suffered grievously as the result of air-raids, although the damage to the fabric of the Abbey Church itself was slight.

On an October night in 1940 a bomb fell outside the House of Lords, destroying much of the glass in Henry VII's Chapel, causing one of the pendants of the roof of that chapel to fall and pitting the outside walls of the east end of the church.

---

1 In the lyric 'To Althea from Prison'.

Far more serious, however, was the damage caused by incendiary bombs on the night of 10 May 1941. The roof of the church was set alight but fortunately the fire was extinguished before it got too firm a hold – not, however, before the roof of the lantern (over the central space between the choir and the sanctuary) had crashed to the floor beneath. There the fire burnt itself out, doing very little damage except to the roof itself and to the pews below. At the same time further incendiary bombs set fire to part of the Deanery, and to some of the houses round the Little Cloister, together with the College Dormitory, the Great Hall ('School'), and the seventeenth-century Busby Library of Westminster School. All these were completely gutted and only the Abbey Library, which had also been set on fire, was saved.

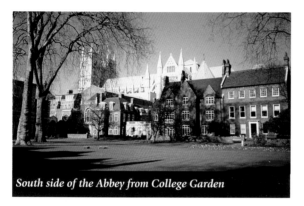

South side of the Abbey from College Garden

COLLEGE GARDEN

A passageway from the south-east corner of Little Cloister leads to **College Garden**, thought to have been in continuous cultivation for over 900 years. In monastic times this was the garden of the Infirmarer, who grew here the herbs and other medicinal plants used to care for the sick and elderly.

The garden occupies a little over an acre and is bordered to the north by canons' houses, on the south and east by the fourteenth-century walls of the monastic precinct, and on the west by the College Dormitory (p. 113). In the south-west corner is a statue of the Crucifixion by *E. Plazzotta*, given by the sculptor's family in 1993. The five magnificent plane trees were planted in 1850.

WESTMINSTER SCHOOL

From early times there was a school for novices within the monastic precincts, but it is not until 1363–4 that we find mention of the 'almonry boys', who had a separate school, called the 'Sophouse', which formed part of the almonry, on a site near the junction of Victoria Street and Great Smith Street. By 1386–7 these 'almonry boys' were distinct from others called the 'grammar boys'. In 1461 some of the latter were moved to a house (now No. 19 Dean's Yard) which then formed part of the monastic guest house, and a lay headmaster was appointed. By 1479–80 the singing boys or Choristers had a separate establishment with a master of their own. The 'almonry boys' were still taught by a monk, probably in the west cloister. Both almonry and grammar

boys were absorbed into one under Henry VIII, and re-endowed in 1560 by Queen Elizabeth I who is revered as the foundress of what has become a great public school. The connection between the scholars and choristers was not finally severed until 1848, when a separate Choir House was built. Westminster School has remained in close association with the Abbey ever since its foundation. The Dean is *ex officio* chairman of the Governing Body; a service for the school is regularly held in the choir, and the Queen's Scholars (wearing white surplices) attend some Sunday morning services. Since the accession of James II the King's (or Queen's) Scholars are present in the Abbey at every coronation and have the right to be the first to acclaim the sovereign on entry into the church.

LITTLE DEAN'S YARD

In Little Dean's Yard are grouped the principal school buildings, which have gradually replaced the monastic offices. Thus at first the Second Master was lodged in a tower, close to the present entrance into this yard, over a gateway which was adjacent to the monastic granary. The granary itself, a long room built on stone arches, was used as a dormitory for Queen Elizabeth's forty scholars and remained in their occupation for nearly 200 years. By the end of the seventeenth century the room was practically in ruins and, before Queen Anne's death, Dean Atterbury, in conjunction with Sir Christopher Wren (himself an Old Westminster) planned a new dormitory, and collected a sum of money which he added to a legacy left by an Old Westminster, the Queen's oculist Sir Edward Hannes, for the same purpose. The present site in the College Garden was chosen but, owing to the opposition of the Head Master, Dr Freind, and of some of the prebendaries, the building was not completed until after the deaths of the architect (1723) and of the Dean (1731) who was in exile for his political opinions.

In 1936 part of the east side of Little Dean's Yard was reconstructed, and a new wall erected with an ornamental gate of wrought iron opening into the College Garden. At the same time the cement which had covered the wall of the adjoining dormitory was removed and the original brickwork revealed through the generosity of the Pilgrim Trust in commemoration of the Jubilee of King George V (1935). The **fountain** was given to the school in 1971 by the Westminster School Society in honour of **John Dudley Carleton**, b. 1908, d. 1974, and to commemorate his long association with the school (1922–70). He was successively: educated there (1922–7); Assistant Master (1932–41 and 1945–9); Under Master and Master of the Queen's Scholars (1949–57); and finally Head Master (1957–70).

THE GREAT HALL OR 'SCHOOL'

At the foot of the steps leading to School is a stone gateway erected in 1734 probably from the design of Lord Burlington. School itself formed part of the monks' dormitory, but was adapted for the use of the school about 1600. From that date until 1884 when extra form-rooms were built, the entire school was taught in this room. It had an exceptionally fine sixteenth-century hammer-beam roof which was unfortunately destroyed by an incendiary bomb in 1941. At the same time the panelling with its painted coats of arms and the whole of the interior was gutted and only the walls remained. It was rebuilt, with a modern roof, etc., after the war and formally reopened by HM The Queen in November 1960 as part of the quatercentenary celebration of the refounding of the school by Queen Elizabeth I in 1560. In the rebuilding the opportunity was taken to restore the semicircular apse, at the north end which, formerly known as the Shell, gave its name to the form taught in front of it and was subsequently adopted as the name for a form by many other schools. New panelling was also put up on which has been painted the coats of arms of famous Old Westminsters, but it was not possible to restore the many hundreds of names which were formerly painted on the walls.

The lower portion of the walls of School and some of the windows date from the late eleventh century, but much of the walling was altered and rebuilt by Wyatt at the beginning of the nineteenth century. The room is roughly divided by an iron bar from which used to hang a curtain which separated the Upper from the Lower School. It is over this bar that, by an ancient custom, the College cook tosses a pancake on Shrove Tuesday. It is scrambled for by a boy selected from each form, and the boy who retrieves the largest portion of it receives a guinea from the Dean.

The Head Master's chair is traditionally said to have been presented to the famous Head Master, Dr Busby, by King Charles II. In front of it is the Rod Table also dating from this time, and two ancient chairs which were used by the masters from the reign of Henry VIII to that of Queen Victoria. At the south end of the room is a seventeenth-century organ case formerly used in the Abbey, and also the memorial to those Westminsters who lost their lives in the two world wars. This replaces a memorial in the form of an oak screen designed by the late *Sir R. Lorimer* in 1921 to commemorate the First World War.

The **Busby Library**, which adjoins School, was 'built and fitted' by Dr Busby at his 'own great coste and charges' between 1660 and 1680. It had an elaborate domed ceiling surrounded by wreaths of fruit and flowers. The bookcases were also of the same period. The library was completely destroyed by an incendiary bomb in 1941. It was rebuilt after the war, and it was found possible from photographs exactly to reproduce the ceiling, bookcases, etc., so that the room has very much its original appearance. The valuable collection of books was fortunately saved.

THE SCHOLARS' DORMITORY

The College Dormitory, situated on the west side of the College Garden, was originally designed by Sir Christopher Wren and the foundation-stone was laid in 1722. However, the Earl of Burlington somewhat altered the original design and the building was not completed until 1733.

The façade towards the garden is of Bath stone, and the dormitory was internally a copy of the old dormitory in Dean's Yard which had once been the monks' granary. The boys were lodged in one long room which filled the whole of the first floor, while the vaults beneath the old granary were represented in the new dormitory by an open cloister giving on to the garden. From about 1730 to 1938 the dormitory was the scene of the annual Latin play, a custom which dated from the reign of Queen Elizabeth I who had ordained that such a play should be acted annually at Christmas by the

scholars for 'the encouragement of good elocution'. Before 1730 it was acted in the College Hall. The dormitory was remodelled in 1846 when the cloister was closed in and converted into living-rooms for the boys.

The interior of the dormitory was gutted by an incendiary bomb in 1941, but the original façade survived. The dormitory was then rebuilt internally on a different plan, and was formally reopened by King George VI in June 1950.

ASHBURNHAM HOUSE

This beautiful seventeenth-century house is on the north side of Little Dean's Yard and incorporates part of the Prior's House, which seems to have been built and added to at various times from the twelfth to the sixteenth centuries. It contained a large hall erroneously identified with the monks' misericorde. The refectory was situated behind this hall, and the wall which separated it from the south cloister still exists. Embedded in it are remains of eleventh- and fourteenth-century work and a thirteenth-century doorway leads into the cloister. South-west was the 'misericorde', an upper chamber resting on vaults, where the monks were allowed to eat meat, and where the grammar school boys had their meals.

After the dissolution and during the ten years (1540–50) when there was a Westminster bishopric, Bishop Thirlby lived in the Deanery and the Prior's House was occupied by the Dean (Benson). It was afterwards let to various persons of note connected with the Court in the reigns of Queen Elizabeth and the first Stuart kings. The house is said to have been rebuilt or remodelled by Inigo Jones, when Sir Edward Powell, Master of Requests under Charles I, was the tenant (1630–40). A later and less trustworthy tradition assigns the rebuilding to Webb, Inigo Jones's pupil, after the house had passed into the hands of Colonel William Ashburnham (1662), a noted Royalist and personal friend of Charles II. In 1730 his descendant, Lord Ashburnham, leased it to the Crown, and the King's and Cotton Libraries were kept there until, in 1731, a disastrous fire broke out, when the precious books and MSS were rescued with great difficulty. The beautiful staircase and panelling, which belong to the Inigo Jones period, fortunately remained intact. In 1739 the house was bought back from the Ashburnhams by the Dean and Chapter, and divided into two prebendal houses.

After the Public Schools Act of 1868 the school was empowered to purchase three houses from the Dean and Chapter when they next became vacant. These were: Ashburnham House, then occupied by Lord John Thynne, Sub-dean of the Abbey; the part already divided from it, where the Abbey Organist (1831–82), James Turle, was living; and No. 18 Dean's Yard, which is said to have been the Monk Bailiff's house. The beautiful seventeenth-century rooms on the first floor of Ashburnham House then became, and have since remained, the school library.

The College Hall, described below, is in the Deanery Courtyard.

THE DEANERY COURTYARD

Entering the cloisters from Dean's Yard, a dark arch on the left leads past the front door of the Deanery into a small courtyard. To the right of the archway leading to the Deanery is a monument to **Captain James Cornewall, RN**, b. 1699, killed 1744 in a victorious action against the French off Toulon. His monument, the first voted in Parliament to commemorate a naval hero, was removed here (1932) from the nave. Sculptor: *Sir R. Taylor*. Facing the entrance are some sixteenth-century rooms built by Abbot Islip, including the Jericho Parlour, which leads into the Jerusalem Chamber; on the left is the College Hall, on the right is the other part of the Abbot's House, used since the dissolution of the monastery as the Dean's residence.

THE ABBOT'S HOUSE OR DEANERY

The 'Abbot's Lodging' as it was called, has been added to and altered at various times, but much of the original house, dating from Litlyngton's time, still remains. Part of a wall of a much earlier date runs along one side of the abbot's long room, which has a western window overlooking the Dean's Yard entrance. The eastern portion of the long room has a fine fourteenth-century window and was no doubt the abbot's private chapel; below the modern floor are fragments of tiles, of the same style as those in the Chapter House. The Abbot's House was also known at one time as Cheyney Gates Manor. Elizabeth Woodville lived in the Abbot's House, while her husband, Edward IV, fled into temporary exile at the return of Henry VI, and here in 1470 her eldest son, Edward (afterwards Edward V), was born. In 1483 the widowed queen again took refuge here, with her younger children, and while in sanctuary was persuaded to give up her second son, Richard, to his uncle, the Duke of Gloucester. In 1486 she appears to have leased the Abbot's House, and lived here again for a time. In 1640 the Irish Archbishop Ussher inhabited the Deanery when he came to attend the Long Parliament. During the Commonwealth John Bradshaw, President of the Council, leased the Deanery and died in the house. In the triforium is a little room which is traditionally called Bradshaw's Room, where he is supposed to have kept his books and retired to study.

THE COLLEGE HALL

The College Hall was built by Abbot Litlyngton in the late fourteenth century (1369–76), and was the abbot's state dining-room. Shields with the abbot's arms can be seen held by the angels on the corbels which support the fine timbered roof. The minstrels' gallery at the west end dates from Tudor or Jacobean times. Until the middle of the nineteenth century the room was warmed by an open fire in the centre of the hall, the smoke escaping through a louvre or lantern in the roof, which still exists. According to tradition it was in this hall that Elizabeth Woodville and her daughters, with the boy Prince, Richard of York, 'sat alow on the rushes all desolate and dismaied' when she claimed the abbot's protection in 1483 for the second time. The tables of oak are traditionally supposed to have been made from the ships of the Spanish Armada, which were wrecked on our shores. The wainscoting dates from the middle of the eighteenth century, when the Hall was 'beautified and adorned', and new paving added. In earlier times the walls were hung with tapestry. Above the high table are the arms of the College (i.e. the Abbey) of Westminster, the two colleges with which Westminster School is closely connected (Christ Church, Oxford, and Trinity College, Cambridge), and the Order of

the Bath, the Dean being *ex officio* Dean of the Order. The Tudor ships in each corner were inserted by Dean Robinson, High Almoner to the King, and represent the Seal of the Royal Almonry. In 1972 the hall was restored with the help of a grant from the Goldsmiths' Company and the Pilgrim Trust. After the dissolution the hall became the College Hall and is now used by the Queen's Scholars and other boys of Westminster School for their meals.

The Latin play was acted here until 1730, when it was moved to the new dormitory. The stage was under the gallery, and dresses were hired from the Office of the Revels and brought here in barges. The expenses of two plays 'plaied by the Children of the Grammar School in the Colledge of Westminster before the Queene's Majesty' in 1564 have been preserved among the Abbey muniments. Elizabeth must have been well pleased, as she came again the following year.

THE JERUSALEM CHAMBER

The approach to this historic Chamber is through a smaller room, added with the apartments above it by Abbot Islip in the early sixteenth century; it is known as the **Jericho Parlour** and contains some fine linenfold panelling. In the vestibule is a little niche which once held a lamp, and there are remains of paintings and inscriptions on the wall. The **Jerusalem Chamber** itself formed part of the Abbot's House or Lodging and is of late fourteenth-century date. It probably took its name from the original tapestry hangings. The room was restored in the time of Dean Stanley (1864–81), who uncovered the original roof and repanelled the walls with cedarwood brought from Lebanon. In this Chamber Henry IV died, and the traditional story dramatised by Shakespeare in the play *Henry IV* – which credits Henry V with putting on his father's crown before his death – is connected with this room. The two busts of the king and his son were placed here by Dean Stanley. Henry IV was preparing an expedition to the Holy Land in 1413, and visited the Abbey on the eve of his departure. 'While he was making his prayers at St Edward's shrine to take there his leave and so speed him on his journey, he became so sick that such as were about him feared that he would have died right there. Wherefore they, for his comfort, bore him into the Abbot's place and laid him

The Jericho Parlour

The Jerusalem Chamber

down before the fire in this chamber. On coming to himself and learning that he was in the chamber named Hierusalem, then said the king, "Laud be to the Father of Heaven! for now I know that I shall die in this chamber, according to the prophecy made of me beforesaid, that I should die in Hierusalem," and so he made himself ready, and died shortly after.' The Chamber was redecorated by Lord Keeper Williams, Dean of Westminster in the reign of James I. His arms, combined with those of Westminster and Lincoln (he was also Bishop of Lincoln) may be seen on the carved cedarwood overmantel, which he erected to celebrate the betrothal of Charles I – then Prince of Wales – and the French Princess Henrietta Maria (1624), when he entertained the French Ambassador with a banquet in this room. The Chamber has been the scene of many gatherings. It was used by those engaged upon the Authorized Version of the Bible in 1611, on the Revised Version of 1885, and on the New English Bible (New Testament) of 1961. The Upper House of Convocation has frequently met there and in it many famous persons have lain in state.

The tapestries in the Jerusalem Chamber, which are sixteenth and seventeenth century in date, have been cleaned and repaired and the subjects identified. The Circumcision of Isaac and the fragments of the Return of Sara from the Egyptians belong to the 'History of Abraham', which is in the Great Hall at Hampton Court. The right-hand part of the Circumcision is now in one of the Deanery rooms known as Cheyneygates. The borders of all these pieces are missing except a strip from the Sara series which is hanging between the windows. The 'Rebekah at the well',[1] opposite the Circumcision, belongs to a later and inferior set. The healing of the lame man by St Peter at the 'Beautiful Gate' of the Temple[2] is from a series called the 'Acts of the Apostles', apparently made in England by a weaver using a Flemish mark; these are distributed in different places, including Boughton and Haddon Hall, and have not all been found. Some of the subjects, like this one, are based upon Raphael's designs, but are very much simplified. Other pieces of tapestry in the Deanery, similar to that near the High Altar, are thought to belong to a set at Holyrood of Flemish manufacture of the sixteenth or seventeenth century.

---

1   Given by the Sub-dean, Lord John Thynne, in 1871.
2   Also given by Lord John Thynne.

The Communion, Altar Plate, & Processional Banners

None of the present plate in the possession of the Dean and Chapter dates from monastic times; such pieces as still existed after the dissolution were broken up or sold under the Commonwealth, and new vessels and ornaments were presented after the Restoration.

Among the more important pieces of plate, some of which may be seen in the Pyx Chamber, are:

A chalice and paten presented to the Dean and Chapter (1918) in memory of Lieutenant Cyril Dupe, an Oxford undergraduate, killed in the First World War. They were found in the river near Oxford, and are thought to have originally formed part of the plate belonging to one of the college chapels, date about 1570.

A pair of large plain chalices, with covers forming patens, and a pair of similar flagons, all London made; initials of maker R.A., date 1660.

A pair of chased chalices, dated 1671, no maker's name or hallmarks, given by John Sudbury, Dean of Durham, who was a Prebendary of Westminster (1660–1).

A pair of tripod candlesticks and a pair of embossed flagons, London made; an embossed centre salver and alms-dish, combined, London made; two smaller alms-dishes, one dated 1684, the other about the same period.

A straining-spoon, date 1697.

Two silver-gilt alms-dishes inscribed 'given to Westminster Abbey by Their Royal Highnesses Princess Elizabeth and the Duke of Edinburgh to mark the occasion of their wedding on 20th November 1947'.

Two pairs of modern chalices and various ornaments have been presented to the altars of St Faith and St Edward at different times. A silver-gilt cross and a pair of vases were given by Lord Rosebery for the High Altar in 1899, after his elder daughter's marriage in the Abbey.

A silver-gilt alms-dish was presented by Colonel Sir Charles Wyndham Murray, KCB, Gentleman Usher of the Scarlet Rod, and Lady Murray, at the second installation of the Knights of the Bath in Henry VII's Chapel on 18 May 1920.

In 1928 the citizens of Westminster, in recognition of Dean Ryle's constant efforts to bring the City and the Abbey together, presented two richly carved alms-dishes in his memory. Made by *O. Ramsden*. An official stall with the arms of the City of Westminster above it has been since assigned to the Lord Mayor 'in perpetuity'.

On the altar in St Edward's Chapel are a pair of silver candlesticks, seventeenth-century Italian work, presented by the Duke and Duchess of York (afterwards King George VI and Queen Elizabeth) in commemoration of their marriage on 26 April 1923. A crucifix designed by *K. Redfern* to match the candlesticks, was given by Miss W.M. Bull and Miss P. Bull in 1979. On either side of this altar are tall standard candlesticks of sheeted silver, given in 1924 by the Order of Crusaders.

In St Faith's Chapel is a lamp of silvered copper; a silver-gilt chalice and paten, given by the Society of St Faith; a parcel-gilt chalice and paten given by Lady Hudson in memory of the late Sir Robert Hudson. Also used in this chapel are two silver chalices and patens given by the Girls' Friendly Society and the late Admiral Sir Austen Moore.

THE PROCESSIONAL BANNERS

These are displayed in the sanctuary on great festivals and consist of: the Banner of Our Lady – presented by the Girls' Friendly Society, 1922; the Banner of St Martin – presented by the Church Lads' Brigade, 1921; the Banner of St Peter – presented by the Mothers' Union, 1926; the Banner of St Oswald – presented by the Church of England Men's Society, 1938; the Banner of St Edward – presented in 1942 by Miss Eulalie Buckmaster in memory of her father, Walter Selby Buckmaster; the Banner of St George – presented by Mrs Louise Beatrix Itterson-Pronk in 1948.

The Painted Glass

There is very little left of the ancient glass except the east windows in the clerestory, two windows at the west end of the nave, and the plain glass with the initials H.R. in the Henry VII Chapel. In the Jericho Parlour and vestibule are collected fragments of the early thirteenth-, fourteenth-, and fifteenth-century glass which filled the windows of the church before the Reformation; those which remained intact after the fifteenth century were no doubt destroyed by the Puritans two centuries later. In the museum are six small panes of thirteenth-century glass of special interest formerly in the Jerusalem Chamber: the scenes depicted are the massacre of the Innocents, the stoning of St Stephen, the martyrdom of St John the Baptist or St Alban, the descent of the Holy Spirit at Pentecost, St Nicholas and the false pilgrim, and the Ascension.

THE EAST WINDOWS

These are a collection of ancient and modern glass. The older parts were probably pieced together in the seventeenth century when the blank spaces were filled up with glass of that period. Early in the eighteenth century the whole window was repaired by Wren, when Surveyor of the Fabric, and the glaziers scratched their names with the dates of their work (1702 and 1706) upon the modern pieces. There is some pot-metal in this window, which includes thirteenth-, fourteenth-, and fifteenth-century fragments. The central figures of St Edward holding out the ring to his patron saint, St John the Evangelist, who is in pilgrim's dress, date from about 1490, with the exception of the king's head which is later. The figures to the north are thought to be those of

Christ and Our Lady, to the south St Augustine and Bishop Mellitus. (Several early shields of arms are intact and are now in **St Edmund's Chapel**. These include the three lions of Henry III, the arms of his father-in-law Raymond, Count of Provence, and of his brother-in-law Richard, Earl of Cornwall.)

The **east window in the triforium** shows Queen Eleanor of Castile, the wife of Edward I, and Lady Margaret Beaufort, with their coats of arms above them. This window was designed by *Sir Ninian Comper* in 1951.

The four-light window immediately above the **Henry V Chantry Chapel** is filled with glass salvaged from a window in the south transept made by *Messrs Burlison and Grylls,* which was severely damaged in the Second World War. It was designed by *Edward Woore* and shows four kings, Henry III, Edward III, Henry V, and Henry VII with their coats of arms.

At the **west end of the nave**, the figure in fifteenth-century glass under the south tower is traditionally supposed to represent the Black Prince. The corresponding figure under the north tower is made up of fragments of various dates, and represents an unidentified bearded saint. In 1922–3 the glass from all these windows was releaded, repaired, and cleaned under the direction of the Victoria and Albert Museum.

THE ROSE WINDOWS & THE WEST WINDOW

In 1722 the **rose window in the north transept** was remodelled and new glass inserted under Dean Atterbury's directions a few months before he was arrested for treason and sent to the Tower. The previous year the artist, *Sir James Thornhill* (d. 1734), who had already been employed on the paintings inside the dome of St Paul's, received £100, by Atterbury's orders, for designing '16 large figures 7 feet high of the Apostles and Evangelists on Canvasses and Frames in proper Colours for the glass painter to work by' for the great north window. It may be noted that Judas Iscariot is omitted and only eleven Apostles are shown. *Joshua Price*, the glass-painter, was paid £442 16s. for carrying out this design, and in December 1733 *William Price*, his son received another sum of £400 from the Dean and Chapter, on commission for his work on the **great west window** at the end of the nave, the design for which was in all probability sketched out by Thornhill the year before his death. This window, created in 1735, has the figures of Abraham, Isaac and Jacob, together with Moses, Aaron and the twelve Tribes of Israel. Beneath these are the arms of George II flanked by those of King Sebert, Queen Elizabeth I, Dean Wilcocks, and the City of Westminster.

Both these windows were put up at the time when Sir Christopher Wren and his successor, Nicholas Hawksmoor, were restoring the stonework on the north front and completing the west end with the new towers.

In the late nineteenth century, the Abbey architect, *J. L. Pearson* (q.v.), completely remodelled the tracery of the rose window on the north front.

During the Second World War the glass in the six lancet windows below the north rose window, which commemorated seven officers who gave their lives in the Indian Mutiny, was destroyed. In 1958 these windows were replaced by a series, designed by *Brian Thomas*, representing the six acts of mercy described in St Matthew's Gospel.

The **rose window in the south transept** is the largest of this type, the stonework outside was remodelled under *Sir Gilbert Scott* in 1849–50. The glass by *Messrs Ward and Nixon* which had been placed in the window in 1840 was removed in 1901, and the present window substituted. The money was raised, by public subscription, as a memorial to **Hugh Lupus (Grosvenor), 1st Duke of Westminster**, b. 1825, d. 1899. *G. F. Bodley* superintended the work of the glass-painters, *Messrs Burlison and Grylls*, and Dr M.R. James, Provost of Eton, drew up the scheme of subjects. Dedicated 26 September 1902.

Thirty-two figures in the outer circle were chosen to represent the preparation of the world for Christ. In the upper half are sixteen Jewish prophets. In the lower half: (from left to right) Enoch, Abraham, Moses, David, Solomon, Job, Ezra, Sirach – representing the Chosen People, while Plato, Aristotle, Æschylus, the Sibyl, Zoroaster, one of the Magi, Virgil, and Seneca represent seekers for the truth in the pre-Christian world.

In the inner circle, round the central figure of Christ, are sixteen figures, symbolical of the virtues and the orders of angels. In the lower spandrels is the Annunciation, represented by St Gabriel and the Blessed Virgin. Adam and St John the Baptist are in the upper spandrels. The twelve trefoiled lights below contain great representative teachers of the Greek and Latin Church; in the upper range: St Clement of Alexandria, St Athanasius, St Chrysostom, St Jerome, St Augustine of Hippo, St Gregory the Great. In the lower range the Christian teachers of our own islands: St Alban, St Ninian, St Patrick, St David, St Augustine of Canterbury, St Aidan. In the upper range of lights are the emblems of St Peter and St Paul on either side of the royal arms. The shields above the figures in the lower range are those of St Edward the Confessor, the Abbey of Westminster, the City of Westminster, the Duke of Westminster, the Dean and Chapter, and the royal arms.

In the **east aisle of the south transept** is a window, glass by *Clayton and Bell*, given in 1869 by Dr Nathaniel Rogers, to represent the poets of the Old Testament (David) and the New Testament (St John). Above are the arms of St Edward the Confessor.

The **Poets' Corner window** (above Chaucer's tomb) was unveiled in June 1994 as a memorial to **Edward Horton Hubbard**, b. 1937, d. 1989, architectural historian; presented by his father, Jack Hubbard. The window was designed by *G. Jones* and continues the commemoration of poets and writers now that wall and floor space is limited. Four authors have been commemorated to date: **Alexander Pope**, b. 1688, d. 1744, poet and satirist, author of *An Essay on Man* and *The Dunciad*; buried at St Mary's church, Twickenham. **Robert Herrick**, b. 1591, d. 1674, one of the finest of English lyric poets; buried at Dean Prior, Devon. **Oscar Fingal O'Flahertie Wilde**, b. 1854, d. 1900, playwright and aesthete. His name was added to the window on 14 February 1995, the centenary of the first performance of his comic masterpiece *The Importance of being Earnest*. Buried at Père Lachaise cemetery, Paris. **Alfred Edward Housman**, b. 1859, d. 1936, poet and classical scholar; his name was added in 1996 to mark the centenary of the publication of *A Shropshire Lad*, his best-known collection of poems. Buried at St Lawrence's church, Ludlow, Shropshire.

During the nineteenth and twentieth centuries various memorial windows were presented to the Dean and Chapter or put up by them.

In the wall of the **west aisle of the north transept** is a window to the memory of the officers and men drowned in the shipwreck of **HMS *Captain***, off Cape Finisterre on 7 September 1870. Glass executed by *Clayton and Bell*.

Next to this is a window dedicated on 25 January 1912 to the memory of **John Bunyan**, b. 1628, d. 1688, designed by *Sir Ninian Comper*. The subjects were taken from the first part of *The Pilgrim's Progress*.

In the **north choir aisle** a window erected in 1862 commemorates **Robert Stephenson**, b. 1803, d. 1859, engineer. The name of his father **George Stephenson**, b. 1781, d. 1848, inventor and founder of railways, was added in 1948. Designed by *William Wailes*, amended by *Sir Gilbert Scott*.

In the next bay to this is a window in memory of **James Turle**, b. 1802, d. 1882, Organist at the Abbey for fifty years, with portraits of himself and his wife, put up by his son. Glass by *Clayton and Bell*.

In **St Benedict's Chapel** was a window commemorating officers and men of the Queen's Westminster Rifles who fell in the First World War. This was destroyed by blast in 1940, and has been replaced by a window to the memory of those **Citizens of Westminster** who gave their lives in the Second World War. It was designed by *Hugh Easton* and was unveiled by HRH Princess Margaret on 7 November 1948. The window depicts St George and St Michael with the arms of the City of Westminster and various badges and emblems representing the armed forces and other organisations in which the citizens of Westminster served during the war.

On the **north side of the nave** is a series of windows, designed and carried out by *Sir Ninian Comper* (see also the Bunyan Window) after a scheme originally drawn up by Dean Armitage Robinson (1902–11), which embodies the kings and abbots, in whose time the Abbey was gradually built, with their coats of arms and badges. From the west they commemorate:

Sir Frederick Henry Royce, Bt, OBE, b. 1864, d. 1933. The first aero-engineer to be commemorated in the Abbey. The window shows King Edgar and St Dunstan, d. 988. Under these figures are the arms of Royce and the city of Derby. In the canopy above the figure of King Edgar is a scene from a drawing by St Dunstan himself, of Our Lord enthroned and St Dunstan kneeling before him. In the right-hand window St Dunstan reads the Scriptures, while an angel plays his harp. The scene in the tracery quatrefoil shows King Edgar sailing into Chester with six kings, with whom he had made peace. Dedicated 1962.

The **Royal Army Medical Corps**. This window, presented in 1927, has for its subject King Edward the Confessor, the founder of the Abbey. His left hand holds the ring which he gave to St John who appeared to him in the guise of a pilgrim and from the wrist of the right hand hang tablets inscribed with the opening words of the king's charter to the Abbey. Beside him is Abbot Edwin, d. 1071. A panel has been added commemorating those who fell in the Second World War.

Sir Charles Parsons, OM, KCB, b. 1854, d. 1931, marine engineer. The figures represent King Henry III and Abbot Richard de Ware, d. 1283, in whose time the eastern half of the present Abbey church was built. Dedicated in 1950.

Sir John Wolfe Barry, KCB, b. 1836, d. 1918, past President of the Institute of Civil Engineers. The figures represent King Edward I, in whose time the new building begun by his father, Henry III, was carried on as far as the second bay of the nave, and the contemporary abbot, Walter de Wenlock, d. 1307. Within the canopy above there is a statuette of the abbot giving the heart of Henry III to the Abbess of Fontevrault, a scene which took place in the presence of Edmund Crouchback, the king's brother, and of William de Valence, his uncle, whose statuettes are in the niches below. Dedicated 1922.

Sir Benjamin Baker, b. 1840, d. 1907, a distinguished engineer, the builder of the Forth Bridge, a small picture of which is on the glass. The figures represent King Edward III, and Archbishop Langham, d. 1376, Litlyngton's predecessor as abbot, whose munificent bequest enabled his successor to carry on the building of the nave and the cloister. Dedicated 1909.

Donald Alexander (Smith), 1st Baron Strathcona and Mount Royal, b. 1820, d. 1914, a great Canadian imperialist and philanthropist; the king in this window is Richard II with Abbot Litlyngton, d. 1386, who devoted the whole of his time at Westminster, first as prior then as abbot, to continuing the rebuilding of the monastery and church begun by his predecessor, Langham. Dedicated 1919.

William (Thomson), 1st Baron Kelvin, b. 1824, d. 1907, whose grave is below. The figures represent King Henry V, a generous contributor to the western bays of the nave, and William of Colchester, d. 1420, the abbot in whose time the work was carried out. Dedicated 1913.

A window in the **north choir aisle** commemorating **Prisoners of War** who died in Germany, 1914–18, completes the series. It was presented (1926) by James W. Gerard, American Ambassador in Berlin, 1914–17, in charge of British interests. The window shows King Henry VI and Abbot Harweden, d. 1441. Statuettes above show Henry's patron saints and include some of his family.

Two eminent civil engineers are commemorated in nineteenth-century windows. Both windows were moved from their original positions on the north side of the nave to give room for the Comper series. The window to **Richard Trevithick**, b. 1771, d. 1833, the father of the steam locomotive engine, is now under the **north-west tower**. In addition to figures of nine Cornish saints, outline drawings of his inventions are shown in scrolls held by angels. Executed by *Messrs Burlison and Grylls*.

That to **Isambard Kingdom Brunel**, b. 1806, d. 1859, is now on the **south side of the nave**. It depicts Old and New Testament scenes concerned with the Temple. Brunel assisted his father, Sir Marc I. Brunel on the Thames Tunnel and designed the Clifton Suspension Bridge. He also designed the *Great Eastern* steamship. Window originally erected 1868. Glass by *Heaton, Butter and Bayne*.

Also on the south side, above **St George's Chapel** is a window given in 1875 by George William Childs, citizen of the USA. It commemorates **George Herbert** and **William Cowper**, both religious poets and both Westminster scholars. Glass by *Clayton and Bell*.

Above the **Abbot's Pew** is a window unveiled May 1922 in memory of the officers and men of the **'British' Flying Corps** who fell in the First World War. The design is by *Harry Grylls*, carried out by the firm of *Burlison and Grylls*; the theme is flying men and wings, illustrated by passages from the prophets Isaiah and Ezekiel. The armour and weapons borne by them are: the breastplate of righteousness, the shield of faith, the helmet of salvation, the sword of the Spirit (Ephesians 6: 13, 17). In the tracery above is the Archangel Michael, the patron saint of Airmen. The window was presented by Mrs Louis Bennett, of West Virginia, whose son, a pilot of the RFC, was killed in France.

West of the cloister door is a window, presented by an anonymous donor as a memorial to the services rendered through the **Young Men's Christian Association** during the First World War, and in memory of its founder, **Sir George Williams**, b. 1821, d. 1905, two portraits of whom as a young and older man appear at the base of the glass. The design is by *Dudley Forsyth*. The subjects are the Sermon on the Mount and the Transfiguration of Our Lord; above are Saints Michael and George; below these are the royal arms, and the collegiate arms. In the quatrefoil above is Our Lord in glory, and surrounding this are types of the soldiers from all parts of the Empire who served their country during the First World War, with the shields and arms of various British Dependencies. Dedicated on 14 November 1921.

In the **Islip Chapel** there is a window, by *Hugh Easton*, which was presented in 1948 by Dr Alan Don, the then Dean, as a thank-offering for the deliverance of Westminster Abbey and St Margaret's church from the perils of the Second World War and in remembrance of John Islip, sometime abbot, and of Paul de Labilliere, sometime Dean (q.v.).

It depicts Abbot Islip, d. 1532, kneeling in prayer, holding in his hand a model of the Islip rooms which survived the destruction of the greater part of the Deanery by enemy action. Above is inserted a diamond-shaped piece of medieval glass with the abbot's rebus – an eye and a slip. In the panel to the left is a cherub holding a model of the Abbey from which flames ascend to commemorate the fire that destroyed the roof of the lantern tower in May 1941. Above are the arms of Dean de Labilliere, who was Dean throughout the war. The other central figure represents St Margaret of Antioch. In the panel to the right is a cherub holding a model of St Margaret's church, Westminster, the chancel of which was rebuilt by Abbot Islip. Above are the arms of Dr Don, who was rector of St Margaret's from 1941 to 1946. In the lights at the head of the window are (1) the cross keys of St Peter with the ring of Edward the Confessor, (2) the arms of Abbot Islip, (3) the emblem of St Margaret, (4) the arms of the Abbey of Westminster.

In the **upper chantry of the Islip Chapel** is a window designed by *Hugh Easton*, in memory of the **nurses** who gave their lives in the Second World War. It shows a nurse with her arms outstretched to the Holy Family. The lower part of the window is filled with the emblems of the nursing organisations and the countries from which they came. Unveiled by HM Queen Elizabeth The Queen Mother on 2 November 1950.

HENRY VII CHAPEL WINDOWS

The heraldic **west window** contains the initials, cyphers and coats of arms of donors to the Abbey's Restoration Appeal 1973–1995, those concerned with the fundraising, and some of those directly involved in the restoration work. It especially honours **Sir John Templeton**, b. 1912, a major benefactor.

Royal Army Medical Corps window

In the centre are the arms of HM The Queen as Sovereign of the Order of the Bath, flanked on the left by those of HRH The Duke of Edinburgh (President of the Westminster Abbey Trust) and on the right by those of HRH The Prince of Wales as Great Master of the Order of the Bath. Devised by *D. Buttress* and *H. Chesshyre*, designed by *J. Lawson*, made by the firm of *Goddard and Gibbs*. Unveiled by HM The Queen at a service of thanksgiving for the completion of the restoration, 19 October 1995.

At the east end is the chapel dedicated to the memory of the men of the Royal Air Force who died in the **Battle of Britain**. The principal part of the memorial is the stained and painted glass window designed by *Hugh Easton*. This was unveiled by King George VI on 10 July 1947. In the lower lights are the badges of the sixty-eight squadrons that took part in the battle. In the centre, between the royal arms and the badge of the Royal Air Force, are the flags of the countries from which the men who died came. Grouped round these are four panels showing figures in the uniforms of the Royal Air Force, representing Dedication, Sacrifice, and Triumph through Resurrection. In the upper part of the window winged seraphim raise their hands to Heaven.

The stained glass windows in the lower lights of the north and south apsidal chapels honour those **donors** who gave substantial sums of money to the Westminster Abbey Restoration Appeal 1973–1995. Designed by *A. Fisher* and *P. Archer* of Chapel Studios, the glass was in place for the service of thanksgiving for the completion of the restoration of the Abbey in October 1995. Further windows will be added to the series.

The following windows were either destroyed or seriously damaged by bombing in the Second World War:

Henry VII's Chapel, south apse chapel, commemorating Lady Augusta Stanley, d. 1876 (see p. 67).

East end of choir, erected by Archdeacon Bentinck, b. 1784, d. 1868, to commemorate fifty years as a Canon of Westminster (1859).

Henry V's Chantry Chapel, commemorating John Ireland, Dean of Westminster, b. 1761, d. 1842.

St Michael's Chapel, commemorating officers and men who died in the Ashanti War, 1873–4.

Six lancet windows below the north transept rose window, and one in the west aisle commemorating seven officers who lost their lives in the Indian Mutiny.

St Andrew's Chapel, commemorating **Vincent Novello**, b. 1781, d. 1861, musician. In 1965 the British-Italian Society presented an eighteenth-century organ by John Snetzler as a further memorial to Novello to replace the destroyed window. The organ usually stands in Henry VII's Chapel.

East wall, south transept, commemorating Geoffrey Chaucer and Edward the Confessor.

Nave (removed), commemorating Sir William Siemens, b. 1828, d. 1883, electrician, and Joseph Locke, b. 1805, d. 1860, engineer.

THE CHAPTER HOUSE WINDOWS

The windows of the Chapter House were largely reglazed by *Miss Joan Howson* after they had been extensively damaged by air-raids in the Second World War.

The previous glass in the windows was by *Messrs Clayton and Bell*, and was given as a memorial to Dean Stanley in 1882. It was found possible to incorporate some undamaged panels of this glass, which are easily recognisable, in the new windows, but the opportunity was taken to fill some of the windows with coats of arms set in clear glass, thus reverting to what is known to have been the way these windows were originally glazed.

The arms include those of sovereigns, other royal personages, and great benefactors of the Abbey, as well as those of abbots who added to the fabric. Among the abbots thus commemorated are Langham, Litlyngton, Islip, and Feckenham.

In the south-west and south-east windows are the devices of the medieval master masons, Henry de Reyns who designed the present Abbey church, and Henry Yevele who rebuilt the nave. Other eminent architects and officials connected with the Abbey and Palace of Westminster are also commemorated. These include William of Wykeham, Bishop of Winchester and sometime Surveyor of the King's Buildings, Geoffrey Chaucer, poet and Clerk of the King's Works, and Richard Whittington, Mayor of London and Treasurer for the rebuilding of the nave.

The arms of later architects include those of Sir Christopher Wren, Surveyor of the Fabric, Sir John Vanbrugh, and Sir George Gilbert Scott, Surveyor of the Fabric, who restored the Chapter House in 1865.

There are also the arms of three First Commissioners of Works: Lord Mount Temple, who held office at the time of Scott's restoration; Lord Eversley, who was First Commissioner when the previous windows were inserted; and Lord Llanover (Sir Benjamin Hall), after whom 'Big Ben' is named. His arms are encircled with a clock-dial.

The Bells

There are twelve Abbey bells; two of them were cast in the reign of Elizabeth I and are now used for the chiming which precedes Matins and Evensong. In 1971, as a result of a legacy from Dr Eric Perkins, brother of the late Dr Jocelyn Perkins, six of the then eight bells were recast and four new bells were added to make a peal of ten. The new bells were named 'Elizabeth' (in honour of HM The Queen), 'Laetatus' (in honour of the city of Westminster and of Parliament), 'Jocelyn' (in honour of the late Sacrist) and 'Jubilate' (in honour of the Precentor and of the secretary of the Company of Ringers, Mr H. N. Pitstow). The last occasion when the bells were recast was in 1919 and King George V and Queen Mary were present at the foundry. HM The Queen was present in the Abbey at the dedication in 1971 and struck the 'Elizabeth' bell. The 'sermon bell', technically called 'the tenor bell', strikes forty times whenever a sermon is to be delivered. In addition there is a small bell, known as the 'Saints' bell', cast by Thomas Lester in 1738; it is rung before early celebrations of Holy Communion for fifteen minutes on Sundays and five minutes on week-days. On the occasion of the death of a member of the College the eighth bell is tolled every half-minute for half an hour; on the death of a member of the Royal Family or of the Dean the tenor bell is tolled every minute for one hour. After a funeral or memorial service the bells may be rung half-muffled.

Index